Maya Nationalisms and Postcolonial Challenges in Guatemala

Coloniality, Modernity, and Identity Politics

Emilio del Valle Escalante

School for Advanced Research
Santa Fe

School for Advanced Research Press
Post Office Box 2188
Santa Fe, New Mexico 87504-2188
www.sarpress.sarweb.org

Co-Director and Executive Editor: Catherine Cocks
Manuscript Editor: Kate Whelan
Designer and Production Manager: Cynthia Dyer
Proofreader: Sarah Soliz
Indexer: Catherine Fox
Printer: Cushing Malloy, Inc.

Library of Congress Cataloging-in-Publication Data:

Valle Escalante, Emilio del.
    [Nacionalismos mayas y desafíos postcoloniales en Guatemala. English]
    Maya nationalisms and postcolonial challenges in Guatemala : coloniality, modernity, and identity
politics / Emilio del Valle Escalante. — 1st ed.
        p. cm. — (School for Advanced Research global indigenous politics series)
    Includes bibliographical references and index.
    ISBN 978-1-930618-13-8 (pbk. : alk. paper)
1. Mayas—Guatemala—Politics and government. 2. Mayas—Guatemala—Ethnic identity.
3. Mayas—Guatemala—Government relations. 4. Mayas—Civil rights—Guatemala. 5. Civil rights
movements—Guatemala. 6. Postcolonialism—Guatemala. 7. Nationalism—Guatemala.
8. Globalization—Political aspects—Guatemala. 9. Guatemala—Ethnic relations—Political aspects.
10. Guatemala—Colonial influence. I. Title.
    F1435.3.P7V3513 2009
    305.897'4207281—dc22
                                    2009016871

 This book was printed on 10% PCR paper with soy-based inks.

Cover illustration: Detail backstrap woven huipil, Guatemala, © Steve Burger, 2007, iStockphoto.com

We don't need permission to be free.
—From a mural in Chenalho, Chiapas, Mexico

I dedicate this book to the women and men
who sacrificed their lives in the recently ended civil war in Guatemala
so that we, Mayas, would have a voice.

Contents

Acknowledgments

I would like to thank the following institutions for their generous financial support for this project: the Center for Latin American Studies at the University of Pittsburgh, the Pittsburgh Foundation, and the Andrew W. Mellon Dissertation Fellowship, for research and writing, and the Romance Languages Department at the University of North Carolina at Chapel Hill, for the translation of several chapters. I also thank and commend Paul Worley for his work on the translation of these chapters.

Several people gave me support and encouragement over the course of writing this book. To Gerald Martin, Alejandro de la Fuente, Jerome Branche, Connie Tomko, and several graduate students in the department of Hispanic Languages and Literatures at the University of Pittsburgh, thanks for the stimulating ideas and conversations. Elizabeth Monasterios and John Beverley offered me much appreciated encouragement, guidance, critical insights, and ideas that illuminated my own thinking. I am also grateful to José Cal Montoya, who encouraged me to publish it in Spanish in Guatemala. He opened the door for the book at FLACSO. In Chiapas, Mexico, during half of 2002 and the summer of 2003 I was lucky to work at Edupaz with Bernarda López, María Elena Tinoco, Father Oscar Salinas, and my friends at the *Frente Chiapaneco Contra las Represas* (Chiapanecan Front Against Dams). This project reflects many of our conversations about "free trade agreements" and indigenous rights. *Maltiox chiwe*, thanks to all of you. I also thank Sherry del Valle for her support and useful comments on some of my ideas. For their endless support and encouragement, thanks to my family, particularly my aunts Gloria, Olimpia, and Elvia, and most especially, my late grandmother, Felipa Lima, and my mother, Dora Felicita Escalante. Their immense sacrifices paved the way for my development. My son Dakota has been my source of inspiration and keeps me from losing my way. I hope, when he is old enough to read this, he'll get an idea of our struggle.

I am also grateful to James Brooks and Catherine Cocks at SAR Press for embracing and supporting my project. Thanks are also extended to Kate Whelan, for her valuable feedback and wonderful work in copyediting the manuscript, and to everyone who collaborated in the production of the book. Their critiques and suggestions offered me useful insights for making my ideas more coherent. Needless to say, the end result is my responsibility.

Some sections of this book have been published in Spanish and English. I want to acknowledge the permission to reprint them here. An earlier and modified version of the section, "Maya Nationalism and Political Decolonization" in chapter 2 appeared in English in *Latin American Caribbean and Ethnic Studies* under "Maya Nationalism and Political Decolonization: Luis de Lión and El tiempo principia en Xibalbá" (2006), and in Spanish in *Revista Iberoamericana* under "Discursos mayas y desafíos postcoloniales en Guatemala" (2006). A modified version of the first section of chapter 4, "Rethinking Modernity," appeared in Spanish in *Revista de Estudios Interétnicos* under "Globalización, Pueblos indígenas e identidad cultural en Guatemala" (2006). Finally, the English translation of citations from Spanish texts in this book is my responsibility unless otherwise noted.

Introduction
Globalization, Coloniality, and Social Movements

In January 2000 the Ecuadorian indigenous movement overthrew President Jamil Mahuad. Three years later, in October 2003, Bolivia's Gonzalo Sánchez de Lozada suffered the same fate at the hands of the peasant movement, which has a high incidence of indigenous participation. The Zapatista Army of National Liberation's campaign against the Institutional Revolutionary Party (PRI) in Mexico was a key factor in the PRI's defeat during the 2000 elections, after a little more than seventy years in power. In Guatemala, a month before the last round of elections in 2003, the two presidential candidates, Álvaro Colom and Oscar Berger, were surprised by a mass mobilization in which seventeen Maya organizations demanded "to be included in the administrative structure of the next government."[1] The protestors expressed this demand making reference to other Latin American governments that had fallen as a result of pressure from indigenous peoples. Guatemala's 2007 elections also witnessed the candidacy of Rigoberta Menchú, which, although she did not win, demonstrated the political gains that have been made by Mayas in Guatemala.

In the past few decades, indigenous movements throughout the Americas have become the cornerstone of popular mobilizations. These movements have made their mark in diverse institutional and political landscapes, ranging from public participation in popular protests to participation in the mass media, literature, parliaments, ministries, mayorships, and even a presidency (I refer to Evo Morales in Bolivia). Although this prominence has

1

been considered a recent phenomenon, it is but the latest example of the ongoing creativity of indigenous peoples in their efforts to achieve civil rights and legal recognition as differentiated cultural entities. Their struggle has changed the makeup of Latin American nation-states to the point that these can no longer be conceived in conventional terms, that is, as culturally and linguistically homogenous.

If we are to celebrate these social irruptions in the name of indigenous rights, it is also important to ask ourselves, What are these movements proposing? Where are they directing us to go? Where are these new political and ideological currents situated in relation to the phenomena of globalization and neoliberalism? What kind of nation is being (re)constructed? What social and interethnic relationships do these movements propose to their mestizo (Ladino in the case of Guatemala), criollo,[2] and black counterparts? This book explores these questions by focusing on the emergence and political-cultural implications of Guatemala's Maya movement.

Being of Maya K'iche' ethnicity myself, I am interested in examining the Maya movement's efforts toward revitalizing and affirming indigenous cultures, through a study of the discourses of literature, journalism, testimonial narratives, educational projects, and other cultural texts about or produced by the representatives of the movement. My primary interest lies in exploring how, since the 1970s, indigenous peoples have been challenging established, hegemonic narratives of modernity, history, nation, and cultural identity as these relate to the indigenous world. For the most part, these narratives have been fabricated by non-indigenous writers who have had the power not only to produce and spread knowledge but also to speak for and about the Maya world. I argue that contemporary Maya narratives promote nationalisms based on the reaffirmation of Maya ethnicity and languages that constitute what it means to be Maya in present-day society, as well as political-cultural projects oriented toward the future.

The importance of analyzing the Maya movement and the recent debates surrounding it resides in the fact that the movement offers an opportunity to reflect upon a new relationship between indigenous peoples, the nation-state, and its hegemonic narratives. There is no doubt that the movement has brought about a significant opening in its historic, social, cultural, and epistemological implications. In many cases, however, instead of offering an opportunity for dialogue and intercultural coexistence, this opening has initiated misunderstandings and political anxieties regarding the movement. These cannot be overlooked; they must be clarified. Here, I will reference one particular case.

Charles Hale, for example, reminds us of the October 1992 edition of the Guatemalan magazine *Crónica*, an issue dedicated to Rigoberta Menchú

Tum after she had been awarded the Nobel Peace Prize. The cover title, "Indigenous Power," is followed by the subtitle "What Are Their Objectives? Integration or Division? Revenge or Justice? Peace or Conflict?" (Hale, *Más Que un Indio* 19). It is not difficult to perceive that these questions display a sentiment of anxiety about the prominence achieved by indigenous peoples. It is curious to note that this attitude can be compared to that of white intellectuals in the United States who responded to the continental movement of black revitalization in the 1960s by asking a similar question: What do blacks *want*? Lewis R. Gordon responded to this question by quoting the words of Jean-Paul Sartre in "Black Orpheus," which can also be related to the Maya movement and the anxieties expressed in *Crónica*: "When you removed the gag that was keeping these black mouths shut, what were you hoping for? That they would sing you praises? Did you think that when they raised themselves up again, you would read adoration in the eyes of these that our fathers had forced to bend down to the very ground?" (38).

To what extent do we find "praises" of and "adoration" for whites, criollos, and Ladinos in Maya discourses? To what extent does the Maya movement seek a kind of "vengeance" against those who have "forced" Mayas "to bend down to the very ground"? It must be said at the outset that, in effect, certain confrontational indigenous discourses go so far as to propose a nationalism that epistemologically places the other in a position of subalternity. Equally, there are more moderate revolutionary narratives of cultural revitalization, as well as those that, despite recognizing a Maya locus of enunciation, opt for an elitist, neoliberal Mayacentrism that excludes populations in conditions of subalternity. The primary intent of this book is to examine the texts of the Maya movement's intellectuals in the context of the debates the movement has generated. I also compare these texts with the words of those who have considered themselves lettered authorities in representing the indigenous world. I suggest that focusing on these debates will enable us to understand what the movement is responding to. More important, this will demystify anxieties and skepticism about the indigenous world and its proposals, helping us to appreciate its contradictions, ambiguities, and material and ideological contributions to the Guatemalan nation.

In general terms, the emergence of the Maya movement is the result of a long political struggle that, to the present, has coincided with a period of profound, generalized economic crisis and the failure of the models of development of the Guatemalan nation-state. According to Demetrio Cojtí (*Configuración; El movimiento*)[3]—a member of the movement and one of its most widely recognized intellectuals—the movement began in the 1970s as the result of significant events. Cojtí mentions, among other factors, the participation of Mayas in the Guatemalan armed struggle (1960–1996); the progressive awakening of the rural sector, leading to the emergence of the Committee of Peasant Unity (CUC) in 1978; and the decision of a group of educated intellectuals—schoolteachers, health promoters, doctors, lawyers, notaries, and the like—to reaffirm their cultural identity and history from a Maya perspective. Also, experiences of economic and ethnic inequality generated the need to change indigenous peoples' material conditions of existence. For Cojtí, these processes challenged the nation-state to assert "the recognition of the Maya as a Nation or a People…and propose solutions and means to achieve such recognition" (*Configuración* 45). In this context, the movement has responded to a colonial situation based on oppression, racism, exploitation, and marginality. Its primary objective is, obviously, to change the structures of the nation-state, proposing a new model that acknowledges the Maya as a political and differentiated cultural entity.

From the time of the movement's consolidation in the 1990s, it has pursued many objectives. For example, it has actively worked in favor of human rights, especially cultural rights, since the end of the 1970s; it has stimulated national and continental debates about the 500th anniversary of the so-called discovery of the "New World"; since 1991 it has advocated a continental campaign called "500 Years of Indigenous, Black, and Popular Resistance"; it has consolidated the world leadership assumed by the Nobel Peace Prize winner Rigoberta Menchú Tum, who in the last elections ran for president of the country; it has institutionalized the declaration of the International Year of the Indigenous Peoples initiated by the United Nations in 1993, and this declaration, in turn, served as grounds for the ratification of the Agreement 169 on the Indigenous and Tribal Peoples of the International Labor Organization (ILO); and in March 1995 it achieved the consolidation of the Accord on Identity and the Rights of Indigenous Peoples that was later ratified with the Peace Accord Agreement signed in 1996 between the Guatemalan National Revolutionary Unity (URNG) and the government, putting an end to Guatemala's thirty-six-year civil war.[4]

The movement has gradually developed two ideological tendencies representing two complementary and, at times, contradictory paths. The first of these tendencies has been defined by some as the Maya cultural rights group (*Maya culturales*). This group is composed of Maya intellectuals (the majority of whom are professionals) and indigenous organizations that prioritize an ethnic adscription and the vindication of indigenous cultural specificities. For instance, the group advocates the revitalization of a Maya (not "Indian") identity, Maya *traje* (traditional dress), and indigenous languages and religion. The primary objectives are to explore and question racism and to elaborate pedagogical materials that emphasize the affirmation of indigenous cultural identity and history. The group's organizations include the Academy of Maya Languages of Guatemala (ALMG), an institution that has produced dictionaries and grammars in Maya languages, and the Association of Maya Writers of Guatemala (AEMG), which has produced didactic materials and educational curricula relevant to Maya culture.

The other tendency can be identified as the Maya popular rights group (*Maya populares*). According to some scholars, this group understands "Guatemalan society in terms of class" and "assume[s] the indigenous identity as secondary" (Bastos and Camus, *Abriendo caminos* 29). Rather than focus political efforts on cultural demands, these intellectuals and organizations denounce the effects of the violence—past and present—against rural and urban communities (Maya and non-Maya). Their members include widows, relatives of the disappeared, people displaced by the civil war, refugees, and communities in resistance that question the nation-state's violation of human rights (Bastos and Camus, *Abriendo caminos* 27–28). Their organizations include the aforementioned CUC and the National Coordination of Guatemalan Widows (CONAVIGUA).

The two groups of the Maya movement have experienced tensions and even rupture, especially after the 2000 elections, which were won by the Guatemalan Republican Front (FRG). To illustrate, in that year certain Maya intellectuals decided to accept jobs in some of the official party's institutions. One of these was Demetrio Cojtí. Until that time, he had engaged in denouncing the politics of genocide against the Maya population during the civil war and had rigorously questioned the Guatemalan nation-state, which he saw as sheltering the structures of internal colonialism. Cojtí's credibility and the confidence he had earned fell apart.[5] It was not so much his decision to become part of the government that caused controversy, but rather that he chose to become part of a government that housed "General" Efraín Ríos Montt as one of its leaders. Ríos Montt is a general who held the Guatemalan presidency during a short period from 1982 to 1983. In the recently ended civil war, his government perpetrated some of the worst massacres against the country's rural population, specifically the Maya, the most affected by the war. The general attempted to return to power in the 2003 elections, running for the presidency, but failed, in great measure because of a campaign of civic consciousness-raising led by Rigoberta Menchú.

Menchú initiated a project called "We Are Guatemala" (a slogan countering that of Ríos Montt, "I Am Guatemala") to promote the vote against the general. On one occasion, the Maya K'iche' activist was attacked for bringing a lawsuit in the Guatemalan Constitutional Court against the general, accusing him of racism and genocide. After this incident, many Mayas questioned the morality of intellectuals like Cojtí who became part of the FRG.

The late activist Amanda Pop, in a letter titled "What will you do now, Dr. Cojtí?" ("¿Qué hará doctor Cojti?"), asked him, "You, who for many years dedicated yourself to denounce and write about the racism that we Mayas suffer, what will you do in protest against the violent racist attack of the official party [the FRG] against our sister Dr. Rigoberta Menchú and, consequently, against our people?"

By seeing the tensions within the Maya movement, we can notice the ambiguities in and contradictions between its "cultural" and "popular" tendencies. These insights demystify many of the perspectives—at times overly celebratory—on the Maya movement, pushing both its members and scholars to rethink it and understand it in ideological and political terms. By focusing on some of the debates that the movement has generated, this book explores the political complexities in Guatemala's reconfiguration as a multilingual, multiethnic, multinational country. While recognizing the similarities and differences between cultural and popular Mayas, this book also extends, broadens, and works with the notion of "indigenous movement" developed by Maya Pérez Ruíz. She proposes that a movement is not a well-defined and delimited entity, but rather a project that stems from an entire political process in which one sees the convergence and involvement of organizations of varying hierarchy and trajectory. Leaders and advisers, in an individual way or through their own organizations, participate with their own distinct orientations. A social movement

> should [not] be understood as a predetermined essence, but as something that is forged as a product of complex internal processes of interaction and negotiation, in which decisions are made, leaderships and interests confront one another, and diverse modes and forms of communication and participation are at stake.... It is generated in conflict and interaction with adversaries, competitors, and even allies who, in large measure, contribute to define the field of opportunities.[6] (Pérez Ruíz 277–78)

In this same vein, I do not assume that the "Maya movement" denotes a series of analogous ideological and political objectives and aspirations, nor do I suggest that all of the movement's intellectuals fully coincide in their causes and goals. It is worth mentioning that the Maya nationalisms I study here derive from a concrete reality: the recognition of a colonial condition and the quest to realize indigenous peoples' historical demands. Nonetheless, Maya intellectuals approach these problems in diverse ways and in diverse fields, many times taking directions that produce tensions, as Cojtí did.

When I speak about Maya nationalisms, I refer to how indigenous intellectuals are not only reimagining Guatemala but also developing proposals and political strategies to reconstruct the nation within and outside the indigenous movement. The debates I study and the existent tensions that emerge from these, in one way or another, make reference precisely to an unfinished colonial experience and the efforts to eradicate that experience *via* nationalist discourses. These nationalisms operate, as Partha Chatterjee would argue (42), within a structure of knowledge derived from Europe and appropriated specifically to repudiate colonialism and propose a new national order. In the case of the Maya, this means materializing a recognition and place within the structures of the nation-state and modernity. Thus, their voices and activism can pave the way for a future in which their prominence and their differences (languages, cultural specificities, spirituality) acquire a dignity that has not been recognized, a future in which they become part of the decision making of the nation. But if we recognize this project's breadth and ambition, then, upon close examination of the practices and local proposals of Maya intellectuals, we will find similarities, contradictions, and ambiguities regarding their nationalisms. For example, de Lión's radical project of mayanization is different from but complements that of Menchú's; in turn, these two projects contradict those of Maya intellectuals such as Estuardo Zapeta and Cojtí. I consider it important not only to analyze the relation between those who defy Maya nationalist proposals but also to consider the nationalist contradictions within the indigenous movement itself.

Critics, for the most part foreign, have acknowledged the complexity that any study of the Maya movement represents. First, in general terms, most of the existing bibliography highlights the historical context of the Maya movement and the growth of an influential Maya intellectual class with a nationalist authority since the post-war period.[7] Second, these studies explore the challenges that Mayas face in a new age of economic and cultural modernization, as well as the tensions and contradictions between Maya culturales and populares. Third, they emphasize the movement's efforts to revitalize languages, Maya dress, and political self-determination. Some scholars have even questioned the movement's exclusion of Maya women from its organizations, its reluctance to encourage their participation. Others have been concerned that Maya intellectuals put too much emphasis on cultural aspects while neglecting issues of race and class and, in doing so, recycle capitalist systems of oppression.

Despite these valuable contributions, I feel that certain gaps need to be filled. Although these studies concentrate on the post-war period and question fundamental aspects ignored within the movement itself, I feel that they still privilege the movement's demands and politics of cultural and linguistic revitalization without giving enough attention to the reproduction of existing relations of power, nor the political-institutional order that continues to recycle a normative and cultural frame of colonialism and coloniality. In other words, I feel that these studies lack a rigorous questioning of modernity—now called globalization—and its intimate relationship with epistemologies that continue legitimating colonialism and coloniality to maintain a hegemonic status quo. My project aims to complement and engage the studies outlined above, by focusing on the challenges that the movement faces in its efforts to eradicate its condition of subalternity through nationalisms that rethink Guatemala in its cultural, political, and economic dimensions.

This book departs from understanding the category of "modernity" as an institution that presupposes and shelters a colonial order in relation to the American continent. Following critics and theorists who have focused on the theme of colonialism and coloniality,[8] I depart from the assumption that globalization is a process that has reproduced and developed more sophisticated forms of financial, commercial, communicative, and informational domination over the realities of the so-called Third World.[9] Through the expropriation of resources, military and political hegemony, and the institutional control of local economies, modernity has as its dark side coloniality (Mignolo, *The Darker Side*; *Local Histories*). Because discussions of colonialism and rigorous interrogations of categories like "modernity," "development," "hegemony," and "nation" as colonial constructions are evident in the textual production of Maya discourses, I situate the debates surrounding the movement within the political and epistemological context of what the Peruvian sociologist Aníbal Quijano and, later, Walter Mignolo (*The Darker Side*; *Local Histories*) have called the "coloniality of power."

Quijano and Mignolo explore the forms by which the West and its agents have constituted a model of power that, at present, is globally hegemonic. This model supposes that, despite the end of "colonialism" as a formal political system, coloniality "has not stopped being the central character of contemporary social power" (Quijano, "'Raza,' 'etnia' y 'nación'" 168). The hegemony of dominant groups, according to Quijano, continues being legitimated through coloniality. Sustaining this are Eurocentrism and the idea of race—the supposed structural, biological difference that places the "Indian," the "black," and the "yellow" races in a natural situation of inferiority to their "white" counterparts. Quijano argues that, alongside colonialism, another conquest has taken place: the "colonization of the imagination of the dominated" ("Coloniality and Modernity/Rationality" 169). Through the expropriation of knowledge and through the repression of modes of signification, social structure, modes of knowing, and the production of knowledge, this coloniality imposed "the rulers' own patterns of expression, and of their beliefs and images with reference to the supernatural. These beliefs and images served not only to impede the cultural production of the dominated, but also as a very efficient means of social and cultural control" (Quijano, "Coloniality" 169). This hierarchical articulation and imposition of power are what Quijano calls the coloniality of power; it characterizes the other face of colonialism (military campaigns, genocide, the plunder of lands). In a "peaceful way," it has served to legitimate a structured control of the workforce, natural resources, and products, based on capitalism and the global market. These models were imposed on all structures of control and material production and reciprocity in existence before the conquest of America (Quijano, "Coloniality" 534).

According to Quijano, the category of the coloniality of power operates through a classification and reclassification of the world's populations, established by institutions with the capacity to articulate and codify meaning and knowledge. The state, the church, the media, and the school, among others, impose a Eurocentric epistemology on dominated populations in order to define peoples, territories, and spaces according to the political, ideological, and economic objectives of the dominant groups. For instance, the conquest of the Americas and the consequent creation of the viceroyalties initiated the first phase of the coloniality of power. The introduction of the alphabet and writing constituted the first exercise of domination, serving as the basis for administering and classifying the territories and the First Peoples of the "New World." The first guidelines of this process are revealed by Christopher Columbus. Believing that he had arrived in India and justifying his authority in the name of the sword and the cross, Columbus culturally defined the first populations of the Americas as "Indians." From that moment on, the diverse peoples of the "New World" were incarcerated within this discursive construction that was conceived a priori.[10] For centuries, it has kept indigenous peoples in a condition of subalternity.[11] Equally, the "new" territories, even when recognized as having been named already by native populations, received different names in order to become part of the Spanish Empire. For example, Columbus mentioned the following when writing to the Spanish king and queen: "'this [island] of San Salvador' (October 14); 'this [island] which I named Santa María de la Concepción' (October 15); 'which I named Fernandina' (October 15); 'which I named Isabela' (October 19)" (quoted in Lienhard, La voz 40).

The same colonial attitude of "naming" the First Peoples and territories was adopted with even bloodier violence by the conquistadores who came after the admiral. No one better illustrates these experiences than Bernal Díaz del Castillo. In describing Hernán Cortés and the storming of Tabasco, in what today is México, he writes:

> *Cortés, having thus made himself master of the town, took formal possession of it for the crown of Castile. He gave three cuts with his sword on a large ceiba tree, which grew in the place, and proclaimed aloud, that he took possession of the city in the name and behalf of the Catholic sovereigns, and would maintain and defend the same with sword and buckler against all who should gainsay it. The same vaunting declaration was also made by the soldiers, and the whole was duly recorded and attested by the notary. This was the usual simple, but chivalric, form with which the Spanish cavaliers asserted the royal title to the conquered territories in the New World. It was a good title, doubtless, against the claims of any other European potentate.* (Prescott, History 264–65)

As can be seen, the attitudes and actions of the admiral, as much as those who followed him, suppressed an entire series of knowledges that were previously held about this "New World." Thus begins a colonial and epistemological violence that, along with new illnesses, the exploitation of labor, and the theft of lands, "organizes the totality of space and time—all cultures, peoples, and territories on the planet, past and present—in a great universal [European] narrative" (Lander, "Modernidad, colonialidad" 84).[12]

The imposition of the Latin alphabet elaborated an epistemology that spread and legitimated the first Spanish imperial enterprise. Language and writing—"the companions of empire," according to Antonio Nebrija (i)— gave Spaniards the power to divide the "Indians" racially and territorially through documents that derived their legitimacy from "God" and the king and queen. In this way, writing constituted an institution that disseminated an epistemology affirming Spain as the culturally dominant power in the native imaginary. Spain imposed its values and norms on indigenous peoples' forms of social cohesion, knowledges, and forms of writing. What the "Indians" offered culturally (in the broadest sense of the word) was inferior because it lacked the supposedly "universal" legitimacy of Spanish values and written documents.

For Quijano, the second phase of the coloniality of power takes place in the nineteenth century when England and France established their hegemony on a global scale. The "independence" of Spanish America from Spain enabled these centers of power to spread the cultural categories already established in the first phase by the agents of "civilization" in the Americas: the criollos. In the second phase, cultural categories such as "Indian," "race," "nation," and "ethnicity" were reconfigured to create a new epistemology that divided and affirmed the hegemony of these centers of power as places where scientific knowledge was privileged. Here, the well-known dichotomy of civilization/barbarism, spread by Domingo Faustino Sarmiento (*Facundo*), legitimized a cultural and civilizing project based on the promotion of Europeans immigrating to Argentina, as well as the extermination of indigenous peoples and blacks who did not convert to "civilized" subjects.

With the category of the coloniality of power, then, Quijano and Mignolo guide us toward studies that examine relations of power (cultural, economic, racial/ethnic, gender) and the diverse epistemological mechanisms of establishing and maintaining hegemony used by institutions to recycle the elements of colonialism. That is, the idea of the coloniality of power continues to determine the relationship between hegemonic institutions and peoples in conditions of subalternity. Today's indigenous cultures, for example, still serve as "objects of study," whereas the West serves as the "authority" that produces concepts to categorize these objects of study. The coloniality of power also exposes the fact that Latin American modernity and nation-states, as well as their institutions, perpetuate Eurocentric colonial legacies. Starting from the dark side of modernity contributes to the elaboration of discussions that force a confrontation with the colonial experience and the relevance of this experience to indigenous peoples in Latin America. This is especially true today as the United States leads a new Western hegemonic expansion: that is, the West continues to superimpose the universal and economic "narrative" that seeks to absorb subaltern peoples into a hegemonic system based on the Universalist narrative of Europe.

If the coloniality of power is modernity's dark side, then how is this being resisted or recycled? How does the Maya movement propose to alter the established narratives of the nation, citizenship, and modernity? What do Mayas propose as means of overcoming the adversity represented in the coloniality of power? These are precisely the questions that this project focuses on and problematizes by analyzing the ongoing debates between Mayas and non-Mayas. My contention is that any discussion involving indigenous peoples and the ideas of "modernity," "nation," or "citizenship" as referents must confront the coloniality of power in order to reconceptualize such categories. Within these epistemological territories, we encounter not only the diverse ideological and political objectives of indigenous rights movements but also, most important, an immanent battle and debate about competing national imaginaries. I feel that an examination of these discussions reveals unresolved tensions that will allow us to reflect upon possible paths to follow in forming an intercultural Guatemalan nation-state.

Some readers might argue that beginning with these unresolved tensions implies advocating a "division" based on differences. However, would not turning the page on modern Guatemalan history be an act that consciously or unconsciously supports racism and the marginalization of indigenous peoples? Is that not a way of continuing to divide Guatemala?

I feel that departing from these tensions and conflictive intercultural relations is precisely the first step in the creation of a more fruitful, interethnic dialogue. In this sense, my book echoes the sentiment of Gerald Graff when he says that instead of evading conflicts, we should confront and discuss them ("Teach the Conflicts" 58).

This book is divided into two parts. The first (chapters 2 and 3) deals with questions of literature and *testimonio*. During the recently ended civil war in Guatemala, a large number of Mayas participated in the armed struggle. However, we know little about what this struggle meant to the indigenous population. My focus here is the category of "revolution." I hypothesize that the objective of the "revolution" for Mayas, more than replacing the government, was their own "national liberation" (Fanon, *The Wretched of the Earth*), as well as the decolonization of Maya culture, subjectivity, and knowledges. In this first part, I primarily examine the works of the first Maya Kaqchikel writer, Luis de Lión (chapter 2), and his efforts to disarticulate previous representations of Mayas in literature authored by non-indigenous writers. I pay particular attention to his novel, *El tiempo principia en Xibalbá* (Time Begins in Xibalbá), his dialogue with the Nobel Prize novelist Miguel Ángel Asturias, and his narrative construction of an alternative Maya nationalism. Chapter 3 focuses on Rigoberta Menchú. First, I examine the debates about the "veracity" of her testimonio, *I, Rigoberta Menchú* (Menchú and Burgos), generated by David Stoll's *Rigoberta Menchú and the Story of All Poor Guatemalans*. Then, I focus on Menchú's second book, *Crossing Borders*, and explore her efforts to promote interculturality through human and civil rights activism in Guatemala and internationally.

The second part (chapters 4 and 5) revolves around discussions on modernity and identity politics. Chapter 4 examines the "intercultural" or "interethnic" debate in Guatemala over the past two decades. Through an examination of Mario Roberto Morales's *La articulación de las diferencias* (The Articulation of Differences) and Estuardo Zapeta's *Las huellas de B'alam* (The Jaguar's Footprints), I show how emerging Maya and non-Maya discourses postulate a new, multicultural Guatemalan identity that can better embrace the challenges of a global order. I point out some of the limitations in these perspectives and offer alternative reflections, especially regarding (inter)cultural identity.

Finally, I turn to the question of education in Guatemala (chapter 5). For many reasons, education has become the practical, concrete way to carry out a project of interculturality that promotes indigenous perspectives and languages in our country. In 2002 the Guatemalan Ministry of Education began an educational campaign to teach Maya languages in various kindergarten and elementary public schools in rural and urban areas.

First, I provide a historical context for the discourse of education in Guatemala and its relationship to indigenous peoples. Then, I examine the new Diseño de reforma educativa (Educational Reform Design) of 1998, outlining the specific objectives of the previous and current discourses on education in Guatemala. Some basic questions I explore are, Does the new intercultural program demystify or reproduce the role of public schools in the production of the "ideal" Guatemalan citizen (for example, a citizen who is linguistically and culturally homogenous) for the globalized era? How are other identities consigned to or rescued from the margins? What kind of "nation" or "intercultural citizenship" is being projected for Guatemala?

Before proceeding, I should clarify a few things. I am familiar with the debates on postcolonialism in Latin America and elsewhere.[13] I make use of the concept "postcolonial" to converse with those who have questioned and analyzed "European territorial conquests, the various institutions of European colonialisms, the discursive operations of empire, the subtleties of subject construction in colonial discourse and the resistance of those subjects, and, most importantly perhaps, the differing responses to such incursions and their contemporary colonial legacies in both pre- and post-independence nations and communities" (Ashcroft, Griffiths, and Tiffin, Post-Colonial Studies: Key Concepts 187). I feel that postcolonial and subaltern studies have best problematized the category of "culture" and the ways in which culture has been used to develop a politics destined to marginalize Maya, even when these politics are well intentioned. In referring to "Maya nationalisms" with regards to the postcolonial, I hope to create and locate epistemological and political spaces in which to question and counteract the identities imposed upon the "dominated." Not only do I contest the existing and historic deformations and distortions of Maya cultures, but also I clarify the economic policies that have maintained their subalternity.

I should also point out that I acknowledge the "essentialism" into which I might fall in referring to the "West," "Europe," and "Ladino" as categories. I understand that many subjects feel (and will feel) interpellated. I do not suggest that the West, Europe, and Ladinos are locations and identities in which all the world's evils are situated, but rather I attack Eurocentrism as a fundamental principle legitimating the domination of indigenous peoples. By making these references, my aim is to center a history of colonialism and the coloniality of power, which have not ended for indigenous peoples. At the same time, to begin with the debates that the Maya movement has spawned situates current conflicts and tensions within a broad historical context that reveals the movement's transformations from the colonial period to the present. As Robert Stam observes, a critique of the "West," in itself, seeks to expose "Europe's historically oppressive relation to its internal and external others" (193). Such a critique also can criticize "the assumption of a 'natural' European right to dominate others, whether through force, as in colonial times, or through domineering financial institutions and ethnocentric media, as in the present" (193). Eurocentrism is not a political position that is consciously assumed by anyone. No one announces himself as "Eurocentric." On the contrary, Eurocentrism is an implied ideology that needs elucidating, a pattern to which even some Mayas have fallen prey. From this derives the importance I find in the category of the coloniality of power; it is a theoretical framework that invites reflection on discourses that, consciously or unconsciously, have recycled these ideologies and attitudes.

Maya discourses and nationalisms, especially those that assign a capital role to Maya cosmovision (chapters 2 and 3), are situated in a new epistemological and political field that enables alternatives to a project of modernity that recycles the coloniality of power, as well as a critical perspective on this. For the most part, some of these discourses can be understood as a search for what Dipesh Chakrabarty calls "provincializing Europe." With this notion, Chakrabarty seeks to construct "a politics and Project of Alliance between the dominant metropolitan histories and the subaltern peripheral pasts" (42). One strategy that the Indian thinker proposes is to counteract notions of European modernity and historicity by inscribing in the history of modernity "the ambivalences, contradictions, the use of force, and the tragedies and ironies that attend it" (43) and also "other narratives of human connections that draw sustenance from dreamed-up pasts and futures where collectivities are defined neither by the rituals of citizenship nor by the nightmare of 'tradition' that 'modernity' creates" (46).

As I will make clear, the movement's epistemological and political perspectives and contributions to the project of "provincializing Europe" are situated precisely within the effort to materialize "a project from subalternity" (Guha, *Elementary Aspects*) based on Maya cosmovision. Despite the diverse meanings and even lack of meaning that this notion has acquired for some,[14] I use the term *Maya cosmovision* to refer to the use that intellectuals, writers, activists, and indigenous and non-indigenous subjects have made of the sacred K'iche' texts, *Popol Wuj*, with the goal of rearticulating a political and epistemological locus of enunciation against anything that threatens the values and struggles of indigenous peoples. That is, the reconceptualization of *Maya cosmovision* seeks to reference ancestral values in order to articulate them in the present, thus maintaining vital aspects of indigenous communities such as language, spirituality, and dress. Furthermore, this cosmovision demonstrates indigenous people's intimate relationship with Mother Earth and Mother Nature, their defense of these, their value of the community and the collective over the individual and competition, and, finally, their articulation of the histories of the sacred texts to show not only a historical and cultural epistemological connection but also a simultaneous cohesion between the past, the present, and the future of Maya peoples.

Centralizing the role of Maya cosmovision also implies centering the important role that interculturality plays in these reflections.[15] As chapter 4 makes apparent, speaking of interculturality brings up contradictions: at times, we fall into the trap of recycling the coloniality of power. This becomes especially clear in the second part of the book, where you will see how "interculturality" acquires diverse connotations, depending on who is talking about it. In some cases, the intellectuals in the interethnic debate merely end up proposing an intercultural perspective that is intimately related to neoliberal multiculturalism.[16] My goal, especially in the second part of the book, is to problematize the discussions on interculturality between Mayas and non-Mayas to clarify the contradictions, tensions, and limitations of this category with regard to the themes of nation, citizenship, and modernity in Guatemala. These facets of the debate elucidate what is at stake in the discussion on interethnic politics. Highlighting these enables us to recognize those Maya discourses that originate from a subaltern locus of enunciation. We can then propose a *politics of the possible*, that is, approaches and dialogues for an intercultural national formation and coexistence.

Another clarification I should make has to do with the categories of "Indian" and "indigenous" employed in this book. I am aware of the colonial precedents that these categories imply, as well as the efforts on the part of indigenous movements to reconceptualize cultural signifiers like "Maya," "Aymara," and "Quechua" in order to affirm their respective identities. When I use categories like "Indian" and "indigenous" in this book, I do so in a spirit similar to that of Frantz Fanon in his use of the category "black" (*Black Skin, White Masks* 109–40). Fanon recognized the potential of inverting and rearticulating this category in a positive way to establish an epistemological, political, and differentiated locus of enunciation. We find this same spirit in Menchú when she uses the category "Indian" in order to invert it. According to her, being Indian represents a permanent, anticolonial, antiracist struggle and ancestral values: "I am proud of my roots. I feel that I am a granddaughter of the Mayas, and I am proud of what the term 'Indian' means to us" (Yáñez 98). Sometimes, I put the category in quotation marks to indicate a pejorative use, but for the most part, it holds the positive value attributed to it by Menchú.

The reader familiar with the Maya movement in Guatemala will wonder about the absence of other key intellectuals participating in the country's current interethnic debates. Among these are Humberto Ak'abal, Víctor

Montejo, Luis Enrique Sam Colop, Gaspar Pedro Gonzáles, Rosalina Tuyuc, Irma Alicia Velázquez Nimatuj, Maya Cú Choc, Arturo Arias, and Rigoberto Juárez Paz. My aim is not to present new literary faces,[17] nor to shed light on Maya and non-Maya politics in a Guatemalan context, nor, even less, to open up a discussion about more well-known Maya and non-Maya intellectuals. Nor am I suggesting that I do not consider their activism and texts substantial in the national interethnic debate. There is no doubt that these intellectuals have made valuable contributions to the formulation of Guatemalan interculturality, and they have certainly developed sound criticism toward eradicating racism and political exclusion. One incident in particular, involving Humberto Ak'abal, attests to their participation in the interethnic debate.[18] In the present study, however, I have selected texts that, according to my criteria, stress those elements of the movement that are more militantly nationalist, because they demonstrate ongoing tensions about cultural identity, modernity, and the colonial experience in the country. The discussions upon which I focus here do not represent *all* Mayas and Ladinos in Guatemala. Rather, they best represent the unresolved tensions that have prevented (and continue preventing) the construction of a truly intercultural project.[19]

One limitation of this book is that it does not center on the role of the country's Xinka and Garífuna populations.[20] From the Maya perspectives studied here, especially in the first part, I hope to at least open up the possibility of a dialogue not only with Ladinos but also with Xinkas and Garífunas, who, I imagine, have much to say about their experiences of colonialism and the coloniality of power. In general, I would venture to say that, like the Maya, they would agree with questioning the state's repressive and ideological apparatuses. As with the Maya, the Xinka and Garífuna have been perceived and interpreted from Eurocentric perspectives, their material conditions of existence and their cultures measured by the signifiers of "civilization" and "modernity."

My foremost objective resides in proposing Maya-ness as an alternative locus of enunciation for Guatemala. I present the challenge of constructing an epistemological, political axis that destabilizes the presently constituted hegemonic systems of knowledge and classification established around categories that still presuppose elements of colonialism. More important, I seek to situate Maya-ness as a space that allows the construction of a more inclusive and democratic nation-state.

For some readers, my use of a Maya "we" in this book might seem paradoxical or contradictory. Despite being "outside" my national and communal environment, I speak from an indigenous locus of enunciation, and I identify with a history of anticolonial and antiracist struggle. For me, this development of an anticolonial and antiracist consciousness has involved a return to and reclamation of a cultural identity that was denied to me in my childhood—by a system of values that, instead of reaffirming my indigenous subjectivity, taught me to hate and even destroy it. Part of my adolescence was spent negating my past and ethnic origin. But later, after sharing struggles, books, and discussions about my ancestral past, the Western values were inverted and defied, making my voyage (and, in large measure, this project) something very personal. This book expresses a favorable point of view on the Maya movement. Writing it has involved my sensibilities and affectivities toward the indigenous world. From these, I think, act, and articulate my reflections in order to respond to that history of marginalization, racism, and exploitation, as well as to the struggle to eradicate these. I yearn for a better future for "we" Maya and also for a subaltern "we" in general. By this, I do not want to imply that I am holding back any criticism I might have of the movement. On the contrary, despite an understanding that this project is the fruit of specific and legitimate historical demands, there is also a necessity to analyze and question the movement's causes and the alternatives it offers—not to undermine the movement, but in the spirit of animating a more global, critical debate that favors an indigenous "we" and a multiethnic, multicultural collective as well.

This project is the result of three periods of research about Maya education, social movements, and political activism for human rights over the past decade in Guatemala and in Chiapas, in southern Mexico. This project became more clearly defined in 2002, when I took an eight-month research leave from the Department of Hispanic Languages and Literatures at the University of Pittsburgh, where I did my doctoral work. I participated in various workshops on indigenous and popular education and human rights in San Cristóbal de las Casas, Chiapas. In addition, I did volunteer work in Cómitan, Chiapas, with Education for Peace (Edupaz), an organization founded by the diocese of San Cristóbal de las Casas. On these occasions, I had the opportunity to work with various Maya communities on projects promoting self-sufficiency, cultural and linguistic revitalization, and peaceful solutions to conflict. My conclusions here reflect these activities, as well as additional research that resulted in my doctoral dissertation. Many of the thoughts developed in that project have been expanded, even re-elaborated. The end result is this book.

Finally, being Maya, I feel that this project is important simply because it seeks to overcome the prejudices, anxieties, and fears of class and ethnicity, in order to promote a dialogue about interculturality and the historical problems and challenges that indigenous peoples have confronted in the era of globalization. I hope that my reflections contribute to such a dialogue.

Part One

2 From the "Indian" as a Problem to the Indian as a Political and Social Agent
A First Light of the Maya Movement

Decolonization…continues to be an act of confrontation with a hegemonic system of thought; it is hence a process of considerable historical and cultural liberation. As such, decolonization becomes the contestation of all dominant forms and structures whether they be linguistic, discursive, or ideological. Moreover, decolonization comes to be understood as an act of exorcism for both the colonized and the colonizer. For both parties it must be a process of liberation; from dependency, in the case of the colonized, and from imperialist, racist perceptions, representations, and institutions which, unfortunately, remain with us to this very day, in the case of the colonizer…. Decolonization can only be complete when it is understood as a complex process that involves both the colonizer and the colonized.

—*Samia Nehrez, quoted in* Black Looks: Race and Representation *by bell hooks*

For the past five hundred years in so-called Latin America, the indigenous world has been interpreted and represented as an object of study under a gaze all too often lazy, at best. This representation of the "Indian" and the Indian's sociocultural environment has been fabricated in his absence, an absence due to (among other things) his limited access to the means of representation, such as literature, theory, and mass media. In the past few years, these cultural appropriations have resulted in a tension between what indigenous peoples say about themselves and what other people say and write about them (Attwood and Arnold ii; Beckett 205). In literature, through what is known as *indigenismo* or *indigenista* discourse, the Latin American intelligentsia elaborated a conceptual and theoretical frame that grounded the category of the Indian. Later, indigenismo informed specific policies that—instead of honoring the Indian's rights, languages, and political demands—collaborate, consciously or unconsciously, in maintaining a politics of domination over indigenous peoples. This literary discursivity proceeds from the 1889 publication of *Aves sin nido* (Birds without a Nest), by the Peruvian novelist Clorinda Matto de Turner (Cornejo Polar, *La novela peruana* 11). Among its most notable characteristics is that indigenismo has been written, for the most part, by non-indigenous authors.[1] Many of these writers have never experienced the racism, political marginalization, and exploitation that the Indian has lived, despite their sympathy for the Indian's condition of existence—in some cases, a sympathy that goes so far as to be paternalistic. Contemplating indigenous reality from the outside, they pretend to understand it as well as, and at times even better than, Indians themselves understand it. Furthermore, indigenista writers have defined the indigenous world as a "problem" to be resolved. The cultural and linguistic specificities of our communities have been seen as obstacles to the desired dream of modernity, which requires eradicating those specificities in order to materialize it. As a solution to the "Indian problem," *mestizaje* has been proposed as an ideology that can, supposedly, redeem the Indian and also spread the idea of a nationally, culturally, and linguistically homogenous subjectivity.

Another characteristic of indigenismo is that it has represented the indigenous world as frozen in time, uncivilized, premodern. For example, the Mexican Revolution (1910–1917) provoked a cultural explosion that sought to redefine Mexico's "national soul" by reclaiming its pre-Columbian origins. In this "recuperation" of the indigenous past, we are presented with harmonious images and a world suspended in time, reminding us of what Johannes Fabian calls the "negation of coevalness": "a persistent and systematic tendency to place the referent of anthropology [or literature] in a time [space] other than that of the present of the producer of anthropological [literary] discourse" (*Time and the Other* 31).[2] In short, this literature, together with the social sciences, has created the illusion that Indians are not contemporaneous with the present or with modernity, but rather with the past. The greatest problem is that these representations, while idealizing and admiring the pre-Columbian past, look down upon the Indians of the present as "barbarous," "uncivilized," or "traditional" subjects.

Finally, indigenista literature has represented the Indian as a subject incapable of agency. Alcides Arguedas, in his book *Pueblo enfermo* (Sick People)—a revealing title—writes that the indigenous "race" is "submissive, fatalistic, sad, enduring a vile subservience without complaint" (57). He later adds that Indians are an exhausted race, "fallen, and worn out physically and morally, incapable of perpetrating any violent vindication of its rights, having given itself over to alcoholism in an alarming way" (65–66). Miguel Ángel Asturias echoes Arguedas when, more than a decade later in his master's thesis, he writes about the Indian's supposed psychic decline: "from the time when he was the indomitable race that died or fled to the mountains in its majority rather than surrender, or bravely fought unequaled heroic battles for his independence, to the condition he is found in today: yesterday courageous, today cowardly" (*Guatemalan Sociology: The Social Problem of the Indian* 91).[3]

Although Asturias would change his perspective to align more with a political ideology proposing to vindicate the Indian through cultural mestizaje, his later literature nonetheless contains similar passages. It is interesting to point out that these authors suggest, besides a lack of agency on the part of the Indian, a resignation to the exploitation and oppression he suffers. As we see in Asturias, this is even attributed to "cowardice" for not acting like the rebel of the past.

Perhaps neither Asturias nor Arguedas could have imagined that in a not too distant future there would be an uprising of indigenous intelligentsia and indigenous militancy. Not only would these events challenge indigenista perspectives and narrative constructions, but they would also reclaim the Indian history and knowledge misappropriated by the other. Imagine the reaction of an indigenous *letrado* (intellectual) familiar with indigenista literature who finds himself confronted by claims to understand his world, or portrayals of it as a problem. What is more, he reads descriptions of himself containing adjectives like "coward," "submissive," "sad," and "fallen," as in the writings of Arguedas and Asturias. What kind of answer could an Indian give to these or similar representations? For some, the answer would be a passionate and angry demand to disarticulate indigenismo and to proclaim the end of mestizo culture.

In this new stage of struggle for the peoples generically called "Indian," what marks *the* difference in the current debates about indigenous issues is their own participation as mediators of collective demands in academic and intellectual terrains. "Indians" must revisit and debate indigenismo because this discursivity has occupied an extremely important space in the colonial order. It has reduced the agency of Indians as historical and political actors, and the knowledge constructed through this discourse has misrepresented their realities, necessities, and demands. Many times, other dominant groups have used this "knowledge" to justify hegemonic control over these populations. Strictly speaking, much of the knowledge concerning the "Indian" is still dependent on indigenista representations racializing the indigenous social body and promoting imaginary worlds. At various historical moments, these narratives have translated into political consequences, influencing policies and governmental practices that have determined Indians' material conditions of existence.[4] Consequently, it would be a mistake to see indigenismo as something that is merely "aesthetic" or confined to the academic environment. Every day, flesh-and-bone "Indians" are being exposed to racism, being excluded politically, being reduced to "objects of study," subjects without history, pictures on postcards, exhibits in museums. Like the notion of orientalism elaborated by Edward Said (*Orientalism* 27–28), indigenismo should be understood as a hegemonic system of theory and practice that has filled the structures of a Latin American national (that is, colonial) order with elements that continue recycling colonialism.[5]

Focusing on literature, in this chapter I show how indigenous peoples have responded to the hegemonic systems that have fabricated their world. I critically examine the literary and militant writings of the Maya Kaqchikel writer Luis de Lión (1939–1984),[6] who, according to some, wrote the first Maya novel in Guatemala, *El tiempo principia en Xibalbá* (Time Begins in Xibalbá).[7] De Lión's poems, stories, and novel are significant because they are among the first epistemological and political manifestations of the Maya movement in Guatemala. Both his life and his work, as I will show, enable us to consider the movement's emergence within the context of the recently ended Guatemalan civil war and to explore the Maya nationalism forged out of this armed struggle.[8] I first consider de Lión's implicit dialogue with Asturias, one of the fathers of modern Guatemalan and Latin American literature. What this dialogue demonstrates is a struggle over the representation of the indigenous world (in the sense of speaking for it) in which the Maya Kaqchikel writer challenges and seeks to disarticulate the indigenista vision in Asturias's representation of the Indian. Any consideration of this dialogue must begin with Asturias's perception of the indigenous world, as well as some of the debates surrounding his works. The first part of this chapter therefore focuses on *Men of Maize* and other, nonliterary texts that demonstrate Asturias's indigenista ideology and his "transculturation" (mestizaje) solution to the "indigenous problem" in Guatemala. In the second section, I concentrate on de Lión and his narrative, beginning with the sociocultural and political contexts in which he lived. My goal is to elucidate the intimate connection between literature and political militancy. De Lión's project is not simply the demystification and disarticulation of indigenismo, but, first and foremost, the articulation of a Maya nationalism as a political alternative for an anticolonial and antiracist struggle in Guatemala.

Asturias: Mestizaje, the Indigenous World, and Interculturality

Men of Maize has many merits. In both its aesthetic and political dimensions, it is one of the most important and revolutionary novels in Latin American literature. It has been characterized as having inaugurated magical realism in Latin America and as setting one of the most significant precedents for the continent's literary boom. The novel has also been said to define the culminating moment of modern Latin American literature's maturity; it is the first writing to suggest that the only hope of safeguarding the continent's chaotic modern civilization resides in the capabilities of hybrid societies (Martin 174–77). I am not so much interested in pointing out and problematizing these merits as in discussing the controversy that has arisen over the past decade about the novel and its representation of the indigenous world. Some of the questions I address are, To what extent can *Men of Maize* be representative of indigenous peoples? To what degree does the work reflect the political demands and aspirations of the Maya? To what degree, as suggested by critics of Asturias's work, does the author transcend the racism that we find in his master's thesis? Problematizing these questions will illustrate how *Men of Maize* reaffirms Ladino consciousness, as well as the indigenista discourse. By bringing up this criticism of Asturias's work, I do not suggest that his textual production and his thought lack merit or should be discarded. On the contrary, I seek to highlight some of the Ladino author's contributions to the interethnic debate in Guatemala—not with regards to his representations of the indigenous world, but rather his criticism of capitalism and his reaffirmation of Ladino subjecthood.

Men of Maize has often been seen as a "vindication" of Indians and even as an "authentic" representation of the Maya. For example, Adelaida Lorand de Olazagasti felt that the work "penetrated" the personality of the Indian, portraying him in a positive light. In her 1968 reading of the novel, she observes that Asturias places himself within the indigenous world, presenting us with "strong Indians, alive, tall, mud lemon color face, with luminous dark hair, teeth of white powdered coconut, *stinking like piston and goat; he smokes and drinks because he is a man. The woman is beautiful with jasmine teeth, plump lips, an erect nose, dimples on her cheeks, smelling like a well"

(Lorand de Olazagasti 105, emphasis added). Far from providing "positive" images, Asturias's novel creates and displays stereotypes. In a 1967 interview with Luis Harss, Asturias acknowledged that his version of the indigenous world, instead of being a vision from within, was an "intuitive and speculative" incursion (Harss and Dohmann 89). This acknowledgment goes hand in hand with his appropriation of the indigenous world in order to promote literary indigenismo and mestizaje to construct a modern Guatemala.

The novel presents the struggle between an indigenous community and Ladino invaders who seek to transform the cultivation of corn into a capitalist enterprise, evoking the general evolution of the conflict between indigenous people and the agents of capitalism, the Ladinos. The novel's vision of indigeneity is strongly influenced by the cosmology revealed in foundational indigenous texts, especially the *Popol Wuj*. Through the use of stories in the K'iche' text, for instance, Asturias depicts the epic vengeance of the indigenous world against its oppressors in the form of curses that lead to the erosion of Ladino ways of life, such as the loss of moral and ethical values. At the same time, the author exalts aspects of Maya culture such as respect for nature and the spirit that maintains ancestral cultural ties.

In its epic representation, however, the novel falls into stereotyping. For example, within an oppressive capitalist system, the indigenous world is reduced to a "primitive" world that represents modernity's counterpart. This often entails constructing this culture as frozen in time and its people, owing to their alienation, as incapable of being political actors. In the chapter "Coyote Postman," this vision comes through most clearly. Here, Asturias introduces the character of Don Casualidón, a Spanish priest who, in his desire for wealth, leaves a Ladino community for a community of "fifty thousand indifferent Indians" (*Men of Maize* 239), who are exploited to produce "nuggets of gold" (239). These new surroundings cause the priest to have doubts about becoming rich because he begins to realize that the process of "producing gold nuggets" legitimates the exploitation of the indigenous workforce. It is not this exploitation that I am interested in highlighting here, but rather the new sociocultural environment to which Don Casualidón adapts himself.

Alongside the indigenous people, Don Casualidón partakes in "the happiness of those good folks, tied to the earth, to their goats, their maize, their silence, their water, scorners of the golden nuggets" (*Men of Maize* 263). Moreover, in this community the Indians were "indifferent to the world which blinked outside" and, "beneath the stars, were sleeping out the weariness of a conquered race" (261).

> He adapted to a primitive existence far from that civilization which his

abstemiousness and sobriety taught him was merely an accumulation of useless things. The natives were poverty-stricken Indians who wanted for everything because their families were large and the wealth which passed through their hands in the placers or in the fields did not belong to them. Wretched wages kept them sick and feeble, always drunk. At first, Don Casualidón would have liked to inject them with energy, with the health that he himself was lacking, as Don Quijote would have said, shake them like puppets to bring them out of their contemplative renunciation, their meditative silence, their indifference to the earthly world in which they lived. But now, with the passing of time, he not only understood them but had come to share their attitude, half dream and half reality, in which existence was a continuous rhythm of physical needs, without complications. (Asturias, Men of Maize 262)

These passages illustrate a dichotomy of civilization/barbarism ("primitive existence") in which the supposedly positive aspects of barbarism go against the grain of civilization. In describing Don Casualidón, Asturias emphasizes this objective: "content with his poverty among those poor children of God, whom he called natural, to differentiate them from civilized men, who should be called artificial" (263). This representation of the Indians reveals an entire series of contradictions and ambiguities: they live happily in their condition as exploited, "sick and feeble," "always drunk," "poverty-stricken" subjects, distanced from civilization, which has become degraded by the "accumulation of useless things." In these conditions of material existence, the Indians have lost any possibility of agency, remaining anchored in the past, "indifferent to the world which blinked outside." The "vengeance" against the West does not reflect their own thinking, nor a possible motivation derived from their condition as exploited subjects, but rather mythology: the Indians "avenged themselves on their oppressors by putting the gems of perdition [gold nuggets] in their hands" (263). Another character in the novel says, "Those people are sacrificed so that the legend may live" (199).

Independently of its critique of civilization, this Asturian discursive construction does nothing less than deploy temporality as an indicator of difference between Ladinos and indigenous peoples. It suggests that these Indians are at the margins of civilization's temptations, "tied to the earth" (263) and supposedly living a life "without complications." Instead of being subjects of the present or of modernity, the Indians are "primitive," a paradigm of originality or antiquity that defines a kind of historical or traditional artifact, an ancestral community in ancestral lands. In one form or another, indigeneity becomes a place that Ladinos have left aside in order to assume the mantle of "civilization" and to enter into modernity. Indigenous peoples represent the past, the origins or childhood of humanity; Ladinos represent the modern or civilized world that has trampled on this origin. Modernity seems to be an experience particular to Ladinos or Europeans and involves the indigenous world only in that modernity destroys its ways of life. Because this representation can be negative or positive, progressive or regressive, the Indian is constructed as a noble being, tolerant, incapable of acting, thinking, or responding politically. In this discursivity, the relationship of knowledge/power does little to alter the colonial relations between dominant and dominated. It is a discourse in which indigenous peoples have lost control over their own destiny and are culturally and biologically immutable.

In another sense, the character of Don Casualidón evokes a nostalgia and sadness, a paternalism that basically seeks to undo the posture that Asturias took in his master's thesis. That is, despite its limitations, this representation betrays a desire to provide a more positive vision of the Indian, going so far as to challenge dichotomies of civilization/barbarism like those elaborated in 1845 by Domingo Faustino Sarmiento (*Facundo*). Here, we see a demystification of Sarmiento's project. Far from representing "order," civilization represents a space of "useless things." Capitalist development, with the systematic growth of riches and greed (represented by the gold), has exploited and dehumanized indigenous people. If Asturias's initial desire was to establish civilization through an injection of "European blood," here, years later, the narrator supposedly favors and better "understands" this world "without complications."

In any case, little in this representation truly vindicates the indigenous world. In my opinion, what is at stake is the vindication of Ladino moral values. This representation of the Indian exists only to contrast and critique the world of the Ladinos. Because of greed, people have situated themselves in a modern world that emphasizes the material at the cost of the spiritual. While destroying the Indians, capitalism seduces the Ladinos, who adopt more and more materialistic values that distance them even further from life's fundamental values. With either the civilizing or the modernizing process, of course, the "primitive" world is condemned to extinction, lacking the opportunity to access modern technology in order to survive progress. It can be ventured that Asturias did not even think that indigenous peoples would be able to read his novel. Rather, it is Ladinos whom the novel interpellates.

In *Men of Maize*, to what extent does Asturias distance himself from the perspective presented in his thesis? Has the racism expressed in that document been eradicated? Although he displays a certain level of cultural affection for the Indians, this affection manifests in a paternalism that claims an epic vindication but does not recognize the Indian's own agency. These attitudes are more apparent in later texts, in which the author proposes mestizaje as a solution to the "indigenous problem."

In his thesis, Asturias attributed the Indian's inferiority to racial factors, a problem that an infusion of Western blood could solve. The Guatemalan state, then, should promote European immigration so that these immigrants would racially mix with the Indians. Eventually, however, Asturias declared that experience had taught him differently: the "vindication" of the indigenous world was more complicated than this. Asturias tells us that when he wrote his master's thesis, he wanted "to say something that today…would possibly be said in a different way" ("La tesis" 137). Instead of reaffirming the Indian's "racial inferiority," Asturias recognized indigenous peoples' capacity to adopt Western civilization and also sought to present them in a more positive light:

> For a long time, the Indian was considered an inferior being, if not a true animal. At least, that is what whites who were not mestizo maintained. This, I repeat, has already changed. Today the Indian is no longer a racial problem. His problem, the precise product of flawed policies, is a social problem. He still has not been assimilated in every sense, due to a lack of certain conditions. These are a lack of money, schools, lack of disposition and will. But that will surely change. ("La tesis" 137, emphasis added)

Despite displaying a little more solidarity with indigenous peoples, his words indicate that the Indian continues to be a problem. This problem is no longer "racial," but "social," and can be resolved through educational policies or a good disposition and goodwill. Contrary to his previous posture, what Europe has taught him is that immigration policy cannot solve the "indigenous problem." On the contrary, as he proposes in *Men of Maize*, socioeconomic aspects are what have created the conditions of inequality that have not allowed indigenous people to develop their culture. Moreover, Asturias has realized that the Indian's inferiority is also the product of governmental policies that have not favored "assimilation" or "mestizaje." Consequently, these methods should be institutionalized to solve the "problem."

Again admitting the limitations of his ideological position in his thesis, Asturias adds that it is necessary "to develop the cultural attributes that [the Indian] possesses" ("La tesis" 138):

> The Indian works but does not buy perfumes, nylon socks, or drinks, but returns to his mountain with his meager earnings to buy a small plot of land or a cow. He lives in houses with dirt floors, but they are

clean, and leads a very organized life. Generally, he wakes up at five in the morning, bathes every day, and has a normal sex life.... Why, then, do we not try to develop the Indian's world, all its virtues, all of this that we do not want to see, to be able to elevate him without sacrifice within his beliefs and culture? Once his cultural level has been raised, he himself will transculturate and be an advantageous element for our culture. Now, the danger is that the purity of indigenous life and culture is threatened by tourism. *(139, emphasis added)*

The first thing that draws my attention in this passage is, Whom is Asturias addressing? Who should be with him in trying to develop the entirety of this Indian world? Obviously, he does not address an indigenous reader, nor the tourists who are ruining the "purity of indigenous life and culture." Everything seems to indicate that the message is directed to Ladinos, who should lead the way in developing the Indian's "cultural attributes." This position reiterates—as in *Men of Maize*—the author's view of the Maya as a race incapable of surviving, of sustaining their own cultural values and norms. In other words, Ladinos must frame the orientation of progress and a sense of history defined in terms of Western civilization with regard to its "traditional" counterparts.

In this idea of "authenticity" ("the purity of indigenous life and culture"), Asturias echoes an entire anthropological corpus of the period. This perspective easily leads to a nihilistic construction of the other. It does not take into account historical transformations of cultural identity, nor the answers that these subjects have given to the "threats" of modernity.[9] In its place, cultural opposition between indigenes and Ladinos is based on an almost nostalgic paradigm: indigenous peoples are passive subjects beyond the evolution brought on by modernity. If an Indian purchases perfume or nylon socks, this authenticity or cultural identity is supposedly lost. That is, confronted with the threat to this authenticity, through contact with tourists, Asturias's preoccupation is to protect it and try to elevate it to a higher level of culture without sacrificing that purity. This, in turn, suggests that what is foreign—but not contact with the Ladino world—endangers this supposed authenticity. Ladinos should set the cultural model to be followed, should be cultural missionaries who "elevate" indigenous peoples to a modern way of being. Such a process will facilitate transculturalization so that the indigenous world will finally be an "advantageous element" of Ladino society.

This line of thinking locates the Asturian project of mestizaje/transculturalization within the context of the period's debates on mestizaje, led by José Vasconcelos in his famous book *The Cosmic Race*. Understood in this context, Asturias's intentions derive from an approach to the Indian that regards him as a problem and as inferior not so much in biological terms, but in social terms. His degraded condition has been created by a modernity that justifies exploitation, land dispossession, and the destruction of communities. Tied to this, Asturias sees that both civilizing and modernizing processes threaten to destroy indigenous culture. In the last years of his life, Asturias gave himself the authority to rescue the Indian from this danger. That is, through an immutable conception of indigenous cultural identity, Asturias—implicitly or explicitly—perceived Indians as a diminished or degraded conglomerate that needed to be led or tutored in order to halt its "extinction," whether this extinction was due to external modern influences or to capitalist exploitation.

Asturias's mestizaje, in this sense, is inclusive. He did not, however, consider that his transculturalization also implied cultural genocide or renunciation of one's culture. In his preoccupation with the Indian, Asturias is responding to the necessity of developing the Guatemalan state and the economy to make these compatible with the changes provoked by capitalism and the West. In turn, this caused him to think in terms of promoting education and modernization policies that governments should adopt to protect the Indian. Rescuing what he considered the positive values of the Indian's historical and cultural ways of life would supposedly facilitate the Indian's economic elevation, assimilation, and ability to take advantage of the resources offered by modern technology and "universal" Western culture—measures, it is worth remembering, that governments did adopt.[10]

Notwithstanding Asturias's good intentions, his argument for mestizaje as a redemptive project for indigenous peoples no longer makes any sense from a contemporary perspective. Although it seeks to incorporate the "Indian" into the national project, it does not favor integration through recognition of Indian linguistic, spiritual, and cultural distinctions. Because of this, mestizaje does not open up spaces in which to think of indigenous cultures as autonomous entities with their own historical logic, as well as their own values and political and cultural needs.

We could derive similar conclusions from other theoretical postmodern concepts. Fernando Ortiz's (*Contrapunteo cubano*) and Ángel Rama's (*Transculturación narrativa*) transculturation proposes integrating the subaltern's cultural attributes into dominant culture. For Ortiz, transculturation represents an alternative to the concept of "acculturation."[11] According to him, this implies "the necessary loss or displacement of a preceding culture, what could be said to be a partial de-culturation, and, moreover, signifies the consequent creation of new cultural phenomena that could be called *neoculturation*" (Rama, *Transculturación narrativa* 33). Rama uses the concept to examine Latin American literature in response to the modernizing advances and dependency theory of his time, counterposing the literary styles of the Latin American *vanguardia* (Avant-Garde) and *costumbrismo* (from *costumbre*, or "custom").[12] Because of the advancements of the vanguardia, Rama argues, costumbrismo faces either complete cancellation or inevitable assimilation into the vanguardia. It is the second of these processes that Rama calls "transculturation."

The problem with this approach to literature is that Rama applauds the vanguardia's influence (or rather "modernity's" influence) over costumbrismo. It follows that he sees costumbrismo as a passive entity that only receives the more modern literary influence, incapable of making the vanguardia assimilate any of its characteristics. Rama makes this same reading of the so-called indigenous question when he suggests that, faced with modernization, indigenous peoples have as their possibilities either the death of their cultures or survival through mestizaje. Like costumbrismo, Rama regards indigeneity as something passive in the face of modernizing processes; indigeneity cannot influence modernity. It is no surprise, then, to see this attitude in his final interview. When asked whether "today there is any hope for indigenous culture," he responded, "Without any doubt, but not for indigenous culture, but rather for mestizo culture, because Indian culture no longer makes any sense" (Moraña 343).[13]

Strictly speaking, Asturias's perspective on transculturation and his desire to make the indigenous world something "advantageous" for Guatemalan society are related to the proposals of Ortiz and Rama. These writers consider themselves lettered cultural "authorities" who know what is best for their objects of study, but they propose mestizaje in order to "save" subaltern cultures from extinction. In these intellectuals' interpretation of the subaltern—whether indigenous or black—what stands out is an understanding of these subjects as incapable of using modernity to their own advantage.[14]

In light of this reading and given the colonial dimensions of this representation, I would say that Asturias's contribution does not reside in his depiction of the indigenous world. He gives himself the luxury of appropriating indigeneity in order to uphold indigenismo and construct a modern narrative of citizenship and nation founded on mestizaje.[15] In other words, the indigenous world serves Asturias as a tool or an object of study to critique the Ladino world and capitalism. In addition, it serves him in the creation of a new aesthetic-literary style based on magical realism (Hurtado Heras 22). Martin Lienhard has argued that, in *Men of Maize*, "'indigeneity' serves Asturias in the creation of the appearance of a 'myth'—not indigenous but Ladino. 'Indigeneity' is only interesting to the extent that it will come to form part of a Guatemalan national identity that Asturias, without a doubt, wants to help construct" ("Antes y después" 584). Asturias's goal in *Men of Maize* and in his ideological position is more than an attempt to promote indigenous self-sufficiency and Maya self-determination. It is to promote Ladino or mestizo cultural identity, as well as to transform the discourse of canonical "indigenista realism" (represented by works like *Raza de bronce* [Bronze Race] by Alcides Arguedas and *Huasipungo* by Jorge Icaza) and inaugurate a new literary strategy influenced by surrealism. Moreover, within this aesthetic-literary project, Asturias seeks to redefine the Guatemalan "national" and elaborate a Maya cosmology he can integrate into a political and historical argument.[16]

Rather than divorce itself from indigenismo, this neo-indigenista narrative merely places indigenismo within a new aesthetic-literary paradigm. Like the preceding tradition, it incorporates discursive elements of indigenous origin, but from a perspective foreign to the indigenous world. To continue with Lienhard's argument, the "immediate objective of this operation is putting into play a less openly 'Ladino' perspective or one that tends to show more solidarity, in cultural terms, with the 'indigenous world.' Its literary objective—more or less exotic—is evoked with literary tools developed by end-of-nineteenth-century realism" ("Antes y después" 571)

In demonstrating these limitations of Asturias's thought, I am by no means suggesting that Asturias should be discarded. By reaffirming the Ladino, Asturias complements the intercultural Guatemalan project of the nation. If we recognize that the Maya movement promotes indigenous cultural revitalization, Asturias's project should be understood as one of Ladino or mestizo revitalization. Further, in Asturias's politics of mestizaje, we find the deployment of a politics of difference between a "they" and a "we," leading us to think from at least two loci of enunciation, in two differentiated cultural projects, and to confront a multiethnic Guatemalan reality. Independent of this representation of the indigenous world, Asturias makes other significant ideological contributions. In his representation of Maya cosmology in *Men of Maize*, Asturias uses an indigenous epistemology and a Maya cosmovision to counteract capitalism. This is the principle we will find again in de Lión and Menchú, who, in their respective articulations of Maya cosmovision, construct a locus of enunciation and a subaltern perspective to counteract a colonial modernity (today, globalization). De Lión and Menchú differ from Asturias, however, in that they demystify the Asturian Indian in order to give him agency. In Asturias, we recognize a profound and visionary reflection on capitalism and imperialism that enables us—whether Maya or non-Maya—to understand the situation in which we currently live, facing new imperial threats such as the Plan Puebla Panamá (PPP), the Central American Free Trade Agreement (CAFTA), and the Free

Trade Agreement of the Americas (FTAA).[17] These opulent programs seek to feed themselves on natural resources and cheap labor that are no longer necessarily Maya, but also Ladino.

Asturias's later works raise awareness of the need to respect and defend nature through nonviolent activism against growing modernization threats. Although present in his earliest work, this tendency reaches full maturity in his banana trilogy (*Strong Wind*, *The Green Pope*, and *The Eyes of the Interred*) and *Weekend en Guatemala*.[18] Here, *Men of Maize* can serve as an emblematic example of Asturias's thought. As Gerald Martin suggests (177), the novel can be inscribed as a criticism of capitalist development and expansion that acquires its current hegemony through the appropriation and destruction of natural resources like the Amazon rainforest. Through Gaspar Ilom, Asturias anticipates this threat in native territories:

> Look, Piojosa, the ruckus'll be starting any day now. We've got to clear the land of Ilóm of the ones who knock the trees down with axes, who scorch the forest with their fires, who dam the waters of the river that sleeps as it flows and opens its eyes in the pools and rots for wanting to sleep…the maize growers, the ones who've done away with the shade, for either the earth that falls from the stars is gonna find some place to go on dreaming its dream in the soil of Ilóm, or they can put me off to sleep forever. Get some old rags together to tie up my things, and don't forget the cold tortillas, some salt beef, some chili, all a man needs to go to war. (Men of Maize 10–11)

We could very well read this passage as announcing a new struggle against "the ones that knock the trees down with axes, who scorch the forest with their fires"—metaphorically, the transnational corporations using up natural resources and enforcing, according to Asturias, a new "democratic slavery" (Callan 13) based on exploitation. (Like the land of Gaspar Ilom, the earth keeps falling from the stars in our skies, and it will find a place to continue dreaming the dream of a world that is more egalitarian in social, ethnic, gender, and linguistic terms.)

It is important to underscore that Asturias's genius as the creator of a literary movement is not in question. Neither is his ability to create a new aesthetic language, nor his project to reaffirm Ladino culture, which contributes to the project of Guatemalan interculturality. I do not question his valuable and necessary critique of capitalism. What is being questioned here is a limited representation of the indigenous world that has been used to "understand" Indians and thereby reproduce stereotypes that diminish

Mayas' political prominence. Of course problems arise when this way of thinking is recycled in order to "solve" the interethnic and intercultural conflicts of Guatemala's diverse population. Construed as a political proposal of assimilation, is mestizaje still the answer to the interethnic problem currently being debated in Guatemala? As we will see in chapter 4, some contemporary critics, influenced by postmodern theories of transculturation and hybridity, believe so. However, in my view and as demonstrated above, the interethnic reality demands other political approaches.

To conclude, the problem we find in Asturias is not resolved by saying that the author's experience in Paris suddenly changed his conception of the indigenous world. That is, if the positivism that ideologically permeates his thesis has, in fact, been transcended, the vindication of the indigenous world that Asturias proposes is equally problematic: it now supports the survival of indigenous cultures through mestizaje, which means only *the possibility* of indigenous survival. Asturias does not stop seeing indigenous peoples as a problem. His literary, ideological, intellectual project constructs a Ladino consciousness, not an indigenous one, a project not of Maya cultural and linguistic affirmation and revitalization but of mestizo cultural and linguistic revitalization. We can also find an evolution in Asturias's attitude toward race. Moving from the perspective in his thesis to the experience described in *Men of Maize*, we see an ideological change that should be understood in its historical and social contexts, despite its limitations.

None of this denies Asturias or any other intellectuals of his epoch their merit. In fact, mestizaje facilitated the gradual eradication of discriminatory laws justified by positivism. But if mestizaje fulfilled its redeeming role, then this should be understood as making way for new and more sophisticated ideas to integrate indigenous peoples into the nation. In reality, this new project equally recycled racism. The proposed assimilation intended to "civilize" and eradicate the "backwardness" (erase indigenous languages and anything else "uncivilized") of indigenous peoples. Its form of social integration comprised new rules to which the Indians should submit, rules to give up languages and customs considered "barbarian" or nonmodern. These policies inspired new forms of resistance, giving rise to new indigenous intellectuals. Educated, ironically, in the context of these assimilationist projects,[19] they sought to tell the history of their peoples from a Maya locus of enunciation. We can situate Luis de Lión within this context. Contrary to Asturias's Ladino project, de Lión's Maya nationalism gives agency to indigenous peoples and rearticulates indigenous cosmovision as an anticolonial and antiracist principle, demarcating a transition toward a political role for Maya peoples.

Luis de Lión: Maya Nationalism and Political Decolonization

In Luis de Lión's "It Seems like a Story [Parece cuento]" (in *Los zopilotes*)—perhaps the most militant and political of his texts—he pays homage to his country, Guatemala, and to Miguel Ángel Asturias: "[Guatemala] has dreamlike vegetation, but the greatest of all its landscape is a giant ceiba tree that tells stories to the wind and sings. Its name: Miguel Ángel Asturias" (26). As this passage reveals, de Lión admired Asturias as both a writer and a representative of Guatemalan literature. Over time, however, the Maya Kaqchikel writer would strategically change his posture to situate Asturias in a position of otherness. His ideology would combine the rhetorical language of literature with a militant politics and would inspire an antiracist, anticolonial movement. The novelist and literary critic Mario Roberto Morales relates an anecdote about de Lión that clearly manifests this process.

Morales states that in a literary workshop with the Maya Kaqchikel and other Guatemalan writers, they talked about defining a new aesthetic-literary role for the next generation of Guatemalan writers. Recognizing the immense weight and literary influence that Asturias had among Latin American writers at the beginning of the 1970s,[20] Morales decided to write his text "Let's Kill Miguel Ángel Asturias [Matemos a Miguel Ángel Asturias]." The title, he tells us,

> came from a remark Luis de Lión made and, in fact, had no pretensions of originality because we knew of other previous literary parricides in Latin America. But Luis, because he was indigenous, was very concerned with Asturias and his vision of Guatemala's Indians. It was Luis who said that it was necessary to "kill" Asturias by reading him more, understanding him profoundly, and accepting that his contribution was, above all, poetic and literary and not social or political. (854, n. 2)

This anecdote illustrates a series of preoccupations that define de Lión's project as a committed writer and intellectual. For the Maya writer, it was important to understand Asturias deeply, not with the goal of imitating what he did but rather to overcome his "version of the Indian" by inscribing a self-representation of that world. De Lión also saw that Asturias was less a "committed author" than a writer whose contribution was "poetic and literary and not social or political." In this anecdote, de Lión comes across as an indigenous intellectual motivated to express his cultural identity from his own perspective,[21] we could say, by "killing" Asturias's version of the "Indian." Aside from the story cited at the beginning, de Lión makes no mention of this. Defining the dialogue between literary father and son is an explicit absence in which, according to Tatiana Bubnova (181), de Lión establishes "a relation of rejection and estrangement within his text."

Luis de Lión, as I mentioned earlier, was of Kaqchikel origin, one of the twenty-one Maya ethnic groups in Guatemala. He was born in the small village of San Juan del Obispo, near Antigua Guatemala, Sacatepéquez, in 1939. After elementary school, de Lión left his native community to pursue higher education in Guatemala City. He became a schoolteacher and, eventually, a professor at San Carlos de Guatemala University, where he also became politically involved as a union leader and member of Guatemala's Workers Party (PGT). These experiences as teacher and activist are very significant, for they shaped de Lión's political consciousness and sense of affiliation to his surroundings, particularly to Guatemala's indigenous and peasant communities. In his poems and short stories, the most prominent themes mirror the experience of indigenous peasants and their struggle to change their material conditions of existence.[22] His exaltation of nature and rural life articulates a worldview that is centered on the circumstances of the Indian communities. It is because he came from their world, says Francisco Morales Santos, that de Lión "represents the marginalized, and he is their voice of protest. Luís representa a generation whose anger emerges in the sixties from enduring the weight of obscurantism and injustice" (29).

And that "voice of protest" was perceived as subversive by the government. Like Otto René Castillo, Roberto Obregón, and other politically committed writers, Luis de Lión was "disappeared." This occurred on May 15, 1984. Nothing was known about his fate until three years after the government and the guerrillas signed the peace accord ending thirty-six years of civil war.[23] In 1999 the Commission of the Peace Accords made public the diary of Guatemala's army. The document listed 183 people who were captured in the early 1980s by military units, including Luis de Lión as number 135. The corresponding details indicate that code 300, which is equivalent to "executed," was applied to him on May 15, 1984, after three days of imprisonment.[24]

De Lión is part of the Committed Generation of writers and poets who played a crucial role in Guatemala's armed struggle during the sixties.[25] Through activism and literature, this generation challenged "traditional" intellectuals (in the Gramscian sense) by suggesting that art, more than being an aesthetic instrument, is a weapon of struggle and political critique. According to Roque Dalton (1993), from Miguel Ángel Asturias's phrase "To be a writer is to be the moral consciousness of the people," one could "improvise a small but solid structure of ethical-aesthetic principals: 'To be a writer is to be the moral consciousness of the people'; that is, a writer should write as he thinks and live as he writes; he has a commitment to the people, with their struggles of liberation, with the revolution" (xxv).[26] The Asturian phrase would later be used to criticize Asturias himself when he accepted a diplomatic post in France, especially after the assassination of the poet Otto René Castillo by the Guatemalan army. Roque Dalton writes:

> His extreme adherence to that phrase's content [To be a writer is to be the moral consciousness of the people] brought Otto René Castillo to be tortured and to his own death. The most absolute betrayal of the principles that this phrase invokes has instead led the person who said it and coined it, Miguel Ángel Asturias, to receive the highest honors from the bourgeoisie society: the Parisian embassy of the criminal military dictatorship that killed Otto René Castillo is at the pleasure, use, and benefit of the winner of Nobel Prize for Literature, on the route to which, it should also be mentioned, even the name of Lenin was vilified.[27] (xxxiii–xxxiv)

In his criticism of Asturias, de Lión seems to follow a path similar to Dalton's, perceiving Asturias—as Mario Roberto Morales remembers above—as a writer who, aside from a poetic and literary role, had not made a social or political contribution. Dalton, Castillo, and de Lión, rather than take the role of a "bourgeois" intellectual, which they saw Asturias embodying, all sought to define their own role as committed intellectuals, a role that tragically led to their torture and death. In this sense, these authors' writings and sacrifices should be thought of as a *performance* of their own political ideals in favor of a revolution that would incite national political change: they wrote as they thought, and they lived as they wrote; they were committed to the people and the revolutionary struggle. In contrast to Dalton and Castillo's work, however, de Lión's literature presents other concerns, hand in hand with a revolutionary project: the reaffirmation of indigenous peoples and the construction of a Maya nationalism.

Carol Smith has observed, "We do not yet know what revolution meant to those who joined the insurgency as voluntary participants" ("Maya Nationalism" 32). Keeping these words in mind, we can use de Lión and his literature to shed light on what this armed struggle meant for many Mayas. In effect, as we shall see, de Lión's "revolution" acquires a decolonizing dimension that seeks to materialize and legitimate Maya cosmovision and Maya nationalism in order to challenge the status quo. The model that de Lión proposes in his texts privileges the role of indigenous cultures as an articulating axis to incite a "national liberation" (Fanon, *The Wretched of the Earth*) but also, primarily, to advocate a national project founded on indigenous memory. De Lión's literature shows that, for Maya communities, the armed struggle meant the opportunity to realize—to use the words of the Maya Kaqchikel leader Pablo Ceto—"a conspiracy within the conspiracy" (quoted in Arias, *Taking Their Word* 171). For de Lión, this meant an opportunity to realize social and ethnic emancipation, an opportunity to recover ancestral values by turning to the past to build a new future. To begin, we can see these proposals in some of his short stories. The first of these is "The Sons of the Father" (in *La puerta*).

This short story narrates the history of a polarized society. There exist two "principal" saints, sons of the same father, one of whom performs miracles for the Ladinos and the other who takes care of the indigenous people, "the poor rabble of the community" (de Lión, *La puerta* 13). On Good Friday, the two communities carry their respective saints in procession and encounter each other on a street, before a carpet of flowers. When the Ladinos demand that the indigenous people go to the back, they refuse to do so. The indigenous people, with the approval of their saint, "[raise] their head and, without measuring, without estimating the others, [begin] to walk forward, with the drum and the whistle sounding of war.... The time had arrived" (15). This scene is defined by a context of confrontation and struggle. After centuries of exhaustion and desperation owing to conditions of subordination, de Lión envisions the beginnings of a decolonial project that must inevitably confront the established, hegemonic system. Here, symbolically, indigenous peoples begin to challenge and destabilize the hegemonic system.

Further, de Lión is concerned with portraying the conditions of social inequality in which rural indigenous peoples live,[28] so much so that he challenges epistemological fields that have established Western forms of understanding the world. In his story "The Sandal Wearer [El caitudo]" (in *Su segunda muerte*), for example, an indigenous Jesus decides to rebel against the hegemonic system. No longer limited to defying hegemonic representations, de Lión exalts, politicizes, and gives life to a Maya locus of enunciation. With the appropriation of his cultural heritage, de Lión also demystifies exotic representations of the rural world. The text that perhaps best illustrates this is his "Tarzan of the Apes" (in *La puerta*). This postcolonial political manifesto not only defines a right to self-determination and cultural identity from one's particular locus of enunciation but also develops a critical and militant consciousness regarding the conditions of inequality in peasant communities.

The story's narrator is named Benigno Julián. Reading about the death of Johnny Weissmuller—who portrayed Tarzan of the Apes in films during the 1930s—Benigno is motivated to give his own testimony as the "true"

Tarzan of the Apes. Contrary to the stories told in books, movies, television, and comic books, the real story of Tarzan of the Apes places Africa not in Africa, but in Guatemala in a small village called San Juan. This Africa is depopulated of its animals, deforested of its trees and jungle, for the purpose of "growing coffee for export" (de León, *La puerta* 30). In contrast to the Tarzan of books, movies, television, and comic books, this Tarzan is "so malnourished that one could count his ribs" (31). Moreover, this Tarzan is obligated to "grab his hoe and his machete and go to work on his small farm" (31). According to the narrator, the only things the fictitious and the real Tarzans have in common are that they are barefooted and sleep in similar beds. The fictitious Tarzan's bed is made of branches and rests in the trees; the real Tarzan's bed is made of sticks and rests "on the ground of a dirt-floor shack" (32). Jane is not Jane, but a woman named Angelina Chonay. Cheetah is a dog, not a monkey. The "real" Tarzan also takes care of his father on Sundays when his father gets drunk in the bars. Similar to how Africa's population was dispossessed of its land, a coup d'etat against Arbenz forces the "real" Tarzan to abandon his land.[29] In addition, the real Tarzan's parents and friends were persecuted for trying to recover their land. After the death of his parents, the real Tarzan—the narrator tells us—conscious of the social inequality in Africa, decides to join the revolutionary struggle to regain everything his community has lost and to create a better future for his children. Finally, as the real Tarzan is constantly exposed to more and more representations of himself, he becomes "more and more disillusioned, because they always [caricature] him" (34).

Explicit in this story is de León's allegory of the sociocultural environment in which he lives, as well as his own role as an intellectual committed to regaining an "Africa" (Guatemala) that has been taken from its people. In turn, through the appropriation and demystification of the mass media's representation of "Tarzan of the Apes," the author offers another vision of the world, a "true" one from his own perspective. The story concerns a struggle for knowledge; through self-representation of the peasants' world, de León establishes a subaltern locus of enunciation that bestows cultural and political legitimacy upon that world. It is undeniable that his goal is to defy the media, which have spread stereotypes about the rural world, the indigenous world in particular. These concerns are equally emphasized in his novel (*El tiempo principia en Xibalbá* [Time Begins in Xibalbá]). Besides problematizing the question of representation, de León establishes that in the "revolution" and armed struggle, the primary concern should not merely be the decolonization of indigenous subjectivity and the Maya world, but also the forging of a nationalism based upon a Maya cosmovision. At this point, I will focus on the novel,[30] a work that takes a critical stance in regard to the mass media's role in generating, promoting, and legitimating the coloniality of power.

In my approach to the novel, I will focus on de Lión's profound insight into the coloniality of power and how it dominates an indigenous community through a wooden statue of the Virgin, which becomes the community's religious and sexual icon. My argument is that, in *El tiempo principia en Xibalbá*, de Lión is responding to indigenista discourse—in particular, *Men of Maize*—in order to articulate a Maya nationalism. I will focus on the allegorization of the main characters, Juan and Pascual, as two alternatives for the indigenous world: to internalize or assimilate into the Western world or to initiate a decolonial project that supports a Maya nationalism drawn from indigenous historical memory.

El tiempo principia en Xibalbá is divided into five chapters. The book has a cyclic structure, narrating the stories of Pascual Baeza and Juan Caca. Pascual is an Indian who deserts the army and, after experiencing marginalization and racism in the city, returns to die in his native community. In the village, he feels disappointed that nothing has changed, and he wants to leave again. Arriving at the church to say good-bye to "those people who have bent down their heads for centuries, who have never lifted them up" (de Lión, *El tiempo* 29), he contemplates the wooden statue of the Virgen de la Concepción, "the only Ladina of the town" (64). Pascual decides to stay in order to steal the statue and "rape" it. Eventually, the people from the community find out about his actions and destroy the statue (76). In its place, they consecrate an Indian woman named Concha because she has "the same hair, the same face, the same eyes, the same mouth and even the same size [as the Ladina Virgin]," the only differences being that she is dark-skinned, has breasts, and is flesh and bone (10). Also, she is a whore. Concha is paraded through the town in a procession. She is venerated to the point that men wrangle among themselves to be able to touch her. The fighting ends with their deaths and the total destruction of the community. Everything settles into "final silence" (79).

Juan Caca—who is Pascual, "but the inverse of him" (de Lión, *El tiempo* 66)—has been living in the city since childhood, when his fervently Catholic parents interned him in a seminary in order to make him a priest. After his parents' death, Juan abandons the seminary and goes back to his native village to open a grocery store. In the community, Juan discovers that because he is too "clean" and has never been seen with a woman, there are rumors that he is homosexual. The rumors provoke nightmares in him. In one of them, Juan's mother tells him that he must marry to put an end to the gossip. He decides to marry Concha, who has had sexual relations with all the unmarried men of the village, but the marriage fails because Juan is sexually impotent. Also, Concha accuses him of being a coward for his desire to assimilate to Ladino ways of life and his refusal to support Pascual after the "rape." Juan's sexual impotence ends when, in a dream, he sexually possesses a woman who appears to be either the wooden Virgin or Concha. The reader does not know who the woman is, although there are humorous hints that she is Juan's own mother (88). When he wakes up, he realizes that his penis is rotten. At the same time, he hears the sounds of the fighting and the destruction of the community. He also realizes that he has died. He lies by himself, with "his bones and his recent dead skull" (98).

The stylistic, aesthetic, and literary aspects of Luis de Lión's novel have received much critical attention in and outside Guatemala. Some critics have pointed to the work's literary influences and intertextualities, placing it alongside the "Boom" novels or qualifying it as belonging to the postmodern or postcolonial Latin American canon.[31] Others have focused on the image of the Virgin. Ana María Rodas, for example, emphasizes "the tremendous attraction that the Ladino woman exerts upon the Indian" (11).[32] This perspective, however, downplays the political, ideological, and epistemological agency that de Lión grants to the indigenous world and its social imagery.

If we view the novel's central characters as allegorical, we realize that Pascual and Juan represent two political models for indigenous peoples. Through Juan, de Lión shows the road of assimilation, in this case, to the Ladino way of life. Juan left as "an Indian child…and has returned filled with another world, with other customs" (de Lión, *El tiempo* 81). He does not relate to the community, even though his physical appearance and his family name reflect his Indian-ness (80). Moreover, de Lión links Juan to the symbols of the dominant ideology. For instance, he lives in the *only* "white house" of the community (48), and he is too "clean." When Pascual commits the "rape," Juan is the only person who does not participate in the statue's subsequent destruction by the community. Instead, he condemns Pascual's action. Concha reproaches him for this: "You think as if you were a judge, as if you were the army. It would seem that you are on their side" (80). And when Juan insists that Pascual should have gone to jail for "raping the mother of God," Concha adds, "But she is not our mother. She is a filthy Ladino woman" (80). Consequently, for turning his back on the community, Concha leaves Juan to join the others. She calls him a coward for not getting his hands dirty (81).

Pascual displays the rebellious attitude of someone who wants to change things. Like Juan, he has lived in the city, but he has returned "with his eyes filled with a hated world, a Ladino world that discriminated against him" (de Lión, *El tiempo* 28). While Juan feels alienated within his own community, Pascual is "the only one who thinks, the only one who realizes that things are different" (28). Pascual has returned to act politically. He feels that in the town "nobody dares to speak wrongly of God, nor of His mother and her son," and he says that "new births cannot be a new history because it seems as if the life of the dead repeats itself in the living" (27). Daring to speak wrongly of God, His mother, and her son translates into acting against what is established. Pascual is back in the community not only to reclaim his ethnic roots but also to challenge the colonial conditions that oppress the community. The "rape" is a radical transgression against the dominant world, an act that will culminate in a collective move to destroy the image of domination.

Indeed, as the "only" Ladina in the town, the Virgen de la Concepción wields ideological authority as the "mother of all men" (de Lión, *El tiempo* 63), subliminally maintaining a colonialist status quo. Because of this authority, the image embodies a limited boundary that cannot be transcended. Before Pascual, no one attempted to defy this ideology, with its obvious origins in the colonial period. Its representation in Luis de Lión's novel can be related to Serge Gruzinski's analysis of the role of images in Mexico since colonial times (*Images at War*).

In the so-called New World, Gruzinski argues, as a result of the linguistic and religious barriers encountered by the conquerors, the image has played a crucial "colonialist" role since the sixteenth century. According to Gruzinski, during the colonial period, the missionaries recognized the value of the image as an effective tool to substitute "idolatry" and indigenous "idols" with the Christian gospel for the conquest of souls. To eradicate the religious beliefs of the peoples of Mexico, represented in their images, the missionaries embarked on a systematic destruction of Nahua idols, replacing these with the icons of Christianity in a process that included "the teaching of the Christian gospel, the setting up of altars, chapels, and crosses, and the organization of the service" (Gruzinski, *Images at War* 34).

But it was not simply a matter of religious conversion. The images were also used to legitimize the Spanish imperial enterprise. The conquerors imposed a Western visual order upon the native imagery, spreading the vision of a new society with different ideas of god, the body, nature, and time and space. Gruzinski tells us that this colonial project of Christianization-Westernization started with the substitution of images after the arrival of Hernán Cortés and was later undertaken by the Church. He offers the example of a community in Tlaxcala that received a wooden statue of the Virgin named La Conquistadora, which "supported, legitimatized, and completed the military and earthly enterprise of the conquerors" (Gruzinski, *Images at War* 34).

Gruzinski argues that this generic Western representation has, for centuries, "peacefully" seduced indigenous peoples within the perverse colonialist logic:

> The image unveiled its new body, whose visible flesh covered its invisible soul, to the Indian. Through the use of perspective, the image gave the Indian a spectator's external point of view, but a privileged one; his gaze and body fully participated in the contemplation. He became a spectator ideally endowed with a "moral eye"; free will and faith would enable him to gain mastery over the true image in order to escape the trickery of the demon and the traps of idolatry. While half of Europe sank into Protestant heresy, Mexico offered the promise of a new Christendom. (Images at War 95)

Through images, the conquerors sought to "clear" the minds of the natives and install a Christian order that was endangered in Europe. At the same time, they promoted an imperial project, constituted through the value of the image as a privileged object, to eliminate the Indians' "traps of idolatry."

In de Lión's novel, the image of the Virgin represents an analogous colonial project. The statue of the Virgin becomes the "mother" of the community. It imposes a hierarchical visual order that spreads Western "morality" and prevents the Indians from looking at themselves and their own religious beliefs. The community, writes de Lión, "saw the Virgin as a stepmother and the crucifixes as stepbrothers; but these were no ordinary stepbrothers; they were invaders, land grabbers, future oppressors" (*El tiempo* 64). When Pascual "rapes" the image, the Indians become aware of what the image is: a symbol of colonial power. With the violation and destruction of the image, de Lión symbolizes the spiritual and political decolonization of the community, as well as its rejection of the dominant ideology. Ultimately, this is not simply an attempt to change the conditions of existence of the community, but a thrust to gain freedom from the Western perspective, represented in the Christianity embodied in the image of the Virgin. De Lión writes: "They put aside gospels and apocalypses, genesis and redemptions, baptisms, hosts, chalices, monstrance, fears of the earth...and they took [the statue of the Virgin] out, removed her crown, cloak and dress, and then they spit at her, insulted her with words of *whore* from here and *whore* from there, and chopped her down" (76).

Following this argument, Pascual's desire to possess the Virgin can be related to Frantz Fanon's analysis of the colonized black subject in *Black Skin, White Masks*. In the section "The Man of Color and the White Woman," Fanon describes the black man's desire to possess a white woman: "When my restless hands caress those white breasts, they grasp white civilization and dignity and make them mine" (*Black Skin* 63). Possession of a white woman symbolizes appropriation of a hegemonic system. In this symbol, according to Anne McClintock in *Dangerous Liasons* (97), Fanon develops an anticolonial nationalist project that bursts violently and irrevocably into history as the logical counterpart to colonial power. This national project, McClintock states, arises out of Fanon's understanding of how colonialism took root: it imposed the colony through a reordering of work and the sexual economy of the people in order to deflect feminine power into colonialism's hands. Similarly, we can interpret Pascual's appropriation as the development of a national anticolonial project that disrupts hegemony in order to place power in the hands of the subaltern.[33]

What emerges with the destruction of the Ladino Virgin and the crowning of Concha resembles Ranajit Guha's argument in *Elementary Aspects*. Discussing peasant rebellion, Guha states that "inversion was its principal modality; it was a political struggle in which the rebels appropriated and/or destroyed the insignia of their enemy's power in order to abolish the marks of their own subalternity" (*Elementary Aspects* 75). The statue of the Virgin is a metaphor for the colonial order's legitimization. Its destruction and the subsequent installment of an indigenous Virgin symbolize a political action to "invert," or destroy, the hegemonic order. The destruction of the Ladino Virgin restores indigenous authority. Indeed, with the consecration of an Indian Virgin of flesh and bone, Concha, as the new "mother" of the community, "a new ritual was discovered, there was a new queen, who looked at them, who was going to give them eternal happiness" (75). Concha, given the explicit sexual connotation of her name (in Spanish, *concha* is a slang term for "vagina"), acquires an erotic dimension, as well as a particularity as the "whore" of the community. This Indian Virgin obviously parodies and challenges the wooden one, which stood for the sacred, the religious values of Christianity, and the belief that sexuality is a sanctified practice. Radically breaking away from that perspective, Concha acquires a new epistemological significance: her cultural, spiritual, and erotic authority as a prostitute nourishes and satisfies the men of the community and promises "eternal happiness" (76).

With the celebration of the new Virgin, Luis de Lión suggests a new national project. This project substitutes Ladino values and norms with indigenous. Indeed, de Lión intimates that indigenous peoples must engage in an epistemological and political struggle to break away from the hegemonic modes of seeing, being, and thinking that are blocking their capacity to see themselves as political agents. Instead of depending on the colonizers, Indians must look back at their own cultural heritage, history, and material conditions to reimagine, describe, and reinvent the world in emancipating ways. Crowning Concha as the new Virgin symbolizes an indigenous political alternative. The very title of the novel, *El tiempo principia en Xibalbá* (Time Begins in Xibalbá), alludes to this project.

For Enrique Florescano, Xibalbá is the place where the conflicts between death and regeneration are played out. It is also the place where that which has degenerated transforms itself to be reborn again. Xibalbá provides the stage for the "struggle of the creator gods against the destructive forces of the cosmos in their first three efforts to give life to the universe" (Florescano 33–34). It is here where the first seed of maize grows after Junajpú and Xbalankê, the divine twins, defeat the gods of the underworld. The victory of the God of the divine twins ends the conflicts, leaving the cosmos in harmonious order (37). With the defeat of the underworld gods of Xibalbá, the god of maize emerges. This "symbolizes the beginning of an era of abundance and stability, supported by the farmers, who assume the role of suppliers of human food and sustainers of civilized life" (51).

Following this line of argument, as evident in both the novel's title and the community's destruction, de Lión reaffirms the Maya foundational myth by rejecting other narratives of the creation of life and the universe, such as the Christian Bible. He seems to suggest that, just as the divine twins transformed the earth's interior into a womb for the germination of life, the Mayas of today must undertake a similar task within their society. De Lión, in other words, turns to the *Popol Wuj* myth about the creation of the "men of maize" (to recall the title of Miguel Ángel Asturias's novel) in order to politicize the role of the divine twins in the present. The story of Juan and Pascual, to some extent, can be thought of as an ambitious rewriting of the Maya cosmogony described by Florescano. Thus, de Lión's *El tiempo* tells us that the indigenous peoples must defy the colonialism presently embodied in the hegemonic Ladino ideology. As in the sacred Maya K'iche' bible, the gods of the underworld must be defied in order to give rise to a renewed Maya cosmovision. De Lión's novel expresses this when, after the destruction of the community, a new cycle begins: "And when they realized that they were not dead, they began to reconstruct the community, to reinvent it after the image they had of it in their brains from past centuries" (*El tiempo* 75). The reconstruction of the community can be understood as the reconstruction of the nation based on Maya historical memory. This reconstructing, however, does not reflect a desire to go back to the past, as some critics would have it,[34] but rather, as Frantz Fanon argued, to look to the past "with the intention to open the future, to invite action, to build on hope" (*The Wretched* 232). Like Silvia Rivera Cusicanqui's Andean concept of Nayrapacha, it is a vision of the "past like a future," a renewal of time and space, "a past capable of renewing the future, of reverting the situation that is being experienced" (*Pachakuti* 10). What Luis de Lión ultimately suggests are the conditions of possibility for articulating a new national project incorporating Maya ancestral values and cosmovision.

De Lión's radical attitude toward Ladino ideology is apparent in the destruction of the statue of the Virgin, as well as in his declaration to confront Ladinos in his short story "The Sons of the Father." Can this be interpreted as an inversion of racist paradigms? Jorge Mario Martínez has argued that *El tiempo* reflects "an ideology of Maya fundamentalism" (19). But it is important to take into account the context of de Lión's novel: a polarized world in which the conflictive historical relationship between Mayas and Ladinos has culminated in the subordination of the indigenous peoples. As Rivera Cusicanqui observes, we should not be surprised by radical responses, because they are the result of an asymmetrical dialectic that has inevitably nurtured separatist and confrontational attitudes: "If coexistence is not possible, it is logical to expect that indigenous movements should reproduce an exclusive identity and propose the segregation or expulsion of the invaders as a way to restore their sovereignty" (*Pachakuti* 19).

We can also compare Luis de Lión's radical position to Cornell West's 1993 reading of the ideas about national culture and the project of decolonization endorsed in Fanon's *The Wretched of the Earth*. The works of Fanon and de Lión are responses to the appalling experiences of colonized peoples, experiences, we need to remember, that have been endured for centuries. *El tiempo* articulates a human response to injustice that reaffirms the Maya world culturally and politically, a reaction to having been "degraded and despised, hated and hunted, oppressed and exploited, and marginalized and dehumanized at the hands of powerful, xenophobic" imperial powers (West 260).

In this light, the primary objective for the Maya author is to reimagine a Guatemalan nationhood that, instead of being culturally homogenous, incorporates the indigenous peoples and their cultures on an equal footing. Also, we should not lose sight of the fact that Luis de Lión was trying to develop the critical consciousness of his readers by showing them the face of colonialism and its historic injustices to indigenous people. For him, the anticolonial, antiracist struggle was a central priority because, like Fanon, he understood that colonialism "is not satisfied merely with holding a people in its grip and emptying the native's brain of all form and content. By a kind of perverted logic, it turns to the past of the oppressed people and distorts, disfigures, and destroys it" (Fanon, *The Wretched* 210). In some of his short stories and in his only novel, very possibly influenced by Fanon,[35] de Lión challenges colonialism and the coloniality of power in order to end its "perverted logic," by developing a more militant role for the Indian. Like

the bell hooks reading of black theologian James Cone, we must regard de
Lión's insistence on demonic images of whites and positive images of indigenous culture as part and parcel of his attempt to counteract racism and
white supremacy.

According to hooks (12), from a black epistemological perspective,
James Cone wanted his readers to distance themselves from white suprema-
cist ideologies so that they could not only envision a radically new world
but also question whiteness as *the* only vision of that new world. What Cone
encouraged was the anti-racist reversal of positions that is today advocated
in much of the critical and literary production of cultural, feminist, and
postcolonial studies. We can think of de Lión's project similarly. He wrote at
a time when indigenous people had very limited access to literature or education. It is obvious that the Maya author, assuming that he had a Ladino
readership,[36] wanted to expose this readership to a completely different
worldview. In the novel, there are moments in which de Lión pauses, takes
the first-person voice, and urges the reader to condemn colonialism and the
exploitation of indigenous peoples:

> *You don't know what it's like to wear sandals on your feet, do you? You
> don't know what it's like to have callouses on your hands, do you? You
> don't know what it's like to go out in the early morning with your
> rations on your back, your hoe over your shoulder, or come back in the
> evening with your thrompline round your forehead and a bundle of
> wood on your back, do you? No. Your world was always another world,
> your air was always another air. You were never tied to the land. I
> mean, of course, you go back to it, to the land that you inherited from
> your parents, like the landowner of the city that you are, but not like
> the man who struggles over the furrow. (El tiempo 35)*

Although these words are addressed to Juan, they are also intended for the
"landowners" and all those who have never suffered the pain of exploitation
or the duress of indigenous rural life. De Lión calls upon those who are
responsible for creating those conditions. Similar to Cone, by condemning
Ladino colonialism and doing justice to the indigenous world, de Lión com-
municates a Maya cosmovision that encourages us to denounce class
exploitation and racism in general, but also to imagine another world
besides the dominant one. A world, I would insist, that is anticolonial and
antiracist.

El tiempo should be understood also as an epistemological challenge to
the discourse of indigenismo. In particular, I would argue that the novel is
a direct response to Asturias's *Men of Maize*, which would "save" the indigenous world through cultural mestizaje. De Lión, for instance, had this to say

about mestizaje: "I cannot participate in the so-called mestizaje, precisely because Hispanismo is a negation of my language, of my culture" (Montenegro 8). What emerges from *El tiempo* is not what indigenista writers call the "indigenous problem," but rather a mestizo or Ladino problem. From that perspective, the ideology of indigenismo must be undermined in order to open the way for the Maya. Ultimately, the real issue is "Mayanizing" the nation. Indigenous history must be written not by the Ladino or mestizo mediators who claim to speak for the Indians, but rather by the Indians themselves. Thus, de León articulates the cosmogony of the *Popol Wuj* as a political locus of enunciation. The sacred Maya bible is not only an epistemological tool for a project of decolonization but also the central ideology of the nation.

In "Tarzan of the Apes" and Pascual's possession of the wooden Virgin, de León appropriates the forms of Western-based literary discourse. He aims to compel the colonizers, and the "other" in general—in their own terms—to recognize indigenous peoples' cultural and social differences and specificities. He wants them to understand that, in every aspect of social life, indigenous people have been involved in a constant process of self-modernization in ways generally unrecognized by Latin American Intellectual elites. The contribution of de León and his novel is as much epistemological as it is political. De León ultimately suggests that hegemonic discursivities like indigenismo should be understood as part of the colonization of the Americas. It has not been enough to appropriate land, natural resources, and labor. Through systems of representation—similar to Edward Said's notion of orientalism (*Orientalism* 27–28)—these discursivities have also elaborated a textual hegemonic system that has dehumanized and stereotyped Indians' most elemental attributes through cultural forms of representation such as literature and mass media.

Furthermore, there is de León's political contribution. We can draw connections between the characters of Pascual in the novel and Benigno Julián in the story "Tarzan of the Apes" and de León. The characters' decisions to take political action reflect de León's decision to sacrifice his life in Guatemala's armed conflict. In other words, de León knew that literature was not enough to change the conditions of racism and marginalization in which our peoples lived. Therefore, militancy and political activism were also necessary for Mayas to have a voice and a better future. From his life and his work, we can conclude that these were also the ideals of many other Mayas who joined Guatemala's armed struggle at the beginning of the 1970s. That is, they launched an antiracist, anticolonial revolution in the name of a future-oriented ethnic and political project that defied the Ladino or mestizo nation. In effect, de León's ideals are echoed in the anticolonial perspective of the

Committee of Peasant Unity (CUC), a group that, during this same period, fought the government's military campaigns against indigenous communities, as well as the dominant culture's stereotyped constructions of "Indians." In the CUC manifesto, the members ask the following of the "people of the world": "to give their total support to our just struggle to end once and for all the repression, exploitation and discrimination that we are suffering.... STOP THE GENOCIDE" (Sanford, *Buried Secrets* 165).

Thus, political actions like those of de Lión and the CUC anticipate the Guatemalan Maya movement's role as a regenerator of the Maya world and visionary of a new Guatemala, not as a homogeneous or mestizo country but as one that is intercultural.[37]

From my point of view, the Maya Kaqchikel writer's work offers an alternative interpretation of Guatemalan reality, demonstrating a fervent desire on the part of Mayas to construct a nation that recognizes indigenous cultural specificity and Mayas' desire to be respected. Indigenous peoples want "the other" to understand that indigeneity is not a myth drowned in the past, but a world with an illustrious history, with dreams and visions that can be used in the creation of something better, of a world in which all can coexist in a democratic fashion.

To conclude, in the tense dialogue between Asturias and de Lión presented here, we perceive a struggle over the representation of the indigenous subject. In Asturias, we find descriptions such as "conquered race," "semi-dreamy posture," "cowardly" subjects, and a "race" that is not beneficial to society or lies outside of modernity but can be redeemed through mestizaje. De Lión represents indigenous peoples as subjects thoroughly capable of elaborating a nationalist political program that insists upon a structural change to their material conditions of existence. De Lión strives to repair the agency stolen from indigenous peoples through indigenista discourse. What unites these writers is that their respective reconstructions of the indigenous world advocate—from both Ladino and indigenous perspectives—Maya cosmology as *the* critical locus of enunciation against capitalism. Further, we can conclude that both authors found the cornerstone of Guatemalan nationalism in the Maya cosmovision of the *Popol Wuj*. This dialogue was the beginning of an intercultural, political, and epistemological project that would later be rearticulated by Rigoberta Menchú. We will turn to her in chapter 3, where we will encounter a new idea of "revolution," through a militancy in the name of human rights and, more specifically, indigenous rights. First, we will examine the debate over the "veracity" of the Nobel prize winner's first testimonio.

3 New Colonial and Anticolonial Histories

As is well known, the anthropologist David Stoll challenged the veracity of Rigoberta Menchú's *testimonio*, *I, Rigoberta Menchú*, in his book *Rigoberta Menchú and the Story of All Poor Guatemalans*.[1] From the outset, we should situate the debate Stoll initiated at the very center of discussions about Guatemala's civil war (1960–1996), especially with regard to those studies and critics who have concluded that there was genocide in Guatemala during this time.[2] Among the questions that emerge from Stoll's study are, To what extent were the guerrillas and the Maya responsible for the genocide? Did the decision of Mayas to join the insurgency culminate in the genocide? At the time, were there other alternatives aside from armed struggle? When answering these questions, Stoll claims that his study is founded upon scientific objectivity and truth. However, a closer analysis of his approach and his conclusions reveals specific ideological and political motives (even though he insists otherwise): to justify the genocide of indigenous peoples in Guatemala. Because of this, it is important to explore his arguments rigorously: on the one hand, they obscure and diminish the heroism of Mayas who sacrificed their lives by joining the Guatemalan guerrillas, beginning in the 1970s; on the other hand, they shed light on a colonialist approach that consciously manipulates information in order to neutralize indigenous movements in Latin America.

Starting with the Stoll–Menchú debate, I am interested in analyzing Stoll's reading of *I, Rigoberta Menchú* as a narrative that gives us "the version of events" (Stoll, "The Battle of Rigoberta" 393) of the Guerrilla Army of the Poor (EGP)[3] and that "became a rationale for guerrilla warfare that acquired more weight than the many forms of Maya alienation from this strategy" (395). With regard to Stoll's interpretation of Menchú's testimonio,[4] I particularly focus on the author's "objectivity" and his ideological and political motives for attacking Menchú. Many of the critics involved in the Menchú–Stoll debate have questioned his motives,[5] but I feel that their responses have not been rigorous enough in that they have not emphasized his colonialist discourse and consciousness. In the first part of this chapter, therefore, my analysis of the narrative construction he develops of Menchú's father, Vicente Menchú, demonstrates how this colonialist discourse and consciousness operate in Stoll. As we will see, it is in this narrative construction that Stoll uncovers a malignant political agenda: the appropriation of *I, Rigoberta Menchú* to cast blame for the genocide of the Maya population not on the Guatemalan army or the government, but on indigenous communities and the guerrillas. His arguments, moreover, defend the status quo and obscure any discussion of what the Commission for Historical Clarification (CEH) labeled the "Maya Holocaust."

The second part of the chapter focuses on Rigoberta Menchú. First and foremost, my analysis departs from Stoll's obsession (and that of the critics involved in the debate) with Menchú's first testimonio. I feel that one of the debate's limitations is that it has practically buried other texts by the Maya K'iche' activist, such as the one she wrote with the Committee for Peasant Unity, *Trenzando el futuro, luchas campesinas en la historia reciente de Guatemala* (Weaving the Future: Peasant Struggles in Guatemala's Recent History), and *Rigoberta Menchú, la nieta de los mayas*, translated as *Crossing Borders*. As I will demonstrate, in these texts Menchú anticipates the "suspicions" and questions that Stoll later developed. Further, I suggest that Menchú, far from promoting the ideals of the EGP, advocates Maya cultural reaffirmation and an intercultural politics that enables resistance to the mechanisms of the coloniality of power driven by globalization.

Cultural Representation and Ideological Domination, Justifying Genocide in Guatemala, Revisiting David Stoll's Exposé on Rigoberta Menchú

The power to narrate, or to block other narratives from forming and emerging, is very important to culture and imperialism and constitutes some of the main connections between them.—*Edward Said*, Culture and Imperialism

It is important to begin the discussion about the Menchú–Stoll controversy by interrogating Stoll's motives for producing his book. On several occasions, he has claimed that he does not seek to "destroy" Menchú (quoted in Arias, *The Rigoberta Menchú Controversy* 66) and "hopes" that this study will help "the Latin American Left and its foreign supporters escape from the captivity of 'Guevarismo'" (Stoll, *Rigoberta Menchú and the Story of All Poor Guatemalans* 282).[6] Nonetheless, Stoll's purpose in producing more testimonios is not to "help" Menchú's cause by denouncing the atrocities committed by the Guatemalan army and military dictatorships against indigenous peoples. Rather, his purpose is to produce "evidence" that supports his claim that Menchú "distorted" her experience to represent the "story of all poor Guatemalans" (Johnson 154). In addition, contrary to his claim of wanting to help the Left or indigenous peoples, Stoll's book has been appropriated by right-wing conservatives in order to diminish the significance of Menchú's narrative, her activism, and her efforts to bring military dictators to court.

Stoll's book was immediately embraced by a conservative movement that distributed propaganda against Menchú to silence her by removing her narrative from the list of books to be read in high schools and universities in the United States. For instance, David Horowitz, president of the Center for Popular Culture in Los Angeles, paid $5,000 to publish ads in student newspapers in the most prestigious universities in the United States. These ads described Menchú as an "intellectual fraud," a "Marxist terrorist," and a promoter of communism in academia. With Menchú exposed as a "liar" by Stoll's book, Horowitz states, *I, Rigoberta Menchú* "now stands alongside the Hitler Diaries as the great literary hoax of our age" (quoted in Cook-Lynn 87). In Guatemala, Alfred Kalsmith, the director of the Foundation for Aiding Indigenous Peoples and a columnist for *Prensa Libre*, Guatemala's most popular newspaper, observed that "Stoll's book, the product of ten years of careful and extensive research, acquires credibility while Menchú's book loses credibility" (Arias, *The Rigoberta Menchú Controversy* 384). This statement suggests a displacement of "truth" reliability from Menchú's narrative to Stoll's revisionism.

With this kind of reception, how has Stoll's book helped the Left or the indigenous peoples striving to bring justice to those who lost their relatives in the genocide in Guatemala? How does Stoll's work hold responsible the Guatemalan army and the intellectual perpetrators of such atrocities? How does this book help indigenous peoples achieve cultural and political self-determination? In raising these questions, it becomes necessary to ask why Stoll's book has fueled so much controversy, to the extent of raising reasonable suspicion about a possible involvement with national and international military apparatuses like the CIA. One of the many reasons is the book's rather untimely publication during a significant political transition in Guatemala.

The 1990s were a significant decade for indigenous peoples. Some key moments are worth reviewing here. In 1992 many debates took place around the "discovery" of the Americas and whether what happened to indigenous peoples was "genocide." That same year, Rigoberta Menchú was awarded the Nobel Peace Prize, an act that began to shed light and give credence to indigenous peoples' long history of struggle and resistance to defend their values, traditions, languages, and cosmovisions. This prominent activism led to the United Nations' decision to declare the International Year of the Indigenous Peoples of the Americas in 1993. In Guatemala, these events also served as a first step toward significant changes for Mayas. In 1995 the Guatemalan government ratified the Accord on the Identity and Rights of Indigenous Peoples, which officially recognized the country as multilingual and multicultural. At the same time, it opened the door to the Maya movement as a new political force in the country, which began to question the government and demand political participation in the nation-state.[7] A year later, the Peace Accords to end the bitter civil war between the government and the guerrillas were finally signed, officially ending thirty-six long years of armed conflict.[8]

In all these events, Rigoberta Menchú and her narrative played a key role. Her political activism began with her participation in the Committee for Peasant Unity (CUC)[9] and later became public with the launching of a media campaign during 1981. Menchú, along with several representatives of organizations then residing in Mexico, "toured the United States and Europe in order to alert the world to the ruthlessness and viciousness of the Guatemalan regime, which was implementing a process of 'ethnic cleansing'" (Arias, *The Rigoberta Menchú Controversy* 6). Later, Venezuelan anthropologist Elizabeth Burgos would invite Menchú to record her testimony about what happened to her relatives and community. Menchú, it is important to remember, is also the daughter of Maya K'iche' leader and activist Vicente Menchú, who, on January 31, 1980, along with other members of CUC, took over the Spanish embassy in Guatemala to protest human rights violations and to demand land rights in the Ixil area of the country. This protest resulted in their assassination by the Guatemalan army (Arias, *The Rigoberta Menchú Controversy* 5). Following the example of her father, Menchú opted for a similar path of political activism in favor of human and indigenous rights and against oppression and ethnic marginalization. Her well-known narrative, *I, Rigoberta Menchú*, describes her own experience and that of her relatives during Guatemala's civil war.

It did not take long for this book to achieve international recognition and acceptance.[10] One of its most important achievements was that it penetrated international political circles, challenging not only traditional stereotypes about indigenous peoples but also the policies affecting them, such as US foreign policy in Latin America. According to Elizabeth Cook-Lynn (85–86) and Arturo Arias (*The Rigoberta Menchú Controversy* 6), Menchú's testimonio emerged at a time when conservatives and the Right were trying to discredit human rights organizations around the world, especially those that denounced the US economic and military assistance to armies and paramilitary groups in Latin America, such as the so-called contras in Nicaragua. This was during Ronald Reagan's administration (1981–1989). The Republican administration and its supporters legitimated this complicity by suggesting that the Central American insurgents were "Communist agitators" and part of a global conspiracy that threatened "Western democracies." Menchú's testimonio contradicted these claims, denouncing the local armies murdering innocent people in the name of "freedom" and "democracy," and helped to enlighten international opinion regarding the consequences and injustices of these civil wars.[11]

Contrary to the path followed by Luís de Lión, Menchú and her text opened the way to a new kind of revolutionary struggle by authorizing the word and rhetoric. To borrow the words of the Verso editorial department's 1998 response to Stoll's attack, the text "was doing something which the guerrilla commanders had failed to encompass—she was putting the army's brutal regime on the defensive," pushing the state to resolve the internal conflicts through peace negotiations rather than through military action.[12] Indeed, the eventual decision of the government to negotiate with the guerrillas was, in great measure, a result of this successful moral campaign by those involved in producing Menchú's text. A moral campaign, it should be noted, that Menchú has not ended. Instead, the Nobel Peace Prize has motivated her to continue working for greater human rights causes around the world. Her tireless activism keeps pressuring the Guatemalan state to resolve human rights violations.[13] She has struggled to bring to justice high-ranking army officers who participated in the civil war, such as generals Ríos Montt and Humberto Mejia Vitores. Menchú's criticism of the "War on Terror" in her letter to President George W. Bush takes her struggle in the name of human rights beyond national borders.[14] Indeed, her testimonio and her activism have modified the ways we think about the indigenous world. She has transcended many barriers, and she has enriched discussions of testimonial narratives and cultural and postcolonial studies in Latin America, revolutionizing the way we think about the continent.[15]

Stoll's book (*Story of All Poor Guatemalans*) emerged in 1999 as if in response to the preceding decade of Menchú's political activism and her national and global impact and accomplishments. According to Stoll, his book is the product of ten years of field research. Stoll claims that he conducted approximately 120 interviews from Menchú's community during the late 1980s and early 1990s. The book gained more popularity after Larry Rother's article "Tarnished Laureate" was published in the *New York Times* (Arias, *The Rigoberta Menchú Controversy* 58–65). The article and the book consequently elicited a range of responses both supporting and challenging Stoll's arguments.

In his book, Stoll questions the veracity of Menchú's first testimonio, stating that "much of Rigoberta's story is not true" (*Story of All Poor Guatemalans* xviii). He does not deny Menchú's urgent charges concerning the assassination of her relatives and the genocide of Mayas.[16] But he contends that Menchú had an ulterior political motive: ideologically, to defend the position of the guerrillas in the armed struggle in Guatemala, even when the struggle and the Guerrilla Army of the Poor (EGP) had already lost popular support. Stoll states that Menchú "revised the pre-war experience of her village to suit the needs of the revolutionary organization she had joined" (xx), the EGP. Stoll also revisits an earlier argument in which he suggests that the guerrilla uprising in Guatemala was even unnecessary and that it did not express the aspirations and demands of indigenous peoples. Therefore, it assumes greater responsibility for igniting the war (I will come back to this argument in the next section of this chapter).[17] Stoll also questions the image of Menchú as a political figure who has been used to promote a multicultural agenda in the US academy. He observes, for instance, that Menchú entered the academy "in the name of multiculturalism" (243). Her testimonio helped promote a politics of *political correctness* that represents the Maya as a "victim" and not as an agent of change. Furthermore, he suggests that the use of the text in the academy continues to encourage and justify armed struggle in places like Chiapas and Colombia. He therefore blames professors who use Menchú's book for romanticizing armed struggle in the academy and in high schools.

Critics involved in the "Rigoberta Menchú controversy" (Arias) have suggested that Stoll's objectives, rather than showing what happened in Guatemala, have more to do with rescuing the authority of the social sciences to narrate and represent political events in places like Guatemala, an authority that has been displaced by figures like Menchú. Others have argued that Stoll's book is a critique of the multicultural curricula in the United States and the scholars who have used the text in the academy. Still others have questioned Stoll's lack of analysis of the complicity of the

Guatemalan army, the Church, and the United States in Guatemala's civil war.[18] Taking into consideration these analyses and recognizing their contribution to the debate, I consider that the reflections upon Stoll's narrative have not been sufficiently rigorous in questioning his political and ideological motives. As will be shown in this section, his motives illustrate not only an intimate affiliation with hegemonic state apparatuses but also a colonialist ideology that legitimates the domination and genocide of Mayas in Guatemala.

My analysis of Stoll's book concentrates on the chapters about Rigoberta Menchú's father, Vicente Menchú: chapter 3, "The Struggle for Chimel," and chapter 8, "Vicente Menchú and the Guerrilla Army of the Poor." In the first, Stoll talks about Vicente Menchú's disputes over land not with Ladino landowners, but rather with other Maya peasants. These quarrels over land are, in Stoll's view, "common disputes" in Chimel. He adds, "Far from being peaceful, Chimel was known for being more conflictual than most" (*Story of All Poor Guatemalans* 34). In the second of these chapters, Stoll looks upon Vicente Menchú not as a militant hounded by Ladinos and the Guatemalan army, as stated in Menchú's narrative, but rather as a collaborator with the EGP. Stoll argues that Vicente Menchú welcomed the guerrillas to Chimel, an act that consequently provoked an indiscriminate repression in the region by the Guatemalan army. We shall see that Stoll's narrative construction of Vicente Menchú as "irrational" and "stubborn" raises suspicion that Mayas and the EGP are to be blamed for triggering the violence to their own communities.

In chapter 3, which talks about Vicente Menchú's relationship to his community, Stoll tells us that Rigoberta Menchú emphasizes an "ethnic hatred" toward Ladinos in her narrative, especially when she discusses her father. Nevertheless, his evidence shows that Vicente Menchú had good relations with Ladinos (*Story of All Poor Guatemalans* 39). In fact, his success as a leader is attributed to his good relationship not only with them, but also with the army, the Catholic Church, the National Institute of Agrarian Transformation (INTA), the urban Left, and foreign institutions (39). Stoll's assumption is that Menchú constructed a representation of her father as a revolutionary in order to tell readers that indigenous peoples are constant victims of the state and Ladinos and to promote "popular" images of resistance and struggle. Stoll writes that Vicente Menchú did not suffer "from Ladinos as severely" (38) as from other indigenous peasants, because "Ladinos coexisted peacefully with indigenous around Chimel" (39). Here, Stoll advises his readers to erase ideas about indigenous communities being spaces of peaceful social cohesion. By providing such images, Stoll suggests,

Menchú conceals the damage that Maya peasants do to one another when they "compete" for land (19). Stoll writes that "a heroic view of peasants blinds us to the possibility that they consider their main problem to be one another. It also blinds us to the possibility that instead of resisting the state, peasants are using it against other members of their own social class" (31). He also tells us that the Ladino families damned in Menchú's text "are only peripheral actors" (31).

Stoll then goes on to narrate the "conflicts" that Vicente Menchú supposedly had with his own relatives, saying that five groups of Maya peasants competed for 360 hectares of land in and around Chimel. Of this land, Vicente Menchú claimed 151 hectares. In the dispute, the National Institute for Agrarian Transformation (INTA), Stoll says, had no legal authority to enforce a solution.[19] Nevertheless, INTA became a mediator of the conflict. According to Stoll, INTA suggested that it appropriate the 360 hectares of land and redistribute 2,753 hectares of unclaimed land to those in conflict. Of all the people involved, Vicente Menchú refused INTA's proposal, maintaining his initial claim for the 151 hectares. According to Stoll, Vicente Menchú's refusal to compromise delayed INTA's signing for the bigger land transaction, which deepened the conflict between Vicente Menchú and his wife's relatives, the Tums, resulting in his being beaten and put in jail a couple times.

Stoll states that Vicente Menchú's "stubbornness" angered his relatives and also the INTA representatives. His numerous trips to Guatemala City created constant headaches for the INTA functionaries, who were "not the main impediment" (*Story of All Poor Guatemalans* 32), according to Stoll. Quite the contrary, they showed a desire to mediate between the Menchú–Tums. One of Stoll's informants recalls an incident that emphasizes "Vicente's refusal to compromise" in the land dispute (36). The informant recalls the INTA functionaries appealing to a nationalist logic to solve the conflict: "'You are Guatemalans,' the INTA official pleads, 'the two of you… as well. If one of you was from another country, fine, but that is not how it is. Both of you are sons of the same father, of the same country. So it's better if you do not continue fighting'" (36). According to Stoll's informant, Vicente Menchú's "refusal" became "the basic grievance against Vicente within Chimel" (36–37).

The impression the reader gets from reading about this "conflict" is that, rather than Mayas being under attack by agrarian governmental policies, the state and its institutions—INTA, in this particular case—are the ones on the defensive. INTA is "not the impediment," but rather people like Vicente Menchú who make life impossible for the state and for other Mayas who "compete" for land. Examining Stoll's arguments and "evidence," we find contradictions and significant gaps. For instance, after narrating the supposed land conflict, Stoll admits:

> *My evidence on the assaults and litigation is fragmentary. One reason is that someone burned the judicial archive in Santa Cruz del Quiché (for reasons unconnected to the Menchús) just before I went looking for it. Another is that many of the principals died in the violence, with others tending to reticence.* (Story of All Poor Guatemalans 33)

And then,

> *still another reason these incidents are difficult to recover is that bystanders were confused about exactly who was doing what to whom. By 1972–1973 Vicente was confronting not just the brothers of his Tum father-in-law but a group of opponents within his own village.* (Story of All Poor Guatemalans 33)

Note Stoll's admission that his research is compromised by inaccessible sources and destroyed documents, so his assertions are unsubstantiated. This should make us wary about his claims regarding Vicente Menchú and the "land conflict." He acknowledges that we cannot know exactly who was doing what to whom, that concrete evidence to provide us with answers was "burned." Despite this lack of evidence, Stoll derives general conclusions about "Vicente Menchú," a figure he has constructed based on his very limited interviews and documents. Focusing on Vicente Menchú's seeming intransigence, he concludes that the Maya leader was a stubborn, illogical, and authoritarian troublemaker who refused to negotiate, placing "land" above family relations and community. Having established this arbitrary narrative, Stoll extrapolates that Menchú was a respected leader but also authoritarian: "As the founder of an independent settlement, Vicente apparently saw himself as the community's father and felt he had the right to punish members who disobeyed him" (*Story of All Poor Guatemalans* 38). Stoll presumes that this overbearing authority to punish others led to Menchú's beating and incarceration.

In this narrative construction about land conflicts, there emerge contradictions. For example, we learn that Vicente Menchú was very aware of INTA's poor performance in the past. Through one of the Ladino informants interviewed by Stoll, we find out that Vicente Menchú had good reasons not to trust INTA: "INTA deceived him many times. It would say that his petition had been lost, that his lands had to be surveyed again. It said that it would deliver his titles and not do it. Trip after trip to the capital. Those people, that man [Vicente Menchú], they went through hardships...INTA is completely impossible" (*Story of All Poor Guatemalans* 32). If what Stoll's informant said is true, then why would Vicente Menchú trust this institution and its supposed "generosity" in offering thousands of hectares of land? Why would he not question INTA's motives?

Other important questions emerge from Stoll's reading of the internal conflicts between Mayas in Chimel. Where does INTA's sudden interest in allotting the initial 360 hectares of land come from? If Vicente Menchú's relatives were so eager to accept INTA's deal and move to a new territory, why did they not work out a deal in which Vicente Menchú could keep the 151 hectares he wanted in the first place? Why did INTA not suggest this alternative if it was truly willing to redistribute more land and solve the conflict? In addition, Stoll does not elaborate on the 2,753 hectares of unclaimed land that INTA was offering. Was this land located in Chimel? Was it ready to be cultivated? Stoll does not provide answers for us. Instead, through reductive, ad hominem assertions on the individual rather than the larger principles of community at issue, he diverts our attention from these questions in order to present Vicente Menchú as a person who is "authoritarian" and "stubborn" and "refuses to compromise."

It is precisely this omission of the state's institution and politics that makes Stoll's book suspect. He does not question the state's motives, nor the historic relations of power it has established and exerted upon indigenous peoples ever since the conquest. We agree with Stoll about the Maya world constituting a social body like any other, where internal conflicts and disagreements occur. Nevertheless, it is evident that Stoll's objective is to discredit Vicente Menchú. Indeed, Stoll's narrative, as we will see later, purposefully creates an unreasonable, obstinate figure in order to divert blame for the massacre in the Spanish embassy.[20] He also paints a picture of someone who welcomed the guerrillas to Chimel, which motivated the army's military intervention in the region. Before examining Stoll's reading of Vicente Menchú's supposed relationship with the EGP, let me offer an alternative interpretation to Stoll's narrative within the time period he studies.

If we contextualize the relations of power that have existed between Mayas and the state, we see that the Guatemalan army imposed a political agenda to fragment indigenous communities. In the 1980s the state achieved this goal by providing indigenous families whom they considered influential with land titles in order to win their sympathy. This strategy counteracted that of the guerrillas, who had achieved some success by winning support in many communities. After the guerrillas were defeated, however, General Ríos Montt carried out extensive campaigns in late 1982 to resettle lands by awarding some two thousand land titles to campesinos (peasants) in the most conflict-ridden areas. Patrick Costello states, "While these campaigns helped improve the army's image, they also removed physical evidence of large-scale violence and enabled the army to prevent 'troublemakers' from owning and working the land." According to Costello, this policy of land distribution went hand in hand with economic and political aid from the US government, which, during this particular decade, poured $53.6 million into military and logistic training of the Guatemalan army.

Besides land redistribution and economic aid from abroad, religion played a significant role in dividing Maya communities, especially during Ríos Montt's regime. The general was denounced by the Catholic Church for ascribing religious motivations to the bloody war. Ríos Montt was successful in dividing communities through religious evangelical groups because he influenced important segments of the population that the guerrillas and Catholic Action could not access. Many of those who participated in the paramilitary groups, such as the self-defense civil patrols (PAC), were Protestant, as was 5 percent of the population in Guatemala during this time. This religious context raises a very significant question about Stoll's study, especially his informants. Taking into account that Stoll gathered his "field research" in a post-war context throughout an area still surrounded by military bases, is it not possible that the testimonies and information he gathered came from war survivors who, in the fratricidal experience, allied themselves with the Guatemalan army?

In addition, why does Stoll marginalize a critique of the state and its institutions, INTA in this particular case? Why not question its role and even the United States' involvement in the war? Why write an exposé on Menchú (to recall the titles of Carol Smith's and Kay B. Warren's essays),[21] and why write it at a time when indigenous peoples were gaining ground by achieving some significant political spaces? This lack of questioning of the state's institutions and the United States' role in the Guatemalan war raises suspicions about Stoll's complicity with the status quo and his lack of "objectivity." These suspicions become more justified when we analyze the supposed relationship between Vicente Menchú and the EGP.

In the chapter "Vicente Menchú and the EGP," Stoll alerts us that "there are enough conflicting versions and enough gaps in my information, that I cannot be definitive about Vicente's feelings toward the guerrillas" (*Story of All Poor Guatemalans* 108). Stoll includes testimonies that suggest "that neither Vicente Menchú nor Chimel became involved with the guerrillas" (111). He even includes information from Vicente Menchú himself, who said that he "wasn't there [in Chimel] when they [the guerrillas] came through" (114). Even though Stoll admits that his evidence is "conflicting," that there are "enough gaps," and that he "cannot be definitive" about whether Vicente Menchú collaborated with the guerrillas, once again, his narrative would make the reader believe that, in effect, Vicente Menchú "welcome[d] the EGP to his village" (115). To argue this point would be important for Stoll because collaboration with the guerrillas would legitimize the intervention of the Guatemalan army in Chimel and Uspantan. Also, this narrative would fit his larger hypothesis: those to be blamed for the massacres and the genocide in Guatemala are not the government and the army, but rather the guerrillas and Mayas themselves.

Stoll's approach, to make Vicente Menchú virtually responsible for the massacres in Chimel, enacts a colonialist strategy in that he appropriates testimonies of informants who presume a connection between the Maya leader and the EGP. Stoll later attributes these testimonies to Vicente Menchú. Stoll even includes the testimonies of informants who did not know Rigoberta's father, in order to support his own assumptions about Menchú's welcoming the guerrillas to Chimel. Stoll writes, for instance, "Although our source did not know Vicente by sight, he did remember an *older man saying*... 'If you live up to your word, we are in agreement.' Interpreted literally, this is a conditional welcome, and perhaps only a reluctant one" (*Story of All Poor Guatemalans* 116, emphasis added). Stoll arbitrarily identifies the "older man" as Vicente Menchú and then attributes the words to him.

We also hear from another "source" who supposedly "heard" that Vicente Menchú had talked with the EGP:

> What I heard *is that Vicente talked with them [the EGP] there. Later they came down...they came here and held a meeting over there in the chapel with Vicente. At the meeting Vicente explained to the neighbors that they are helping us, that they are here to support us.... I was watching at a distance, became worried and didn't stay.... At [a later] meeting, Vicente said that* if there is someone who doesn't want to come to the meetings or who wants to inform the army or the military commissioners, this is called a reactionary, this is called an *oreja* [ear, meaning "spy"], and he is killed. *He said that, if one goes to the army, the guerrillas will come another time to kill him. There were several meetings. They [the guerrillas] came several times.*
> (Story of All Poor Guatemalans 111, emphasis added)

The words of this informant are later appropriated by Stoll and attributed to Vicente Menchú in order to suggest that he was frightening the community into welcoming the guerrillas. Stoll then repeats what Vicente allegedly threatened ("how Vicente has been quoted above"): "If there is someone who doesn't want to come to the meetings or who wants to inform the army or the military commissioners...this is called a reactionary, this is called a [spy], and he is killed" (120). It is clear that these are not the words of Vicente Menchú, but rather of Stoll's informant.

The same strategy of misappropriation is used again when Stoll quotes an interview in which an indigenous peasant—"probably Vicente Menchú," according to Stoll—says:

> I was a soldier in the time of [the dictator] Ubico; these ideas didn't exist like what is happening now.... We always went out to inspect something for the head of our unit, but they were always watching us so that we didn't do anything against others. But now it appears that those in the army have no discipline, because they no longer respect our rights as campesinos indígenas. (Story of All Poor Guatemalans 119)

In footnote 11, which accompanies the quotation, Stoll justifies his belief that this indigenous peasant is Vicente Menchú: "I presume this was Vicente because he was known for his good Spanish and the delegation probably did not include another army veteran from the Ubico era" (*Story of All Poor Guatemalans* 297). Again, what we obtain is Stoll's assumption and not concrete evidence. Furthermore, Stoll's narrative strategy to show a relationship between the Maya leader and the EGP is equally based upon innuendo—for instance: "Why would he welcome the FGP to his village *before* the army began kidnapping men from Chimel and San Pablo?" (115). This question insinuates a connection between Vicente Menchú and the guerrillas, again, founded upon Stoll's assumptions and not upon concrete evidence.

In this chapter, "possible," "probably," and "perhaps" are repeated constantly. It is "possible" that Vicente Menchú "was attracted to the promises of the Guerrilla Army of the Poor" (*Story of All Poor Guatemalans* 122), that "perhaps he regarded the guerrillas as friends" (114), and that he welcomed them to his community possibly "because he hoped they would help him against the Tums" (122). Yet another "possibility" is that Rigoberta's father "could have" welcomed the guerrillas because

> peasants are very aware of their lack of power, so they understand the importance of maintaining good relations with whatever faction has the upper hand. The sudden arrival of a guerrilla column, in far greater numbers than government troops had ever manifested themselves, could have impressed Vicente, as could their vision of a new social order. (Story of All Poor Guatemalans 119)

Revealing what resembles Edward Said's discussion of orientalism (*Orientalism*),[22] Stoll subsumes how peasants think—"understand," "are very aware." More important, note how the relationship between Vicente Menchú and the EGP is founded on probabilities.

Stoll finally concludes: "How about Vicente's relation to the EGP? What can be established is that guerrillas held meetings in Chimel, but not much else" (*Story of All Poor Guatemalans* 122). Beyond the guerrillas' presence in the village, then, nothing links the Maya leader to the EGP, except the title of the chapter. Elizabeth Burgos states in her prologue to the new edition of Stoll's book that he verifies "facts with other witnesses and carr[ies] out a historical, sociological and ethnographic survey, *in the best professional sense of the term*" (xvii, emphasis added). On the contrary, as we can see above, Stoll manipulates information: he does not obtain the direct testimonies of Vicente Menchú but instead gathers testimonies from other people in order to invent a narrative to implicate the Maya activist's involvement with the EGP. So much for "truth standards" and "objectivity"!

Stoll also manipulates his readers' sympathies by suggesting that the army's repression resulted from Vicente Menchú's actions. In the end, what this narrative truly shows is Stoll's predisposition against Guatemala's EGP. Several times, he wonders, "Why not report the EGP's visit to the army?" (*Story of All Poor Guatemalans* 115), or "Why didn't anyone in Chimel complain to the army?" (110).

Stoll's narrative construction of Vicente Menchú displays an obvious colonialist affiliation with circuits of power. His narrative strategy even resembles a colonialist literary and ideological tradition founded by Lydia Maria Child and James Fenimore Cooper, whose fictions—unconsciously perhaps—manipulated the histories of Native Americans. Child's novel *Hobomok* and Cooper's *The Last of the Mohicans* emphasize a politics of erasure and historical forgetfulness. These authors appropriated the indigenous world in order to distort it and use this distortion against the peoples of that world. In Child's representation, the "disappearance" of indigenous races is not so much the result of genocide, but rather an auto-disappearance of Indians. The English settlers, according to this narrative, find themselves "amid the fierceness of [Native American] savage warfare" (Child 34). Cooper, besides attributing the "disappearance" of Indians to auto-genocide, adds that the "inevitable disappearance of all these people" is also the result of "the advances, or it might be termed the inroads, of civilization" (vii). He later capitalizes on this point:

> There are remnants of all these people still living on lands secured to them by the state; but they are daily disappearing, either by deaths or by removals to scenes more congenial to their habits. In a short time there will be no remains of these extraordinary people, in those regions in which they dwelt for centuries, but their names. (Cooper 23)

These discursive strategies, which resemble Stoll's, represent the invaders and colonizers as being on the defensive against—according to Child (30)—indigenous peoples' "plan of universal domination." Child does not mention colonial policies of land dispossession or genocide. Similarly, with Stoll's appropriation of Vicente Menchú, he constructs a narrative suggesting that Maya peasants are to be blamed for their own terrible fate; that is, Vicente Menchú's welcoming the EGP in Chimel necessitated the army's brutality in the region. Also, Vicente Menchú's supposed land conflicts are not with Ladinos or the state, but rather with his own people, just like Child's and Cooper's representations of Hobomok and the Mohicans, who had good relations with the Europeans but were at war with other indigenous tribes. In Stoll's view, the Maya leader had "good" relations with Ladinos and the army.[23]

In light of this reading, it is pertinent to ask, To what do we owe this attack on Rigoberta Menchú and this conscious distortion of events in Chimel? Why accuse Mayas like Vicente Menchú, who actively struggled to change the conditions of existence in their communities, of initiating civil war and genocide in Guatemala? In my view, Stoll's analysis shows a political agenda that can be related to what Ranajit Guha calls a "prose of counterinsurgency" (Elementary Aspects 3), because it represents the history of Guatemala from the perspective, and according to the epistemological and cultural apparatuses, of the dominant groups, as well as constructing a bureaucratic and academic discourse in the name of those hegemonic apparatuses. Despite Stoll's claims that he is not an apologist for the army or state institutions like INTA, his reading of the civil war ends up legitimizing and apologizing for these institutions.[24] This prose of counterinsurgency becomes more evident when he mentions the role of the US government in Latin America since the 1960s.

Even though Stoll admits certain responsibility on the part of the US government for supporting military dictatorships in Latin America and for the genocide in Guatemala, his statement rationalizes this support:

> The United States bears much of the responsibility for this tragedy, but it could not have happened without the specter of foreign communism, as provided by the revolutionary theatrics from Cuba. Insurgency would seem to be a remedy that prolonged the illness, by bolstering the rationales of the most homicidal wing of the officer corps in one country after another. (Story of All Poor Guatemalans 279)

Note how Stoll admits the complicity of the United States in Guatemala's fratricidal experience and at the same time justifies it: "It could not have happened without the specter of foreign communism." Furthermore, if guerrilla movements had not existed, there would have not been an "illness" in the first place. Rather than problematize the context of such intervention, he suggests that the causes of the genocide were foreign communism and the insurgencies, not an imperialist desire for political and economic hegemony.[25] This perspective also marginalizes the United States' long-standing support of dictatorships in the region, such as the aforementioned Ríos Montt and Augusto Pinochet in Chile. Even President Bill Clinton admitted and assumed responsibility for the United States' complicity in Guatemala's civil war. In March 1999 he apologized to the Guatemalan people: "It is important that I state clearly that support for military forces or intelligence units which engaged in violent and widespread repression was wrong."[26] Stoll's statement also raises questions: What were the alternatives available to those who suffered under dictatorships in Latin America? In Jennifer Schirmer's analysis of the Guatemalan army, she asks Stoll about such "alternatives": "What kind of politics was possible in Guatemala in the late 1970s and early 1980s? What was one to do to change society at this time? How did one operate with such a powerful army dominating politics?" ("Whose Testimony?" 72).

Thus, Stoll marginalizes a history of oppression, racism, and persecution experienced by peoples who, during the civil war, only thought about surviving, which is what Rigoberta Menchú wanted to communicate. Indigenous peoples have struggled to overcome these systematic assaults ever since the conquest. Stoll's study displays a deliberate colonialist and epistemological attack because it consciously falsifies and misrepresents information, elaborated on the grounds of "empirical and objective evidence." His book may be understood as reaffirming colonialism itself because it takes its authority from a Eurocentric anthropological tradition and discursivity founded on the pacification, domination, and domestication of its object of study.

Indeed, Stoll's book demonstrates the very warning of the International Indian Treaty Consul when it states that "anthropologists and archeologists have continually robbed our graves, perverted our intellectual property, and disturbed our sacred sites to promote 'their' version of history" (quoted in Sanford, "The Silencing of Maya Women" 136). These experiences of cultural dispossession are nothing new. Many critics have sought to demonstrate the colonialist complicity of the social sciences and the West in developing narratives of national, political, and cultural formation by legitimating and deploying the domination of the subaltern, by constructing a racial/ethnic cultural division through "difference" and "otherness."[27] Stoll's study goes against the efforts of those who seek to develop new relationships with the peoples who have experienced political marginalization, oppression, and genocide. Johannes Fabian, for instance, states:

> We will always be liable to be seen (correctly) as old colonizers in a
> new guise as long as we understand critical, emancipatory anthropol-
> ogy as doing our critique to help them—be they the Third World, the
> working classes, the disinherited, women.... Who are we to "help"
> them? We need critique (exposure of imperialist lies, of the workings of
> capitalism, of the misguided ideas of scientism, and all the rest) to help
> ourselves. The match is, of course, that "ourselves" ought to be them as
> well as us. (Time and the Work of Anthropology 264)

By imposing his version of the "truth," and contrary to Fabian's assertion,
Stoll reflects Stanley Diamond with regards to the discipline of anthropology: "It is only a representative of our civilization who can, in adequate detail,
document the difference and help create an idea of the primitive which
would not ordinarily be constructed by primitives themselves" (433).[28]

In this line of argumentation, it is pertinent to remember what Edward
Said tells us about interpretations:

> [They] depend very much on who the interpreter is, whom he or she is
> addressing, what his or her purpose is in interpreting, at what histori-
> cal moment the interpretation takes place. In this sense, all interpreta-
> tions are what might be called situational: they always occur in a
> situation whose bearing on the interpretation is affiliative. It is related
> to what other interpreters have said, either by confirming them, or by
> disputing them, or by continuing them. (Covering Islam 154)

Said helps demystify Stoll in particular and the social sciences in general by
reminding us that there are no "apolitical" readings. When "experts" take
indigenous peoples as "objects of study," there are specific political and ideological objectives, as well as consequences. This point is also reaffirmed by
Martin Nakata, who reminds us that "apolitical readings" about indigenous
peoples by Western experts are suspect because such readings are
"inevitably done in the interest of the West, however liberal their pretensions are, however blind they are themselves to this" (64).

Thus, despite Stoll's claims to empiricism and objectivity, his approach
to the "land conflicts" and Vicente Menchú's "relationship" with the EGP is
nothing more than a trick to make us believe that he is being "objective" and
"apolitical." His narrative construction is deliberate, founded upon his own
privileges as a cultural authority and seeking to legitimate his privileges, as
well as the coloniality of power. He constructs a narrative in which the
Guatemalan army and the government, with the support of the United
States, were defending themselves against insurgents and troublemakers like
Vicente Menchú and therefore the latter were most responsible for the

tragedy in Guatemala. It is pertinent, in this context, to remember the words of Elizabeth Cook-Lynn, who writes of Stoll's study:

> The struggle of the colonized indigenous peoples of the continent to tell their own stories in the twentieth century through politics or literature or revolutionary movements has been the struggle to reveal to the public the hope for a new and remodeled world. The denial of this basic human right, through the development of nationalistic, legal, social, and intellectual systems that make it impossible for a domestic people, or a domestic nation of Indians, to express itself collectively and historically in terms of continued self-determination, is a kind of genocide that is perhaps even more immoral than the physical genocide of war and torture. (86)

In the end, this deliberate attack on Rigoberta Menchú and her father, contrary to Stoll's assertions (*Story of All Poor Guatemalans* 296), confirms that Stoll represents the interest of those in power and the status quo, and not indigenous peoples. His epistemological efforts seek to neutralize narratives and movements of resistance like those of Menchú or the Zapatistas in southern Mexico, because they not only represent a threat but also expose the dark side of modernity. For Stoll, the history of genocide experienced by thousands of Mayas in Guatemala represents a disgrace to Western morality, a disgrace that needs to be removed from the progressive vision of that "modern" narrative. Nevertheless, such an attack is not enough to diminish Vicente Menchú, his daughter, and others who have tirelessly worked to better the conditions of indigenous peoples. Vicente Menchú, like other Guatemalan Mayas who sacrificed their lives in the recent civil war, represents heroism, dignity, and, most important, the aspirations of indigenous peoples to a future in which colonialism, racial oppression, and inequality cease to exist.

To what extent was Stoll successful in his attack on Menchú? Has he stopped Menchú's and other women's activism and denouncement of political injustices? I now turn to these questions by considering Menchú's cultural and political contribution to the Maya movement and her intercultural discourse as a basis to rethink Guatemala's intercultural nationalism.

Rigoberta Menchú: Toward New Intercultural Relations in Guatemala and Latin America

I feel that women's voice, once it is heard, will activate and make audible the other small voices as well.—*Ranajit Guha, "The Small Voice of History"*

Let us return for a moment to Stoll's reading of Menchú's testimonio. According to Stoll, *I, Rigoberta Menchú* validated the premise that "the insurgency…springs from the most basic needs of peasants, for their land [and from] the immiseration or oppression" (*Story of All Poor Guatemalans* 9). She also represents those she knows as "peasant revolutionaries of the kind envisioned by the EGP" (194). With this narrative, then, Menchú not only provided a rationale for insurgency but also "became the revolutionary movement's most appealing symbol, pulling together images of resistance from the previous decade" (7). As such, Stoll suggests that Menchú's testimonio does not reflect her voice, but rather the EGP's objectives. That is, she is a mediator who is directed or manipulated by the guerrilla organization.

From these statements, we can determine that Stoll understands Leftist narratives as being similar to the discourses of Mario Payeras or Omar Cabezas in, respectively, *Days of the Jungle* and *Fire from the Mountain: The Making of a Sandinista*. These texts emphasize guerrilla strategies according to the *foquismo* ideology theorized by Regis Debray and Carlos Marighella, which helped Cuba and Nicaragua achieve their revolutionary objectives. The ideology of foquismo, it should be remembered, consists of an intellectual and political vanguard that assumes leadership of the armed movement by claiming to understand the problems of the oppressed masses and promoting guerrilla warfare as a first step toward their emancipation. The model of struggle that Stoll describes with regard to the EGP, despite his reservations,[29] falls within this characterization. He thus desires to save us from the "captivity of Gueverism" mentioned previously (*Story of All Poor Guatemalans* 282).

In the chapter "After the Controversy: Lessons Learned about Subalternity and the Indigenous Subject" (Arias, *Taking Their Word*), Arturo Arias challenges Stoll's reading of *I, Rigoberta Menchú* as a narrative that endorses the EGP. In Stoll, Arias reads a certain arbitrary authority with respect to the "discoveries" of Stoll's research on the Guatemalan Left. Arias tell us that instead of being something new, Stoll's assumptions (regarding the presence of guerrillas in Maya territory and the consequent incorporation of Mayas in the insurgency) have precedents in the debates that arose within the Left itself during the 1970s.[30] According to Arias, despite the fact that Stoll includes key texts on the debates in his bibliography, Stoll fails to recognize their contributions. Instead, he appropriates them, insinuating "that Menchú might still secretly be a member of the EGP…. He also insinuates that the Guatemalan Left still looks or thinks as it did in the early 1980s and that no Guatemalan had previously published a critique of the Left or a serious analysis of the conditions that led to war between 1954 and the 1980s" (Arias, *Taking Their Word* 121).[31]

From this perspective, Arias suggests that Stoll homogenizes the varied ideological manifestations that existed between organizations like the EGP, the Revolutionary Organization of People in Arms (ORPA), and the Revolutionary Armed Forces (FAR) during the 1970s. Contrary to Stoll's conclusions about the Left, Arias affirms that the military presence in Maya areas was more a question of logistics and that the incorporation of Mayas into the armed struggle "was the result of accelerated modernization and not of centuries of languishing in backward conditions" (*Taking Their Word* 112). Furthermore, Arias indicates that the reading and interpretation that international solidarity organizations obtained from Menchú's text was one of solidarity and awareness about the genocide and not one of endorsing armed struggle. Arias himself relates his experience as a conference participant abroad whose work denounced what was happening in Guatemala during the 1980s.

Besides marginalizing these debates, Stoll omits a discussion of the Committee of Peasant Unity (CUC) and Catholic Action (AC), organizations that Menchú centralizes in her narrative and that played a significant role in her political and activist formation.[32] However, I am more concerned with examining whether Menchú is really spreading a "Leftist" discourse. With this in mind, what are we referring to when we speak of the Left today? What does it mean to be labeled Leftist? How do we interpret the fact that Stoll considers himself to be on the "Left"? It is curious to note that when Stoll made these attacks on Menchú, he did not pay much attention to the text she wrote with the CUC, *Trenzando el futuro: Luchas campesinas en la historia reciente de Guatemala* (Weaving the Future: Peasant Struggles in Guatemala's Recent History), a text that is much more combative than *I, Rigoberta Menchú* and that appeared a few months before she was awarded the Nobel Peace Prize.

In the interview with Bernardo Atxaga that appears in this practically forgotten book within the current Menchú–Stoll debate, Menchú anticipates the emergence of interpretations like the one Stoll makes of her and of the Left:

> *The racist reaction of many people when I first spoke out is incredible. I know many anthropologists or sociologists, and I am not against these professions;* they said that I was manipulated by the Left or that I had been indoctrinated *and that I carried Leftist propaganda because I spoke of the unity among poor indigenous peoples and Ladinos. When I spoke on the topic of human rights, of militarization, when I spoke of the disappeared, some of these people said: Rigoberta is actually indoctrinated by the Left. I am supposed to speak of an indigenous past using*

an exclusive indigenista discourse…here, ironically, there is a certain
message suggesting that indigenous peoples will never get along with
the West.[33] (Menchú and CUC 14–15, emphasis added)

This quote advances some of the fundamental points of Menchú's discourse. As can be seen, she desires to further a political agenda that denounces injustices against human rights—to "speak out" against "militarization," about "the disappeared." She also demystifies the indigenista discourse that imprisons the Maya past by not relating the experience of indigenous peoples to their present. Moreover, as with her first testimonio, Menchú emphasizes the "unity" among poor indigenous and Ladino peoples. These themes are a constant in Menchú's discourse and constitute an early manifestation of an intercultural epistemology that reaches full maturity in her second testimonio, *Crossing Borders*. I will return to the discussion on interculturality in *Crossing Borders* later in this chapter. For now, it is important to highlight how, in this quote, Menchú insists on establishing her own agency—she is neither "manipulated" nor "indoctrinated" by the Left. What is important for her is to denounce injustices committed against indigenous communities. Menchú's agency as a narrator, however, is not something new; in fact, it is also established by Elizabeth Burgos in the prologue to *I, Rigoberta Menchú*.

When Burgos and Menchú were working on the testimonio, the former recognized that the Maya K'iche' activist brought a political agenda with her. Burgos says, "When we began to use the tape recorder, I initially gave her a schematic outline, a chronology.… As we continued, Rigoberta made more and more digressions, introduced descriptions of cultural practices into her story and generally upset my chronology" (Menchú and Burgos xix). Years later, Burgos again alluded to Menchú's agency: "Very quickly I realized that Rigoberta Menchú wanted to talk about herself, to go beyond just an account of repression. I therefore opted in favor of delving deeply into her customs, her vision of the world (as much political as religious), and, above all, her identity" ("The Story of a Testimonio" 55–56). What this demonstrates is that, far from being the "revolutionary movement's symbol" or spreading "Leftist propaganda," as Stoll suggests (*Story of All Poor Guatemalans* 7, 194), Menchú controls the power to transmit her narrative in her own terms. The story, for the most part, is Menchú's. It obeys a discursive strategy devised by Menchú herself, not in order to give us the EGP's "version of events" but rather to give us her own version (Rabasa 232, n. 27), which involves developing and promoting an agenda of cultural revitalization related to the political ideals of the Maya movement.

In the relationship between Burgos and Menchú, it is not difficult to perceive the challenges that the Maya K'iche' activist makes to the authority that Burgos represents as an anthropologist, establishing her own political goals in order to narrate her own story. Even within the stories, in text we perceive a woman who defies the authority of others. Perhaps the most notable and memorable is Menchú's challenge to her own father, Vicente Menchú, when she defies him by taking the initiative to learn Spanish and educate herself within the dominant system. This decision shows her conviction to challenge an entire political system that affects indigenous peoples. That is, learning Spanish has nothing to do with achieving a higher socioeconomic position and turning her back on the community, but rather represents a political strategy or a path to follow in a decolonial struggle similar to that proposed by de Lión in his literature (see chapter 2). These examples show that, throughout her experience, Menchú was taking advantage of each available space to gain political authority in order to establish her own locus of enunciation, to voice her perspective, and to spread the demands and political objectives of indigenous peoples.

The discursive deviations referred to above appear consistent with Menchú's ideals of reaffirming and promoting Maya cosmovision as a fundamental principle of survival. In fact, the emphasis that Menchú places on indigenous cosmovision—especially the intimate and spiritual relationship between the Maya and Mother Earth—is precisely the signature of her discursivity. We find it repeatedly throughout her textual production. Let us compare what Menchú says to us on different occasions.

In her first testimonio, she observes, "We think of the Earth as the mother of man, and our parents teach us to respect the Earth. We must only harm the Earth when we are in need. This is why, before we sow our maize, we have to ask the Earth's permission" (Menchú and Burgos 56). And later: "When we plant seeds, we ask permission of the Earth. We make a ceremony with incense and candles, and we plant a seed of corn. The entire community participates. We pray to the Earth because it is there where God is. So we feel very Christian, but at the same time, very indigenous and loyal to our ancestors" (Menchú and CUC 27). And, finally, in Menchú's Nobel acceptance speech:

> To us, Mother Earth is not only a source of economic riches that give us the maize, which is our life, but she also provides so many other things that the privileged ones of today strive for. The Earth is the root and the source of our culture. She keeps our memories, she receives our ancestors and she, therefore, demands that we honor her and return to her, with tenderness and respect, those goods that she gives us. We have to take care of her so that our children and grandchildren may continue to benefit from her. If the world does not learn now to show respect to

nature, what kind of future will the new generations have? (Menchú and CUC, pg. 15)

The importance that Menchú gives to the relationship between Mother Earth and the Maya is extremely significant; it is a valuable moral and spiritual contribution of Maya culture that she wants to share with the rest of humanity. Not only that, her descriptions define a narrative of local and international resistance. John Beverly, for example, makes reference to this particular aspect of Menchú's discourse, especially in regards to *I, Rigoberta Menchú*, suggesting that her insistence on the authority of her ancestors or on that of "tradition" is "an appeal that is being activated *in the present*, that it is a response to the conditions of proletarianization and semiproletarianization that subjects like Menchú and her family are experiencing in the context of the *same* processes of globalization that affect our own lives" (*Testimonio* 74). We can thus conclude that emphasizing the Maya cosmovision entails, for Menchú, developing an indigenous epistemological locus of enunciation that resists narratives of transculturation and hybridity proposing cultural homogenization and resists and criticizes modernization mechanisms that threaten indigenous values.

It should be made equally clear that when Menchú refers to Maya spirituality or the relationship between indigenous peoples and the Earth, she is not resisting modernity or globalization in order to declare a kind of "return" to the past. In referring to the use of "modern things," she tells us: "I, for example, use a fax machine a lot, and I like fax machines. Should we instead revive the practice of sending messages via mule?" ("Menchú and CUC 15"). As this passage makes clear, what she points to is an understanding that indigenous peoples are also participants and protagonists in modernity, that Maya "tradition" also coexists and is compatible with Western "modernity." By emphasizing aspects of her culture, she dismantles the perception that indigenous values have no place within modernity and suggests that such values can actually contribute to reshaping modernity itself.

With her desire and capacity to center Maya cultural specificities within modernity, is Menchú recycling the "Guevarista" discourse of the EGP? Is she promoting "Leftist" propaganda? In another place, Menchú has also affirmed that, beyond denouncing what happened in Guatemala, she felt it important "to share experiences with brothers from other places" (Yáñez 97), which is why she sees the Spanish language as a powerful mechanism of communication and intercultural exchange (97). We can affirm that, far from "promoting the ideals of the EGP" in Europe, Menchú intended, according to Elizabeth Burgos herself, "to sensitize public opinion to the terrible repression hanging over her country, especially its indigenous communities" (54).

Here, it is also worth remembering that when Menchú narrated her testimo-nio, she was already giving talks denouncing what was happening in Guatemala. Menchú later met Burgos in Paris, where she was planning fur-ther travels in order to continue her activism and political work.

I, Rigoberta Menchú is a narrative that denounces the horrors of war that have plagued thousands of Maya and indigenous peoples in Latin America in the past few decades. As well, it is a narrative that establishes a Maya epis-temology centralizing the survival of the values of present-day indigenous peoples. Indeed, the importance that Menchú places on Maya cosmovision could even be understood as a locus of enunciation that represents a dis-course of resistance, and an alternative, to Eurocentric colonial models, including those of "national liberation" movements that have ignored the importance that cultural, linguistic, and religious values have for indigenous peoples. This is Menchú's contribution to the discussion that Arias mentions in regard to Leftist debates within the Left itself. She is not only a direct or an indirect participant in the armed struggle but also a producer of a dis-course that defies the status quo. She thus establishes a narrative that can be read against narratives of mestizaje or transculturation (Ortiz, *Contrapunteo cubano, Cuban Counterpoint*; Rama, *Transculturación narrativa*), which pro-posed the incorporation of the indigenous population through assimilation. Contrary to those narratives, Menchú emphasizes—as did Luís de Lión—that the integration of indigenous peoples into the nation and modernity needs to recognize their cultural, spiritual, and linguistic specificities and cosmovision.

A more recent response to Stoll's intimations, as well as affirmation of intercultural values from the Maya perspective, can be found in Menchú's second testimonio, *Crossing Borders*. For some, like Georg Gugelberger ("*Stollwerk* or Bulwark?" 49), this text dispels many of the uncertainties that Stoll introduces. For example, in this book Menchú clarifies the significant participation of historian Arturo Taracena in constructing *I, Rigoberta Menchú*. She also talks about her intimate relationship not with the EGP, but with the CUC, an organization that she claims helped shape her principles of life and struggle. She says that in the CUC she learned "to fight as a woman and for the cause of women; she learned to fight for the most ele-mental human values and principles" (Menchú, *La nieta de los Mayas* 254).[34] In this narrative, Menchú also describes how one of her sisters came to be a part of the insurgency (245). Despite this, after leaving Guatemala she did not consider herself to be a voice for the Left (301), but rather that her job was to represent the CUC on an international scale and to draw the interna-tional community's attention to the grave and permanent violations of human rights against indigenous populations in Guatemala. She was "trying to make the Guatemalan situation understood in its totality" (302). Her first book is a "part of the memory of the victims, our right to life" (254).

Moreover, in *Crossing Borders* Menchú provides a significant criticism of "liberation movements" whose ideological foundation is based on Marxist-Leninist ideologies. As is well known, Marxism-Leninism played a central role in giving the defense of the Indian a distinctly revolutionary flavor in Latin America. On the whole, discourses on the Indian had a profound impact on social and political movements that challenged the standing political and social order. Nevertheless, this indigenista discourse was generally not progressive in terms of gender and its approach to Indians, producing stereotypical representations of femininity, masculinity, and the indigenous subject (see chapter 2). While recognizing the contribution of liberation movements toward democratization in the Third World, Menchú suggests that, in their approach to the "indigenous question," their analyses "are very poor...their assertions are limited" (*La nieta de los mayas* 131). Although these movements have pursued better economic conditions for the "people," they have not recognized indigenous people's cultural and linguistic demands. She shows a similar concern regarding "feminism" by suggesting that the struggle for women's equality, besides focusing on the vindication of gender, should support other social causes (131). Menchú had previously touched on the topic of feminism more directly, drawing a link between the struggles of women and indigenous peoples:

> The emancipation of the woman is the emancipation of our peoples. I have always understood that it is not enough to be a woman to have a conscience and it is not enough to be indigenous to have values...the concept of feminism does not exist for me. In my judgment there exists a place for everyone, man or woman, in society. The women of the world, we have specific vindications, but these should be crystallized in the vindication of our society.[35] (Menchú and CUC 9)

What emerges in Menchú's statement is the necessity to develop a collective effort to vindicate society as a whole, a political strategy that embraces the demands of those who, historically, have been oppressed. The specific vindication of women should be included within the demands of indigenous peoples and society in a collective struggle against what we could say represents the coloniality of power.

These critiques on feminism and liberation movements are also echoed by other indigenous activists, who have pointed out a certain arrogance on the part of these movements toward the subaltern. The following demands and criticism of Marxist and feminist paradigms are put forward, respectively, by Lorelei DeCora Means and Janet McCloud, members of the American Indian Movement (AIM). Means states:

> We are American Indian *women, in that order. We are oppressed, first and foremost, as American Indians, as peoples colonized by the United States of America, not as women. As Indians, we can never forget that. Our survival, the survival of every one of us—man, woman and child—as* Indians *depends on it. Decolonization is the agenda, the whole agenda, and until it is accomplished, it is the only agenda that counts for American Indians. It will take every one of us—every single one of us—to get the job done. We haven't got the time, energy or resources for anything else while our lands are being destroyed and our children are dying of avoidable diseases and malnutrition. So we tend to view those who come to us wanting to form alliances on the basis of "new" and "different" or "broader" and "more important" issues to be a little less than friends, especially since most of them come from the Euroamerican population which benefits most directly from our ongoing colonization.* (Jaimes and Halsey 314)

And then McCloud adds:

> *Most of these "progressive" non-Indian ideas like "class struggle" would at the present time divert us into participating as "equals" in our own colonization. Or, like "women's liberation," would divide us among ourselves in such a way as to leave us colonized in the name of "gender equity." Some of us can't help but think maybe a lot of these "better ideas" offered by non-Indians claiming to be our "allies" are intended to accomplish exactly these sorts of diversion and disunity within our movement. So, let me toss out a different sort of "progression" to all you Marxists and socialists and feminists out there. You join us in liberating our land and lives. Lose the privilege you acquire at our expense by occupying our land. Make that your first priority for as long as it takes to make it happen. Then we'll join you in fixing up whatever's left of the class and gender problems in your society, and our own, if need be. But, if you're not willing to do that, then don't presume to tell us how we should go about our liberation, what priorities and values we should have. Since you're standing on our land, we've got to view you as just another oppressor trying to hang on to what's ours. And that doesn't leave us a whole lot to talk about, now does it?* (Jaimes and Halsey 314)

The decolonizing project referred to here values the Earth as its touchstone, as an epistemological and political principle of struggle for the continent's indigenous peoples. In this way, it condemns the Eurocentric character of the "progressive" ideas controlled by the Left and feminism, which—it is suggested—have assumed authority over the epistemological and cultural principles of indigenous peoples. These perspectives, at the same time, emphasize a specific goal: the recuperation of sovereignty.

These positions that question the "progressive" character of the Left and feminism can also be related to the famous debate between Domitila Barrios de Chungara and feminist intellectuals in Mexico, among them Betty Friedman,[36] at the celebration of the International Women's Year Conference. Barrios de Chungara recalls the interventions of various professionals who wanted to homogenize the category of "woman," claiming that it involved the same experiences, the same concerns, and the same struggles toward "equality" for *all* women. At a certain point, Barrios de Chungara entered into a confrontation with Friedman in which some of the event participants prevented her from speaking. They told her to forget for a moment her situation, her poverty, the massacres of miners in Bolivia, and the militarization of the mines, in order to address the common objectives of all "women." Barrios de Chungara then responded:

> All right, let's talk about the two of us. But if you'll let me, I'll begin. Señora, I've known you for a week. Every morning you show up in a different outfit and on the other hand, I don't. Every day you show up all made up and combed like someone who has time to spend in an elegant beauty parlor and who can spend money on that, and yet I don't. And in order to show up here like you do, I'm sure you live in a really elegant home, in an elegant neighborhood, no? And yet we miners' wives only have a small house on loan to us, and when our husbands die or get sick or are fired from the company, we have ninety days to leave the house and then we're in the street. Now, señora, tell me: is your situation at all similar to mine? (202)

All these interventions respond to historical, homogenizing attitudes of racism, sexism, intolerance, paternalism, and xenophobia spread by the discourse of the Left and the feminist movement, which have closed their doors to the epistemological contributions of indigenous peoples. At the same time, these discursive articulations oblige us to think of the "Left" and "feminism" as categories that, similar to "modernity" and the "nation," need to be provincialized (Chakrabarty). That is, these discourses make visible *other* projects concerned with shifting toward decolonial thought, allowing us to

retheorize the social conditions and demands for sovereignty and indigenous rights. Instead of claiming to speak for and about those who live in
conditions of subalternity, these interventions suggest that Leftist and feminist movements should embrace the specific demands and aspirations of the
subaltern. But the demands and aspirations of the subaltern, such as the valorization of indigenous cultural and religious specificities and languages or
the struggle for national sovereignty, do not necessarily go along with the
agendas of feminism and the Left. In spite of the contributions made by the
Leftist and feminist paradigms, these criticisms certainly force us to rethink
their tendencies to overlook the plurality of histories, subject, and cultures
and the collective demands of indigenous women and peoples in their
struggles. Through the emphasis that these organic intellectuals (Gramsci)
place on their experiences of emancipation, their perspectives even redefine
and resignify the structures of power that have excluded them.[37] They reveal
repressive systems and expose the complexities of their own postcolonial
situations. In each of the situations cited above, indigenous women articulate a critical questioning and affirm their locus of enunciation through their
own reinventions as protagonists of history. These women, as Laura
Charlotte Kempen suggests, work toward the creation of a nominative, feminine, singular and plural agent, one that is allied with other women and
men in conditions of subalternity not only within their own cultures, but
also on a global scale. By "bearing witness to their own and others' traumas,
these women rebirth their imprisoned spirit and revitalize it through language, creating and valorizing individual and community identities"
(Kempen 3). In various degrees of radicalism, these indigenous activists
inscribe a criticism of Western progressive discursivities, but most important, they demand that we reread and reconsider the history of the "modern" Americas from their ideological-political standpoint and experiences.

These perspectives also demystify arguments like Stoll's, who suggests
that the struggles of indigenous peoples are imitations or representations of
the struggles of the Left. On the contrary, even if we were to agree with the
assertion that Menchú was a member of the EGP, we could also conclude
that, like de Lión, Menchú used the Left and the armed struggle as a plat-
form to achieve her own political objectives through the narration of her testimonio and her political activism. Contrary to Stoll's suggestions, Menchú's
testimonio and activism, in addition to being a denouncement of the injustices committed against indigenous communities, should also be understood as a narrative and a discursivity that promote the ideals of the Maya
movement—specifically, cultural and linguistic revitalization. The emphasis
and consistency that we find in Menchú's discourse with regard to Maya cultural politics are the result of indigenous peoples' desire to gain prominence

within the hegemonic narratives of the nation and modern Guatemalan history, the desire to revive a political program and an epistemology that can be used to rethink the project of the nation itself, not as a culturally and linguistically homogenous entity but as one that is intercultural.

But what does interculturality consist of for Menchú? Using this discourse, how can we reconcile the narratives of the Maya movement with the historical Ladino narratives of transculturation and mestizaje? How do we reconcile the perspectives of Luis de Lión and Asturias? To respond to these questions, we must return to Menchú's discourse on interethnic relations. I will now focus on her second testimonio, *Crossing Borders*, because it represents, in my opinion, the formation of an intercultural project with precedents in her previous book.

In Elizabeth Burgos's article "The Story of a Testimonio," she criticizes Menchú's second text, arguing that it "simply fails on every count" (60). Burgos disapproves of Menchú's not publishing the text in Guatemala first, nor writing it "with the help of Maya intellectuals" (60) but rather in conjunction with non-indigenous intellectuals (referring to Dante Liano and Gianni Minà): "To have published in Guatemala with the help of Maya writers would in itself have amply justified the book's existence, making it more than simply another mediated exercise" (60). However, as a reading of her book affirms, Menchú's project, beyond establishing the foundations of Maya identity and cosmovision in light of globalization, proposes an intercultural politics in order to build a bridge between indigenous and non-indigenous peoples.

This intercultural project can be traced back to Menchú's very beginnings as a narrator and political activist and became global as she acquired more widespread notoriety. In her acceptance speech of the Nobel Peace Prize, Menchú observed: "If the indigenous civilization and the European civilizations could have made exchanges in a peaceful and harmonious manner, without destruction, exploitation, discrimination and poverty, they could, no doubt, have achieved greater and more valuable conquests for Humanity" ("Discourse of Acceptance"). This passage translates into an incessant search to establish new relationships, not through the domination of some forms of life over others but rather through "exchanges" that serve to eradicate the "destruction," "exploitation," "discrimination," and "poverty" that have affected the majority of humanity. Her emphasis on "indigenous civilizations" seeks to establish a differentiated cultural entity that can contribute to these new and more worthwhile conquests for humanity. According to her, the inevitable path to follow is an intercultural one (*La nieta de los mayas* 189). In this sense, it is no coincidence that, for *Crossing Borders*, Menchú worked in collaboration with Liano (a Guatemalan

Ladino) and Minà (Italian, European), symbolically demonstrating the personal and continental bridge the three of them built with the production of the text.[38] In this same sense, we can recognize the collaboration of other voices in the book, like those of Eduardo Galeano, Esteban Beltrán, and Humberto Ak'abal.[39]

Despite some key differences from her first testimonio, *Crossing Borders* essentially complements the previous text. The book narrates Menchú's life after the Nobel Peace Prize and her work as an activist in prominent institutional spaces like the United Nations (UN). If her first testimonio narrates her life from a position of subalternity, here Menchú, who at this time had established her authority as a political figure, plays the role of a mediator for indigenous peoples in the Americas in front of national and international institutions. As Sarah Penny indicates (514–60), the book is an interesting collection of subjects that includes an account of the events that led to the false kidnapping of her nephew by her own family; the description of who was involved in the narration of her first testimonio and the extent of their involvement; and the importance and influence of other actors in her intellectual formation, such as the Guatemalan writer Luis Cardoza y Aragón, who was living in exile in Mexico, and *Tatic* (Father) Samuel Ruiz, the bishop of the diocese of San Cristóbal de las Casas in Chiapas and mediator in the conflict between the Zapatistas and the Mexican government. In addition, the book narrates her work with exiled Mayas in Chiapas and her tireless legal battles against those who committed the Xamán massacre.[40]

Beyond these anecdotes and experiences, Menchú's book is a profound meditation on globalization and the place that indigenous peoples and the subaltern occupy within its economic and sociocultural processes. Throughout the text, the Maya K'iche' activist is preoccupied with concerns such as "How do we combine Western thought with a communal, millenarian culture that has its own and deep characteristics, that possesses its own symbols and its own communal scheme? How do we weave the basis of intercultural relations with our own peoples? How much time do we need to do that?" (*La nieta de los mayas* 87). When asking these rhetorical questions, Menchú responds to globalization's ongoing violent threats to subalterns and provides some alternatives from the Maya cosmovision. For her, a first step toward establishing intercultural relations means denouncing and disarticulating the "god of war, the god of capital, the god of power" (186), which "places the resources produced by humanity into the hands of a few" (156). According to her, the politics of domination persist through the plundering of resources and property and the unending quest to erase ancestral values and turn men and women into objects of labor and oppression.

Menchú underscores that these globalizing threats are not new; these interminable conflicts have historical-colonial precedents in which the West has imposed its rule upon other subaltern cultures. At present, these conflicts again seek to establish a normative cultural framework of domination, through a market that legitimizes social and economic inequality. At the same time, these neoliberal processes are armed with new and innovative mechanisms for spreading their ideology and covering up the terrible consequences. Menchú's book responds to those who, historically (and now through globalization), have eclipsed or marginalized others. Menchú centers the significant role of the marginalized and the oppressed in the construction of a new narrative of "interculturality" (*La nieta de los mayas* 189).

For Menchú, the construction of this narrative necessarily emphasizes differences in culture and values between an indigenous "us" and a Western "other." However, instead of a harmonious picture of an "us" and "them," Menchú depicts a conflictive relationship based on economic, gender, and political inequalities and the constant violation of indigenous peoples' human rights. The story of the Xamán massacre, which Menchú narrates at the beginning of her text, can even be thought of as a metaphor for the colonial projects that have impeded the sociocultural development of indigenous peoples. Indeed, the war in Guatemala and the Xamán massacre are only two examples of modern processes that have sought to destroy the elementary aspects of Maya culture and prohibit its development. These processes are exemplified in the military occupation of indigenous areas, the usurpation of indigenous lands, the displacement of indigenous communities, the internal divisions provoked by these acts, and the cold-blooded assassination of thousands of Mayas. By highlighting these violent mechanisms, Menchú demystifies the ideas of progress, prosperity, and wellness often associated with the narrative of modernity, casting a shadow over its epistemological landscape. She also states that these violent mechanisms are not particular to Guatemala, but rather are experienced by other people in the world. Referring to the recent genocide of Kurds in Yugoslavia, she observes that "all that cruelty occurs again at a time when everyone proclaims development, when everyone proclaims progress, when everyone proclaims modernity" (*La nieta de los mayas* 186). The very idea of Western modernity is in question. It rejects and tramples upon life, has forgotten service to humanity, and lacks, according to her, a true commitment to the defense of human rights.

In addition to condemning Western violence, Menchú criticizes science and technology. She does not deny or reject their valuable contributions to humanity but rather understands that, historically, they have served the powerful in eliminating human creativity. Rather than foster human unity, Menchú suggests, science and technology have often been used to alienate and fragment humanity. For her, technology should work in favor of humanity and human values, making new generations sensitive to life. Menchú proposes to invert these tendencies in order to develop an exchange of experiences by using the media and technology:

> Rather than the elder narrating his stories to the grandson, he can tell them to society as well.... Television can be the medium to spread traditions without them being manipulated and distorted, ridiculed by folklore. I think that indigenous peoples have a lot of desire to have a computerized web of information. We dream of reaching a brother, sister, mestizo, Ladinos or non-Indians in general; to tell them about our experiences, to share our knowledge and hopes, but from a position of equality and respect. (La nieta de los mayas 154)

Contrary to the accusation that Menchú promotes a "fundamentalist" or "essentialist" discourse or one of "ethnic hatred," she seeks new interethnic relations in a globalized world. The media, instead of manipulating, distorting, and ridiculing, can serve as a cultural mediator that enables the "sharing" of indigenous experiences with non-indigenous peoples.[41] In this way, Menchú presents the fundamental bases of interethnic relationships, respect and equality. This is not a matter of using categories like "Maya" to divide society, but of using the media to reaffirm ancestral values as a fundamental contribution of "our cultures, our identity, so we can come together" (La nieta de los mayas 86). In effect, Menchú believes that "indigenous peoples, in great measure, guard the sacred right of collectivity, the sacred right of community as a foundation of equilibrium" (213). These significant values counteract those of "an opulent, ambitious, stubborn and preponderant circle" (165) that imposes competition—buying, selling, and winning—as the basic principle of survival.

Beyond Menchú's desire that the *others* recognize Maya cosmovision's universal contributions, she emphasizes Maya cosmovision as an alternative to the threats of colonial globalization, a locus of enunciation in itself. For her, this means "revaluing our cultures, revaluing what has been lost, a new dimension of life for all" (La nieta de los mayas 158). This does not mean that Mayas should be concerned only with the specific aspects of their own cultures or with essentializing indigeneity: "In reality, the problem is not in admiring other cultures, the problem is in imposing a culture upon another one" (187). This is the problem with mestizaje in the Americas. Rather than establish a basis for mutual cultural understanding between millenarian cultures and those of the West, mestizaje was proposed as a normative policy to be "imposed" upon indigenous peoples. According to Menchú, this ideology has buried the important contribution of indigenous moral values, culture, thought, and presence, as well as elemental aspects in which these peoples "have contributed with their own blood and their own suffering to build the so-called democracies" (284). This means reestablishing the dignity that has been trampled on; understanding that Maya culture represents a differentiated entity; appreciating that "Maya" is a historical identity that "establishes itself in a tradition, a millenarian culture, in its own vision of life and philosophy" (160). Menchú later suggests that the Maya past should not be reduced to a past of legends but rather "must be the source and support, must also be the pillar of a present and a future" (188).

Drawing on these reflections, Menchú constructs principles based upon a consciousness that denounces the impunity and inequality inflicted by capitalism. She sheds light on reality, giving voice to subalterns who, like her, suffer(ed) the consequences of modernity. She outlines a critical consciousness that should be accompanied by political activism. Everyone is called to contribute in a collective effort emerging from subalternity itself, entailing not only an understanding of "cultural" differences but also an understanding of our role in society as agents of change.

If Menchú emphasizes the collective, she is also cautious in emphasizing the differences that exist among indigenous peoples and so-called minorities. Instead of homogenization, Menchú stresses interculturality as an epistemology and a practice of social cohesion that respects the identities of each individual and of each group.[42] For example, Menchú understands that, on the one hand, the Maya represent cultures that have survived historical experiences of racism, exploitation, and marginalization through a resistance based on millenarian principles and cultural values. Minorities, on the other hand, although in many cases a product of historical conditions of racism, exploitation, and marginalization, do not necessarily base their struggles on ancestral values. In drawing these distinctions, as Ofelia Schutte suggests (1024), Menchú responds to those who confuse and homogenize the struggles of indigenous peoples and of minorities in order to distort the rights and demands of both groups. Menchú states that minorities are

> misunderstood, marginalized, underestimated, repressed...the discrimination that indigenous peoples experience is also experienced by marginalized sectors in society, and the desire to reach a new legal order is also a demand of discriminated sectors. I think that their struggles are similar. The women, indigenous and minorities in the world should definitely come together in the struggle for common interests. We should embrace those struggles because we experience the same

consequences of racism, discrimination, exploitation and the manipulation of our own reality. (La nieta de los mayas 195)

Menchú emphasizes a subaltern perspective in which both minorities and indigenous peoples can interweave their commonalities and struggles, despite their differences. This perspective is Menchú's response to the mechanisms of "marginalization," "racism," and "exploitation." Likewise, Menchú proposes "embracing" political struggles through interculturality, through a collective critical "consciousness" that commands a degree of political prominence.

As a Maya woman who has achieved cultural and political authority, Menchú follows a path in which she assumes a responsibility and commitment to indigenous peoples and subalterns in general, as can be discerned from her interpretations of globalization. This attitude still is articulated during a time in which many no longer consider Menchú to be a "subaltern." However, she has not stopped honoring this commitment.[43] If previously we took her as speaking from subalternity itself, Menchú now occupies, in effect, a space of authority outside the environment from which she came, redefining her commitment as a mediator in institutional spaces. For her, this does not mean turning her back on everything that formed her critical and social consciousness, but rather furthering this consciousness, taking this political prominence to new institutional spaces, and carrying out her work as an organic intellectual (Gramsci) in these new surroundings.

Menchú is concerned with exposing the "dark side" of globalization, which spreads the myth of democracy but does not reconfigure the profound authoritarianism and exclusion endured in subalternity. In addition, Menchú clarifies the mechanisms with which modernity obscures and hinders the collective destinies of subaltern peoples. Of course, Menchú's foremost contribution from the very beginning, despite its limitations, lies in establishing that we cannot ignore the realities of racism, exploitation, and marginalization. She perseveres in suggesting that the necessary solutions to eradicating neocolonial violence reside in the peoples who suffer these experiences. For her, this means encouraging a broader vision of globalization, one that honors public ethics and morals. Our attitude, instead of scorn for humanity, should be one of hope, to "enrich the life of the planet, the life of animals, the life of water, of our rivers, of our seas; but also the life of men and women and the life of our future generations, of our children" (*La nieta de los mayas* 164).

Menchú's contribution, then, should be understood epistemologically and politically. Hers is not simply a politics of nondifference or of the problems that affect humanity. Rather, she is assuming a leading role in accomplishing the structural change to the conditions of existence affecting the subaltern in society. This politics is exemplified more clearly in Menchú's legal battles to imprison the intellectual authors of the genocide in Guatemala. Here, we find a tireless effort that corroborates her discursivity and her human rights activism. Moreover, it reveals a political activism that is not limited to the local but is global as well.

After sending a letter to the president of the United States, George W. Bush, in September 2001, Menchú participated in a protest at the United Nations against the US attacks in Afghanistan. Joining other Nobel Prize winners, such as Mairead Corrigan Maguire and Adolfo Pérez Esquivel, she protested the United States' military eradication of "terrorism." In an interview, Menchú makes reference to the US government's "dual morality," observing that it "seeks to ignore that they themselves trained, armed, financed, and encouraged the twisted minds that have turned on them today" (Oliva García). Although she condemns the terrorist attacks on the Twin Towers, Menchú also condemns warlike actions based on the ideology of an "eye for an eye":

> Today we are confronted by an indescribable injustice in which the richest and most powerful nations of the world have united their most advanced technology and their death machines to attack one of the poorest nations on earth. It offends the intelligence of those in the world who think with their own minds, that the United States and the great powers would expect us to believe that, in order to pursue a group of terrorists, they are justified in destroying whole villages, attacking urban civilian populations and destroying buildings like those of the UN or the International Red Cross in Kabul. (Oliva García)

Menchú felt that more productive contributions to peace would come from "the very people of the United States." In this condemnation, she newly criticizes the Western capitalist order's intrusion on a global level. Curiously, there is a surprising similarity between her perspective on the West and globalization and Martin Luther King Jr.'s (1929–1968) position on the military actions of his country against Vietnam in the 1970s.

In his text "Conscience and the Vietnam War," King declares his decision not to support his country in the war. This invasion, according to King, is nothing but the product of "Western arrogance that has poisoned the international atmosphere" (26). This arrogance characterizes a hegemonic power that feels it has everything to teach to others but nothing to learn from them. King argues that his country's aim in invading Vietnam is global and capitalist, that the West wants to invest "huge sums of money in Asia,

Africa, and South America only to take the profits out with no concern for the social betterment of the countries" (32). King questions these imperial policies and the US support of Premier Diem and the country's landowners and elite classes: "Where are the roots of the independent Vietnam we claim to be building?" (27). On the contrary, with this invasion, says King, the United States has become one of the largest "purveyors of violence in the world today" (24). Referring to the consequences of war in Vietnam, he adds:

> We have destroyed their two most cherished institutions: the family and the village. We have destroyed their land and their crops. We have cooperated in crushing one of the nation's only non-Communist revolutionary political forces, the United Buddhist Church. We have supported the enemies of the peasant of Saigon. We have corrupted their women and children and killed their men. What liberators! (King 28)

In addition, King adopts a subaltern perspective that transcends the frontiers of his own struggles for civil rights in the United States, by suggesting that the poor classes of Vietnam are his brothers. Furthermore, King calls upon people to carry out a "true revolution of values" (32) in which capital is invested in social development programs instead of military defense. He finally calls on *everyone* to protest the Vietnam War.

As we can see, King's call for a "true revolution of values" essentially illustrates Menchú's intercultural perspective on the violence perpetrated by Western civilization yesterday and today. Both these activists take political initiatives that combine their discursive struggles and their pro–human rights activism. What is more, Menchú reproduces an entire tradition of pro–civil rights politics that dates back to Mahatma Gandhi (1869–1948) and was later taken up by King himself. Menchú's activism recalls these historical figures and their respective struggles for human rights, as well as their fights against poverty, racism, and inequality.

In sum, if we find a confrontation in the dialogue between Asturias and de Lión, Menchú emerges as the point of intercultural encounter and coexistence between the two. Menchú shares with de Lión a firm desire to reaffirm and project Maya identity by centralizing indigenous peoples in the construction of the nation-state and modernity. Further, this means reviving Maya cosmovision for a revolutionary purpose: to dismantle the mechanisms of the coloniality of power, which today are driven by globalization and modernity. With Asturias, Menchú shares a criticism of the opulent modernizing projects that intend to bury indigenous values, imposing their own norms, and to halt the cultural development of these peoples, such as their intimate relationship with Mother Earth and nature. What unites these three authors is the importance that each attributes to Maya cosmovision—

represented in the *Popol Wuj*—as a locus of enunciation from which one can resist Western modernity and reconstruct new narratives grounded in humanity. Indeed, the *Popol Wuj* is the fundamental beginning that guides each of their projects, whether literary or political, and each places his or her hopes for the present and the future in this text.

In their respective sociocultural and historical contexts, through Maya cosmovision these authors reaffirm a narrative of resistance that resurges to confront Western modernity (Asturias, Menchú) and assimilation via mestizaje or transculturation (de Lión, Menchú). At present, Menchú promotes the concerns and ideals of Asturias and de Lión, defining an intercultural epistemology that, in Catherine Walsh's terms, "denotes a cultural politics of opposition based not simply on recognition or inclusion, but rather directed toward sociohistorical and structural transformation. A politics and a thought directed toward the construction of an alternative proposal of civilization and society; one that springs from and confronts the coloniality of power and involves another logic of incorporation." In this sense, Menchú's political activism also indicates, as Marc Zimmerman writes ("Rigoberta Menchú after the Nobel"), that her path is not one of armed struggle, but rather—through a nonviolent activism driven by interculturality—a path of *politics of the possible*. Following Doris Sommer, as well as Alice Brittin and Kenny Dworkin, Zimmerman adds that we find Menchú "in some unexplored new space beyond current theorizations. The process by which Menchú projects and shapes her public, revolutionary identity is also the process by which a new, nonreducible collective subjectivity begins to emerge" ("Rigoberta Menchú after the Nobel" 126).

Based on an entire tradition of struggle for civil and human rights, Menchú establishes herself as a model that reaffirms and projects Maya identity and cosmovision as loci of enunciation from subalternity. Confronted with globalization, this identity can be the very place where the oppressed unite, eradicating the coloniality of power through collective action. At the same time, this identity means new forms of seeing, understanding, and acting that are more democratic and more viable than current hegemonic perspectives on globalization. Some see Menchú's participation in state politics as a limitation, but she is articulating the foundations of this new intercultural civilization. Moreover, I feel that Menchú's participation in presidential politics achieved her goal: to shed light on the fact that racism and discrimination against Maya peoples are still rooted in Guatemalan society. As Edelberto Torres-Rivas indicates, despite her limitations as an electoral candidate, Menchú represents "a fundamental break with the history of racist and colonial politics" (40) in Guatemala. She is forcing the world to confront this history.

To what extent is the road paved by Menchú—begun by de Lión and, in some sense, Asturias—the road followed by Mayas and non-Mayas in Guatemala? To what point has the movement carried out in practice this collective and intercultural consciousness that originates from the very heart of an antiracist and anticolonial struggle and a subaltern locus of enunciation? Through an exploration of the interethnic debate between Mayas and Ladinos, I address these and other questions in the next chapter.

Part Two

4 Rethinking Modernity and Identity Politics in the Interethnic Debate in Guatemala

We want a world where many worlds fit.

—*Zapatista National Liberation Army*

In this chapter, I analyze the tensions and limitations in discussions of identity politics that have emerged from the interethnic debate in Guatemala. My objective is to explore narratives that seek to construct an intercultural political and national project. Given that what is at stake in this debate is the formulation of a new cultural and national identity in the age of globalization, my goal is to outline the proposals of two of the debate's representative intellectuals: Mario Roberto Morales and Estuardo Zapeta. I feel that both Morales and Zapeta foreground a series of unresolved tensions between Ladinos and Mayas that must be carefully considered in order to transcend the ambiguities and contradictions in the ideas of modernity and interculturality being proposed for Guatemala. Moreover, examining Guatemala's

87

interethnic debate allows us to broaden discussions of identity politics and modernity in Latin America.

In this chapter, I focus primarily on Morales's *La articulación de las diferencias, o, el síndrome de Maximón* (The Articulation of Differences or Maximon's Syndrome) and Zapeta's *Las huellas de B'alam* (The Jaguar's Footprints). These texts allow us to evaluate a Latinamericanist tradition of mestizaje as an effective response to the demands of neoliberalism (Morales).[1] Also, they introduce us to a new multicultural neoliberalism currently in vogue (Zapeta) that is being appropriated by various indigenous intellectuals on the continent to propose viable solutions to the economic problems and challenges confronting indigenous peoples. Whereas Zapeta endorses this neoliberalism as favorable to indigenous peoples, my reading of his text suggests that it is better to question this economic and cultural model because it recycles the coloniality of power.[2] Analyzing the perspectives of Morales and Zapeta highlights the difficulties that many Mayas and non-Mayas face while trying to establish a politics of interculturality that challenges globalization.

Guatemala's interethnic debate can be traced to discussions about the "Indian problem" and its impact on the armed struggle during the seventies and eighties. The Guatemalan Communist Party (PGT) and liberal intellectuals related to the October Revolution (1944–1954) argued that an existing feudal economy inherited from the colonial period continued to isolate Ladino and indigenous peasants. These intellectuals believed that a politics of agrarian reform and assimilation was the key to national development. Following the example of Mexico after its revolution (1910–1918), they believed that the mestizaje of the indigenous population would result in a "modern" peasants' movement that would fight for its rights and emancipation (Zimmerman, *Literature and Resistance* vol. 1, 60).[3] This ideological orientation of the Left was later questioned during the seventies because it did not recognize indigenous cultural and linguistic specificities. Some critics opposed an ethnic perspective that reduced the "Indian problem" to categories of "class" and "orthodox Marxism" based on the construction of a proletarian class that obscures such cultural and linguistic differences. These intellectuals insisted that recognition of indigenous peoples' rights to their languages and cultural logics and values is indispensable. However, they many times negated models of modernization and transculturation, suggesting that indigenous cultures remained at the margins of development as "closed corporate communities."[4]

In the past few decades, the interethnic debate has been conditioned by the rapid cultural and economic transformations led by globalization, the official end of the Guatemalan Civil War (in December 1996), and the rise of the Maya movement (during the 1990s). On the one hand, the debate involves materializing a utopian project of fusing differences by finding a "unity in diversity" through a democratic process of transculturation, hybridity, and cultural mestizaje. On the other hand, intellectuals involved in the Maya movement propose a differentiated ethnic and cultural perspective in order to promote an expansion of civil rights, economic opportunities, and cultural, linguistic, and territorial self-determination for Maya peoples. In this way, the movement promotes a discourse that demands a rethinking of the Guatemalan nation as being multicultural, multilingual, and multinational instead of culturally and linguistically homogenous. These last two tendencies, to which I later refer, have been discussed in Guatemalan newspapers—usually in the opinion section—since the beginning of the 1990s. Besides Morales and Zapeta, the debate includes among its contributors Irma Alicia Velásquez Nimatuj, Rigoberto Juárez Paz and Adrián Zapata who write their opinion columns in *El Periódico*, Luís Enrique Sam Colop of *Prensa Libre*, Víctor Montejo of *Siglo veintiuno*, and Mario Alberto Carrera of *Siglo veintiuno* and *La Hora*.[5]

Mario Roberto Morales: Articulating Differences or Dynamiting Intercultural Relations?

The context described above conditions Morales's book *La articulación de las diferencias*. Influenced by Nestor Garcia Canclini's *Hybrid Cultures*—John Beverley points out that Morales's book can be read as the "Guatemalan or glocal version, if one wants," of Canclini's book ("Prólogo" 10)—Morales focuses on indigenous peoples, situating the problem of identity politics within the space of consumption and the role of mass media as producers of hybrid, transcultured mestizo identities. He does this in order to rethink the question of representation, in the mimetic sense of "speaking about" and the political sense of "speaking for" (13).[6] Morales is responding to the political role achieved at the national and international levels by the Guatemalan indigenous movement with the signing of the Peace Accords in 1996.[7] He maintains that he is not opposed to regional autonomy or making Maya languages official and he recognizes the difference between indigenous peoples and Ladinos. Because of their binary interpretive logics, however, these discourses are "essentialist," "fundamentalist," or "anti-Ladino" and create cultural divisions or apartheid on a national scale. The problem, according to him, is that the invention of new cultural signifiers of identity—"Maya," in this case—deepens the divisions between the peoples who constitute the nation. The Maya social construct, it is suggested, promotes an ethnic identity that is discursively unchanging or culturally pure because it is based on the pre-Columbian period and that responds only to the necessities and ideological objectives of a bourgeois indigenous intelligentsia.[8] Morales argues that, beyond representing the "voice" of indigenous peoples, the goal of the Maya intelligentsia is not to displace the hegemony of national groups affiliated with neoliberalism or the Guatemalan army, but rather to reproduce a similar hegemonic economic system and to exclude Ladinos from negotiating with globalization.

In addition, Morales argues that Maya identity is a cultural signifier based on Western knowledge and responds to the demands of the market, suggesting that such an identity is constructed strategically to obtain foreign economic support for indigenous organizations. Because this implies financial support and external solidarity (with NGOs, anthropologists, linguists, and Leftist intellectuals), Maya-ness produces a situation of intellectual dependence (Morales, *La articulación* 224), thereby becoming a commodity for foreign consumption.[9] According to this situation of dependence, the narratives and politics of resistance that the movement creates in order to promote Maya identity would be better understood as simulacra created "intentionally for the consumption of its supporting conglomerates" (306). As a solution to the "interethnic problem," Morales proposes an "intercultural mestizaje" in which ethnic differences are abolished, giving way to a shared identity. He tells us that this will create, politically, "an inter-classist and interethnic popular subject capable of being the protagonist in a national-popular political project that is, itself, interclassist and interethnic" (61). Such a process entails an ethnocultural expansion and negotiation through a mestizaje that originates from within the democratic coexistence of cultures. All of this has the simultaneous goals of creating a cultural block that resists neoliberalism and constructing an interethnic alliance that contributes to the democratization of transculturation and mestizaje at a national level.

In the following analysis of Morales's text, I begin with his reading of globalization as an "omnipotent" process that "cancels," "transculturizes," and hybridizes indigenous identities. My argument is that, within his conception of the interethnic question, Morales's arguments condemn both the interculturality proposed by Mayas and any politics that advocates difference as a possible alternative in the rethinking of Guatemalan society. Further, I argue that Morales's perspective on "intercultural mestizaje" betrays a desire to reaffirm a Latinamericanist intellectual tradition founded upon colonialism and the coloniality of power, as well as a cultural, lettered authority that imposes identities upon subjects in conditions of subalternity. What we find in this proposal is the political and ideological recycling of a

Latinamericanist project that insists upon the Ladino or mestizo hegemonic status quo and continues an exclusive ideology that negates Maya peoples' possibilities for self-determination and self-affirmation.

Within the frame of interethnic relations and contrary to policies that argue in favor of difference, Morales begins with the supposition that, for indigenous peoples, globalization implies an inevitable reshaping by culturally homogenizing processes that produce hybridized or "transcultured" subjects, a "cultural homogenization via economic globalization" (*La articulación* 36). Spearheading this homogenization are neoliberalism, protestant Christianity, and the media. These cultural institutions, according to Morales, not only destroy any resistance to their homogenizing mechanisms but also erase traditional identities. Dominant cultures, especially those of economically advanced countries, with their power to spread and transmit information, constitute a threat to subaltern cultures. The media, for example, promotes a

> uniform message… [that] tends to homogenize tastes for certain audio-visual goods, in this way homogenizing the demand for an equally homogenized supply; and, further, traditions tend to be transformed or to disappear as elements that fulfill functions of social cohesion, political legitimation, and the offering of profiles of identity before the uniformed offering of mass culture, which offers new possibilities for cultural identities. (Morales, La articulación 323)

Given these conclusions, Morales brings into evidence his theoretical deductions derived from his visits to an indigenous community in Santiago Atitlán.

What motivated Morales to go to this community was the threatened "extinction" of the ballet-drama *Rabinal Achí*.[10] He claims that the play now lacks the "authenticity" of its uncontaminated pre-Columbian origin (Morales, *La articulación* 353) because of its continual cultural hybridization over the years. In the ballet-drama's current representations, "the heroic men who, since [Luis] Cardoza y Aragón's translation, we imagined as being dressed in pre-Columbian fashion now dance dressed in the garb of Moors and Christians to the rhythm of indigenous sounds, monotonous and sad" (353). Further, Morales observes that, owing to internal problems such as insufficient funds and declining appreciation of tradition, the owners of the performance, as a possible way to rescue it from "extinction," are even open to accepting financial support from national and foreign tourist agencies. Morales concludes that accepting this economic support equates to converting *Rabinal Achí* into a commodity; the play ceases being "traditional" in order to become merchandise in the global market.

A similar fate befalls people living in indigenous communities. In Morales's ethnographic saga, on a second visit to the same community, he notices that not even the townspeople have been spared from the inevitable penetration of modern merchandise that supposedly rids indigenous culture of its specificity. Morales sets the stage:

> While the imposing Catholic procession crossed the plaza and entered the temple, the video arcade in the park was full of indigenous children, for whom the impressive spectacle outside was unimportant and so they played at virtual war, absorbed in the machines. On the walls of many houses, there was graffiti with the unmistakable calligraphy of the gangs, and in one store that sold secondhand clothing from the US (pacas), the indigenous women lined up to buy blouses and jeans. The sound of Techno Music came out of some houses, and the cable television antennas opened onto the sky. In the movie theater, Cine Variedades, they advertised movies with Arnold Schwartzenegger and Bruce Lee, and X-rated films. (La articulación 356)

After describing this new scene of "cultural hybridity," Morales interviews some informants and presents us with their worries about the effects of these (post)modern offerings on the indigenous world. One expresses his disillusionment over the influence of cable television on children and how the *ropa de paca* (secondhand clothes from the United States) has come to be a "harmful influence" on indigenous women because they stop wearing their "traditional" clothing in favor of "Western" dress. The same occurs with the community's young people: "the specific indigenous components (themselves already mestizo) of the structure of these juvenile identities" have been annulled by these globalizing processes (343).

From the interpretation of globalization presented here, one concludes that indigenous peoples cannot avoid cultural "homogenization" or "hybridity," that resistance is not a viable option. Indigenous traditions and cultural specificities seem to have no meaning or future. Indigenous peoples' quest to defend "traditions" that inevitably will be absorbed by modernity amounts to another useless effort. It is then suggested that these elements have survived through a logic of hybridity or transculturation that has transformed and revived them in globalization, not as specifically indigenous but rather as "hybrid." This representation of modernity, however, is guilty of producing a discursivity that not only assigns a place to the Indian in the future of this modernity but also condemns him to accepting hybridity, transculturation, and mestizaje as the *only* possible paths toward his cultural vindication.

To begin, it is not difficult to perceive in Morales a certain cultural authority as an intellectual who seeks to reduce the role of indigenous peoples within these "globalizing" phenomena. In his examination of globalization and in his description of these postmodern scenes, there clearly emanates a colonial attitude of "naming" that is inherited both from the conquest and from an anthropological and ethnographic tradition that takes the Indian as its object of study without taking into account and without respecting the self-definitions of culture and identity of this object of study. Such an attitude is even more evident in Morales's perceptions of indigenous young people and indigenous women. Morales and his informants automatically assume that "Techno Music," the use of "secondhand" North American clothing, cable, and the films of Arnold Schwartzenegger and Bruce Lee negate any affiliation with or affective and cultural sensibilities to the community from which these subjects come. This ethnocultural vision betrays an archaeological gaze prone to limiting the indigenous subject. For example, in the representation of the Indian offered by Morales, rootlessness and deformation displace these young people and these women from a cultural atmosphere that is supposedly "intact," "uncontaminated," and foreign to cultural change. The transgression or entrance of "modern" wares, it is suggested, has come to deform this supposedly "natural" relationship with a new sociocultural environment characterized by homogenization. All contact that the Indian has with the outside world unavoidably cancels out this natural world. Morales proposes indigenous biological and cultural purity as a condition of indigenous existence. This is ironic, given that he presents himself as a critic of the "essentialist" or "fundamentalist" arguments of Maya intellectuals who construct "pure" or "unchanging" identities.

This perspective on the indigenous world is not exclusive to critics like Morales; paradoxically, even indigenous *letrados* (intellectuals) share similar desires for and conceptions of the "authenticity" of their own world, reaffirming Morales's own arguments. For example, among Maya intellectuals, we find objections to who is actually interpreting indigenous identity as being "unchanging" or "frozen in time," but also ambivalence about the perception of indigenous cultural identity. Making reference to the "levels of ethnic consciousness," Demetrio Cojtí seems to agree with Morales to a certain extent when he writes that "illiterate Maya peasants have a lot more practice and *cultural authenticity* and have a consciousness of the pueblo as such; that is, they recognize that they are members of the Maya People (which are now called in Spanish *natural*, *Indian*, *aborigine*, or *indigenous*) and they are socially marginalized and ethnically discriminated against" (*El movimiento Maya* 52, emphasis added). And later: "The educated indigenous middle and lower classes, for their part, *having suffered under a Ladinoizing educative system, maintain fewer cultural practices and have less cultural authenticity*" (52, emphasis added).

As we can see, what Cojtí constructs here is a discourse of "authenticity" in which "traditional," "peasant," "illiterate," and the like equal an essentialized construction of Maya-ness as "real" whereas "urban" precludes an identification with this identity and other cultural modalities. This discursivity operates from suppositions based on access to and a relationship with the land. That is, having lost or having been removed from their land, urban indigenous peoples are now assigned to the margins of a cultural model of Maya-ness, far from "indigenous cultural authenticity."[11] This representation, of course, could lead to the danger outlined by Morales: recolonizing indigenous identity at the level of consumption and folklore, just as tourist businesses and official institutions like the Guatemalan Institute for Tourism (INGUAT) have done.

Cojtí's representation appears to coincide with Morales's argument; he understands modernity to be a mechanism that negates indigeneity (represented by the "*Ladinoizing* educative system"). However, Morales shows that rural areas are not entirely foreign to modernization, but Cojtí suggests that it is precisely in these areas where one finds "authenticity." In other words, there still exists, distant from these globalizing processes, an uncontaminated indigenous culture that practices "Maya traditions" we can emulate.[12] Both perspectives reaffirm an interpretive order implicated historically in spreading representations that collaborate in promoting a desire to maintain or eradicate an "intact" or "uncontaminated" cultural identity, whether this identity be foreign to modernity or surviving within modern processes via mestizaje.

Morales, his informants in the community of Santiago Atitlán, and Cojtí, in their perspective on modernity, all suggest that the relationship between globalization and indigenous peoples entails a certain cancellation of indigenous "authenticity." These peoples are conceived of as passive entities that indiscriminately interpret globalization as a "uniform message," inserting themselves into the logic of globalization only to bury their own traditions. In other words, Morales, his informants, and Cojtí assume a lack of control and lack of ethnic consciousness on the part of indigenous women and young people in these communities and in the city. All of them are portrayed as incapable of appropriating globalization to reaffirm their own identity. Just to illustrate indigenous creativity and control, the following is an anecdote that Roger Bartra tells about an Otomí community north of Mexico City (in Ferman).

Bartra tells us that in this community a group of young people play rock music "like this, with sandals" (quoted in Ferman 44) and are constantly being confronted by officials from the National Indigenist Institute (INI). "You will then see," Bartra adds, "the underdogs, screwed, defending themselves from nationalist outsiders. And what do they use to defend themselves? Rock, as an affirmation of their Otomí being, before these nationalists, who perhaps spoke about being Otomí and about Mexican nationality, in the abstract, but without Otomís realizing it" (44). As can be seen in this anecdote, these indigenous young people have appropriated an aspect of Western modernity not to hide their traditions and their relationship with their community of origin, but to affirm their being Otomí. Indigeneity is located, maintained, and rearticulated in a new geo- and sociocultural context by borrowing the technologies offered by the West, to initiate a new space of resistance and re-accommodation of indigeneity within the nation and Western modernity. Morales and Cojtí, in their own minds, clearly occupy a position of lettered cultural "authority" and, as such, feel that they can determine how Indians in these communities are supposed to think of and recognize themselves within modernity. What we get is the description of a modern club in which indigenous subjects are assumed to have lost their cultural specificities, or they should put them aside if they want to survive in the age of globalization. Entrance to this club entails being condemned to perish or to survive under mechanisms of homogenization and cultural hybridity.

We can also find this position of a lettered, cultural "authority" that decides how Indians should understand and act within globalization in Nestor García Canclini's *Hybrid Cultures*, a book which, as already mentioned, Morales emulates in his own study. It suffices to repeat one of Canclini's anecdotes in order to clarify both his theoretical approach and his cultural authority:

> [E]ight years ago I went into a shop in Teotitlán del Valle—a Oaxacan town dedicated to weaving—where a fifty-year-old man was watching television with his father while exchanging phrases in Zapotec. When I asked him about the tapestries with images by Picasso, Klee, and Miró that he had on display, he told me they started to make them in 1968, when some tourists visited who worked in the Museum of Modern Art in New York and proposed that they renovate their designs. He showed me an album of photos and newspaper clippings in English that analyzed the exhibitions this artisan had done in California. In a half hour I saw him move with ease from Zapotec to Spanish and to English, from art to crafts, from his ethnic group to the information and entertainment of mass culture, passing through the art criticism of a metropolis.

I understood that my worries about the loss of their traditions were not shared by this man who moved without too many conflicts between three cultural systems. (172–73, emphasis added)

Note Canclini's surprise upon seeing that this artisan moves within various cultural spaces. For Canclini, this artisan represents an example of "hybrid cultures": he has incorporated himself into a new modern world character-ized by an entire series of cultural "mixtures" (the paintings of Miró, Klee, moving between various languages and spaces). However, I wonder whether the artisan would have self-identified as indigenous Zapotec or a hybrid subject if Canclini had asked him? Here, it is worth mentioning that instead of turning to the artisan to define his own culture and identity, Canclini worries himself with determining the identity of his object of study.[13] This same attitude surfaces in Cojtí and Morales when they talk about the indige-nous subjects they study.

These lettered attitudes that claim to understand the indigenous world and its relationship with modernity and "tradition," these perspectives that promote an "authenticity" based on "purity of blood" or "cultural purity," are challenged and even put in check when we take into account the cultural self-affirmation of subjects who at first considered themselves "Ladinos" or "mestizos" but later decided to speak from an indigenous locus of enuncia-tion. Here, I am specifically referring to Subcomandante Marcos and José María Arguedas, both of whom represent paradigmatic examples of indige-nous intellectuals, even if critics insist on calling them non-indigenous sub-jects.

In Armando Bartra's essay "Mitos en la aldea global [Myths of the Global Village]," he offers what would later be the prologue to Subcomandante Marcos's *Relatos de El Viejo Antonio* (Tales of El Viejo Antonio). Bartra makes a historical reference to the fact that dominant culture has robbed indige-nous peoples of their word, be it written or oral, for more than five hundred years. In Mexico, in Chiapas, this voice is born again in the mouths of these very peoples, Bartra tells us, through the uprising of the Zapatista National Liberation Army (EZLN), and mediated "by Subcomandante Marcos, the Ladino who helped to straighten out the confused [Ladino]" (38) and who "became a splendid communicator, an amanuensis capable of fusing indige-nous speech and the mestizo's language in a syncretic discourse that has been the amalgam of neo-zapatismo" (39). Here, I am not interested in problematizing the Zapatistas' "syncretic discourse" to which Bartra makes reference, but rather in pointing out how, once again, Bartra categorizes Marcos as a "Ladino" or "mestizo" subject.

Marcos tells the well-known story about his arrival to Chiapas's indigenous communities. He describes himself as an intellectual who wanted to "liberate" indigenous peoples from oppression. He and a few other intellectuals decided to enter the Lacandon Jungle to "enlighten" the Indians. However, his group is confronted by an unanticipated reality. Instead of enlighteners, they become students who learn to listen. What is interesting about this is the assimilation to an indigenous identity. In interviews and other public texts, Marcos has made reference to this process of assimilation, which entailed learning "the language, but also...something more than the language itself: the *use* of the language, of the symbol in communication, all that" (Nash 226). Afterwards, having lived with and learned from Maya communities, the Sub reaches a level of ethnic consciousness that displaces his political affiliation with what is "mestizo" or "Ladino." He adopts an indigenous "I" or "we." In Marcos's spoken and written texts, we find, for example, "*we* who are the color of the land" and "As indigenous Mexicans, *we are indigenous* and *we are* Mexicans. *We want* to be indigenous and we want to be Mexicans" (in *La jornada*, 24 Feb. 2001). And elsewhere: "As indigenous peoples, *we have* come to turn back the clock and thus make sure that the world of tomorrow is inclusive, tolerant, and plural" ("El otro jugador"). In the text to which Bartra refers—*Relatos de El Viejo Antonio* (Tales of El Viejo Antonio)—Marcos also describes how the indigenous world symbolically adopted him: "They sat with me and *took*, in the end, my word and my voice to tell our struggle" (102, emphasis added). From this beginning, from being "taken," it is evident that Marcos no longer sees himself as a Ladino or mestizo, but as an Indian. Why, then, does Bartra insist upon continuing to categorize Marcos as a "mestizo" or "Ladino"? Why does he violate Marcos's right to self-definition and the self-affirmation of his cultural identity as indigenous?

A similar problem can be found in the debates about José María Arguedas, debates that have involved critics such as Ángel Rama (*Transculturación narrativa*), Antonio Cornejo Polar (*Escribir en el aire*), Mario Vargas Llosa (*La utopía arcaica*), and Alberto Moreiras. Arguedas has been used to exemplify theoretical frameworks such as "narrative transculturation," "heterogeneity," and "Archaic Utopia" that have, for the most part, done nothing but subalternize what is indigenous. Rama, for example, says that Arguedas represents "a certain, definite type of *mestizo*" (*Transculturación* 201). Cornejo Polar, in a subtler approach, makes reference to Arguedas's "*misti* [mixed] origin (son of a lawyer and a *hacendada* [landowner])" and how "his later insertion, first into the world of the university in the city and then into the international literary and academic system, *was never sufficient to erase this literally foundational experience* [mixed]" (*Escribir* 208–09). For his part, Moreiras, responding to the "celebratory

telos" of Rama's notion of transculturation, observes that Arguedas's literature can be better thought of as a "mestizo space of incoherence" (216).
These critics' perceptions of Arguedas and his work, however, marginalize
his affective and political affiliation with the Andean world. These are most
evident in his hymn "To Our Father and Creator Tupac Amaru [Tupac
Amaru kamaq taytanchisman]." Invoking the words of the indigenous
rebel—"I will return and I will be millions"—Arguedas emphasizes, "*We*
thousands of millions, here, now. *We are together. We have* assembled town
by town, name by name, and *we are* pressing upon this immense city"
(*Tupac Amaru* 19, emphasis added). One can see that, in this collective call,
Arguedas does not hold himself to be mestizo, or "misti," but indigenous,
and that he identifies with the political struggles of Andean peoples. As with
Bartra on Marcos, Arguedas's critics are incapable of seeing a "certain type of
Indian," or an "indigenous origin," or "an indigenous space of incoherence."
Identifying mestizaje as the only possibility for their theoretical construc-
tions, they fail to consider indigeneity.

Obviously, these perceptions of Marcos and Arguedas are conditioned
by an understanding of cultural identity based on purity of blood. It is supposed that, because of their Spanish "biological" origins, the indigenous
identity from which Marcos and Arguedas claim to speak, this locus of
enunciation has no "authenticity." Ironically, as we saw with Morales, Cojtí,
and Canclini above, it is easy to picture an indigenous person who sheds his
cultural identity by immigrating to the city, by not speaking his native language, by using a computer, or by wearing "Western" clothes. But it is
impossible to conceive of someone like Marcos or Arguedas placing himself
in the indigenous world—emigrating from the city to the Lacandon Jungle,
living in indigenous communities, learning the native languages and symbols, adapting to the communities' way of life, and developing an affective
and political relationship with these peoples!

This entire situation illustrates the inability of Latin American criticism
to accept an inverse transculturation, a transculturation from below.[14] It is
unable or unwilling to accept that the indigenous world penetrates and
influences dominant imaginaries to the point of transforming the cultural,
political affectivities and sensibilities of dominant societies and peoples, as
the cases of Marcos and Arguedas demonstrate. The problem, as we have
also seen, not only resides in interpreting or understanding cultural identity
from biological aspects. It also resides in a conscious or unconscious insistence on the part of Latinamericanist criticism to reaffirm mestizaje—today,
with its postcolonial and postmodern connotations of hybridity, transculturation, and the like—as Latin America's locus of enunciation. With the

exception of Cojtí, mestizaje continues to be the aspiration of all these critics. It is culturally offered in order to resist globalization even when social examples point in another direction (I am thinking of indigenous movements especially). Latin American criticism vehemently anchors itself in an intellectual tradition that is, without a doubt, in crisis. The greatest problem, of course, is that Latin Americanist tradition does not want to accept the historical, cultural, and political prominence of indigenous peoples unless it serves to legitimate the place of the mestizo in history. Beginning in the 1990s, indigenous peoples have attained a cultural and political authority that obligates these "modern" nation-states to confront their own constitutive crises. Indigenous peoples have demanded integration into the very narratives accustomed to marginalizing them. To say it plainly, the Latinamericanist tradition, which celebrates mestizaje, continues disseminating itself with an authority and a paternalist character that subordinates the role of indigenous peoples as political agents of change.

To return to an early metaphor, these perspectives on modernity and cultural identity describe a modern club that denies access to indigenous subjects because of their cultural specificities. To enter this club, indeed to survive, indigenous peoples must submit to the mechanizations of homogenization, mestizaje, and cultural hybridity. But, we must ask ourselves, does globalization affect only indigenous peoples? If this phenomenon "cancels" or "transforms" our identities, what happens to mestizo and Ladino identities? Will they remain immune to such cancellations, or are they capable of co-opting globalization without losing their cultural specificity? And on what is Ladino cultural specificity based? How does Ladino cultural specificity survive this phenomenon? At this point, we should return to Morales because, in the Ladino–globalization relationship, his argument is based on a Ladino identity that is "a political discursive construct that does not have the consensus of all its members but which justly seeks to *build* this consensus through the construction of an identity that is historically nonexistent" (*La articulación* 405, emphasis added). The Ladino identity with which we are familiar, then, is a political "construction" that, contrary to Maya identity, has appealed "*not to thousands of years of ancestry, but to a few centuries of political prominence, hegemony, and domination*" (405, emphasis added). Leaving aside the references that imbue the Ladino with colonial dimensions ("political prominence," "hegemony," "domination"), what merits attention here is Morales's understanding that cultural identity implies a "political affiliation." Ironically, this argument applies to Ladino identity and not to Maya identity in their respective relationships with globalization. To what do we owe these attitudes and this exclusion of a more global study of cultural identity as a social construct? Is this proposal, as opposed to that of "intercultural mestizaje," not a more viable argument for the interethnic debate? I return to these questions in the final section of this chapter. For now, I would like to clarify Morales's ideological and political objectives.

As I suggested at the beginning, Morales's deductions in regards to indigenous cultures and globalization are strongly conditioned by an opposition to, and a desire to silence, the politics of difference advocated by Mayas as political alternatives for Guatemala. This is evident if we carefully analyze Morales's readings of texts produced by organic intellectuals within the movement. In these readings, he concludes that these texts appeal to "archeological criteria" and to an "immutability of the past" with the goal not of promoting the vindication of indigenous peoples, but of giving shape to an "anti-Ladino" identity and promoting "essentialism" and "fundamentalism." Although I do not deny that there is a certain relevance in some of Morales's arguments, this interpretation reaches tendentious conclusions. They not only foment resentment against the Maya movement and its formulations toward a politics of difference but also reduce and dismiss the movement's heterogeneity of thought through categories like "essentialism" and "fundamentalism."

It is not difficult to discern Morales's ideological arbitrariness in his theoretical pretensions of mestizaje being *the only* possible way to navigate through the vague apocalyptic, messianic, global-modernizing storm that threatens indigenous peoples. This celebration of the mestizo talks about indigenous vindication "in terms of a hybridization and a mestizaje that are just and egalitarian" (*La articulación* 328). Rather than explore the indigenous movement's political propositions, I reiterate, Morales wants to dynamite interculturality as a possible national alternative for Guatemala. This objective is crystallized in his readings of indigenous discourses.

Morales focuses on Estuardo Zapeta, Demetrio Cojtí, Menchú, and Humberto Ak'abal, concluding that these intellectuals express a binary, anti-Ladino logic. However, as we shall see, instead of uncovering this "anti-Ladino logic," Morales preoccupies himself with trying to silence and marginalize these discourses. In effect, instead of analyzing these texts, Morales throws low blows at these intellectuals, deprecating their political proposals. He points out, for example, that several of Zapeta's articles are "poorly edited" (*La articulación* 55). Referring to one particular article, Morales observes that "there is an evident and uncontrolled use of the language [Spanish] (syntax, use of vocabulary, gender agreement, etc.), which implies an incorrect use of the inevitable enemy code. This has complicated the debate since it has provoked frequent confusion" (286). In regards to Humberto Ak'abal and his poetry, Morales observes that Ak'abal's image (his traditional dress, his long hair) is his way of selling himself to the international market, by "offering a *Maya look* that does not look out of synch with what the tourist expects of his country and his *cultural heritage*" (370). Turning to Ak'abal's poetry, Morales concerns himself with showing the "Ladino influences," arguing that "Ak'abal's *Maya* poetry owes a greater debt to the mestizo poetry of the Ladino [Luis Alfredo] Arango—an unflagging supporter of indigenous peoples—than to a supposed pre-Columbian poetic tradition that, according to its exegetes, has remained hidden and that he is revealing" (262).[15]

As for Menchú's text, Morales does not acknowledge the possibility that the Nobel winner constructs her own narrative; he maintains that she needs a group of people to help her construct it. From this, he derives his reading of the testimonio as a collective cultural product that is ethnically hybrid (*La articulación* 131). Morales focuses on the process of making the testimonio and on clarifying whose idea it was to write it, arguing that it is a "strategically narrated discourse" (132–33). Similar to Miguel Angel Asturias's *Men of Maize*, it is a discourse that oscillates "between factuality and fiction, these being seen as constitutive parts of the real. And that self-construct their enunciators as mestizo subaltern subjects in different *popular* positionalities, although, given the 'national' situation of each, both are also complementary for the future project of the intercultural mestizo nation" (142).

With conclusions that recall David Stoll's attack on Menchú, although in a more affirmative tone, Morales also specifies that "Menchú's voice consciously and deliberately fictionalizes the brutal reality to which she testifies, with the political goal of winning supporters for her cause, which is all at once Leftist, Christian, and ethnocultural, that is, culturally hybrid and mestizo-ized" (*La articulación* 143). Morales also produces an entire series of discursive recriminations that, instead of legitimating Menchú's agency, reduce her authority as narrator. For example, he tells us that Spanish words like *suplir* (replace) in *I, Rigoberta Menchú* could not have been part of Menchú's lexicon. This must be a product of the "contact that [she] had with the lettered city (through the Left, which helped her to improve her Spanish) and a Western mentality. She could also have learned a large number of these more or less cultivated Ladino expressions when she was working in the capital" (155).

As far as the doubts and concerns that Mayas raise about institutions like the state or the idea of modernity, Morales focuses on Menchú's "rejection" of modernity as proof of an "essentialism" or a "fundamentalism" that seeks to maintain an immutable indigenous identity. Given that the passage Morales cites is open to different interpretations, we should take a look at it.

Menchú says, "They have tried to take our things away and impose others on us, be it through religion, through dividing up the land, through schools, through books, through radio, through all things modern" (Menchú and Burgos 170–71, quoted in Morales, *La articulación* 161).

From this passage, Morales concludes that Menchú is rejecting the foundations of "modernity" offered by Ladinos, in order to "exalt her [indigenous] culture as better and less contaminated by modern evils incarnated by the Ladino: vanity, disloyalty, wickedness, etc." (*La articulación* 160). The conclusions derived from this paragraph are biased in their references to Indians' perceptions of modernity.

It seems to me that what Menchú rejects is a colonial project of modernity, not the idea of modernity itself. The quote makes an explicit historical reference to the reality of indigenous peoples. "Religion," the "dividing up of land," the "schools," the "books," all have been the arsenals for an exclusive "modern" project that has never favored the development and self-sufficiency of indigenous peoples. Let us consider the category of schools, for example. When an indigenous child has attended a "modern," "Ladino" Guatemalan school, this child—until very recently—has never heard his language, his history, or his culture reaffirmed. Instead, these have been denigrated. To paraphrase Menchú, other things have been put into this indigenous child's mind in order to alienate him from what he is and what is his.[16] The same could be said of the divisions of land, religion, and books, which even today presuppose elements of colonialism that affect indigenous peoples' daily experiences. Rather than reject modernity itself, this quote from Menchú's testimonio—like de Lión's posture in *El tiempo principia en Xibalbá*—leads us to reject and radically question colonial modernity, which, in turn, leads us to imagine and construct a different modern project—one that includes equal participation for both Maya and non-Maya peoples.

Morales's readings of Maya texts reveal that he is not interested in listening to what Mayas say about national culture and matters. His study does not focus on the political content of these texts, but on their stylistic and formal construction. His goal is to marginalize discussions about coloniality that arise in Maya discourses so that he can argue how this textual production represents and affirms mestizo agency. He is preoccupied with delegitimizing and reproaching Mayas who challenge the state and the colonial idea of modernity.

Morales's distorted interpretation of indigenous discourses suggests that all Mayas, when speaking of their past or its "archeological criteria," favor a "return" to the past and promote an "anti-Ladino," "essentialist," or "fundamentalist" consciousness. How can a "popular interethnic alliance that strengthens the democratization of transculturation and mestizaje"

(Morales, *La articulación* 61) be constituted under terms that obviously seek to delegitimize the Maya voice? These prejudicial interpretations devalue the intellectual production of indigenous peoples and thereby perpetuate the interethnic problem. Morales does not even attempt to take the movement's proposals into account; he is not open to other possibilities that could be used to think of more viable solutions. Instead, he discusses indigenous vindications in "terms of hybridization and mestizaje": "The Guatemalan nation needs to democratize not only socially and economically, but ethnically and culturally as well, to be able to enter into the era of globalization with some form of *competitiveness* (considering that this is the pivotal point in the national agendas of the third world) and with *some type of popular representation*" (407, emphasis added).

When Morales speaks of entering globalization with some "competitiveness" and with "some popular representation," he leaves the reader in no doubt that he sees "intercultural mestizaje" as the *only* possibility of entering into modernity, the *only* way of being "compatible" in the eyes of the West. As in the work of Bartra, Rama, Cornejo Polar, and Moreiras mentioned previously, indigeneity cannot represent a space of popular possibility, but mestizaje can. This posture is affirmed more clearly—and in a confrontational way—when Morales says, "It is impossible that Ladinos would accept that Guatemala is 'Maya,' although it is feasible that they would consider it as mestiza" (*La articulación* 408).

The *only* way out for Morales, then, lies in nothing less than accepting mestizaje. Of course, this would also maintain the status quo, in which Ladinos continue exercising a hegemonic power in Guatemala.[17] Maya discourses seem to provoke a certain discomfort in Morales. Their rhetoric defies his cultural authority as a lettered subject (Beverley, "Prológo" 19) and seeks a politics of difference that promotes the specificity of indigenous culture. This is why Morales argues that globalization makes no sense for indigenous peoples. Further, he intends to create a new postmodern project that would reaffirm a Latinamericanist intellectual tradition based on the celebration of mestizaje.

In fact, Morales's approach to Maya discourses can be understood as the result of a desire to rescue a Latinamericanist intellectual heritage—it is worth adding, with colonial ties. This intellectual tradition advocates mestizaje as a cultural project that defines what is "American" and what is "modern" in the eyes of the West. It clearly takes shape in Morales's conception of globalization as a project of modernity that implies an inevitable process of cultural homogenization in which the *sole* possibility for survival for subaltern cultures confronted by this devastating modernizing process is mestizaje. This Eurocentric, Latinamericanist intellectual tradition has historically sacrificed indigenous specificity in the name of the Promised Land called "modernity"—and now called "globalization."

Here are some examples that echo Morales's arguments about mestizaje. Armando Muyulema gathers the following observations, within different historical contexts but with analogous objectives:

> *José Carlos Mariátegui: "The principal vindication of our vanguardism is the vindication of the Indian.... Translated in intelligible language ['the Indian problem'] presents itself as the problem of assimilating into the Peruvian nation four-fifths of Perú's population"; Ángel Rama, asked whether there is a place in the future for Indian communities: "Without a doubt, but not for indigenous culture, but for mestizo culture because Indian culture no longer has meaning"; Leopoldo Zea: "Iberian culture and blood, integrated with Indian, African, and Asiatic blood and culture were mixed.... Thus, we await the beginning of a new possible Universal Order that collects the experience of Spain that tolerantly was mixed with the races and cultures of the previously unknown region of the world: 'America'"; Mario Vargas Llosa: "If I were forced to choose between the preservation of indigenous cultures and their assimilation, with great sadness I would choose the modernization of the Indian population because there are priorities.... Modernization is only possible with the sacrifice of Indian cultures."*
> *("De la 'cuestión indígena' a lo 'indígena' como cuestionamiento" 332)*

Morales recodifies and recycles a posture similar to that of these critics. They define a Latinamericanist intellectual tradition based on an ideology of mestizaje characterized by an exclusionary line of thinking. These Latin American critics maintain that this ideology represents "our expression," "our path" toward the West's recognition of Latin America. But what is even worse is the underlying basis of this: the American continent can exist as an autonomous cultural entity *only* if it is recognized by the West. This vision shows the colonial neurosis and inferiority complex that are still present within Latin America. It affirms that "only European culture is rational, it can contain 'subjects'—the rest are not rational, they cannot be or harbor 'subjects'. As a consequence, the other cultures are different in the sense that they are unequal, in fact inferior, by nature. They only can be 'objects' of knowledge and/or of domination practices" (Quijano, "Coloniality and Modernity/Rationality" 174).

In addition, this intellectual tradition would be complicit in the celebration of colonialism and the coloniality of power exercised by the "lettered city" (to use Ángel Rama's words), given that these obscure the concrete realities that indigenous peoples have confronted for more than five hundred years. Cultural mestizaje, no matter how much it is advocated, does not resolve the racial and ethnic conflicts and does not address the profound cultural and social differences separating us. Even less does it liberate the subaltern subjects who have fought for their autonomy and the construction of noncolonial histories. This cultural criticism in *favor* of mestizaje brings to fruition its desire for modernization, a desire not to remain behind the technological and intellectual advances of the West, not caring whether it suppresses other aspirations and political possibilities. As a consequence, this type of criticism is subject to being seduced by a Western ideology that, instead of recognizing actual problems and their most viable solutions, collaborates in obscuring and perpetuating these difficulties.

It should be made clear that no one denies that mestizaje is a natural process and that there are no pure races. Mestizaje has been the rule for the human species. Neither does anyone deny subjects the right to self-identify as mestizo or Ladino, or to "mix" with humans who are culturally different. What I criticize about mestizaje is that it has historically constituted itself as a cultural norm and as a political subjectivity that is superior to others. Mestizaje considers itself to be the only worthy option for the "representation" of a national and continental subjectivity, as well as the only way to respond to modernizing mechanisms. This ideology manifests serious limitations. Through its ideological justification, it constitutes what Martin Lienhard calls a "collective amnesia" ("Kalunga o el recuerdo" 505). It not only suppresses a palpable reality and silences native cultures but also ignores the unresolved traumatic experiences we have inherited from the colonial experience and are still reproduced in the present. In other words, through the diffusion of this intellectual tradition, this class of cultural criticism recycles a neocolonial mode. Its politics of forgetfulness has constantly sought to superimpose new memories in order to avoid confronting the coloniality of power.

The question remains, can mestizos and indigenous peoples resolve the tension by acknowledging a politics of difference? Can the construction of a Maya signifier and locus of enunciation end the interethnic debate? These questions lead me to the ideas of interculturality promoted by Mayas themselves. What are the implications of speaking from a Maya locus on enunciation? What are we talking about when we speak of interculturality? If the Maya movement has brought an idea of interculturality based on the recognition of difference to the debate, then one must explore the implications of this discursivity. I will problematize these questions through an analysis of Estuardo Zapeta's *The Jaguar's Footprints*.

Estuardo Zapeta: (Neo)Liberal Interculturality

Reproducing a Colonial, Maya Modernity?

No doubt the most significant contribution of the Guatemalan Maya movement has been the ethnic and civilizing dimension it introduces to the
indigenous question. This contribution acquires a fundamental importance
insofar as it recasts the "national," turning toward a reimagining and reconceptualization of the nation as being a multiethnic, multilingual, and multinational space instead of one that is culturally and linguistically
homogenous. The movement has declared that it is prepared to continue
defending its recognition as an autonomous and differentiated cultural
entity within the nation-state and to demand the creation of a new multilingual and multicultural national project. For example, the Academy of Maya
Languages of Guatemala (ALMG), in producing dictionaries and school-
books in Maya languages, works "to promote the knowledge and diffusion
of the Mayan languages and culture. This recognition is not the gift of the
government, but is the result of the efforts of an entire People, the Mayan
People, who are seeking the construction of a fully multilingual and multicultural society in Guatemala" (Nelson 153). Victor Montejo (*Maya
Intellectual Renaissance*) also made an important contribution when he
observed, "We must keep our eyes on ethnic diversity in our country and
recognize our ethnic or cultural differences. We must start from this multiethnic affirmation in order to construct a free, just, and democratic
Guatemala. Haven't we spoken and even bragged about having a pluricul-
tural, multiethnic country in our discussions? Now it is time to construct it
and live it as Guatemalans" (9). These ideological manifestations, as stated
in the introduction, have produced debates between the Maya cultural and
popular rights tendencies within the movement.[18] Here, I do not intend to
outline this debate but rather to explore the idea of the new "multilingual"
"multicultural," and "multinational" nation being promoted by both popular and cultural Mayanists. What are some of the implications of this reconceptualization of the nation? What is at play in this politics of difference?
Does this positionality mean the promotion of a national project that
responds to the necessities of *all* Guatemalans in economic, ethnic/racial,
and gender terms? Obviously, those are the fundamental objectives. But is
talking about a politics of difference that recognizes linguistic and multicultural diversity enough to reach those objectives? Should the movement
focus on the interethnic problem merely in terms of cultural and linguistic
revitalization? In this section, I analyze these questions through an examination of Estuardo Zapeta's book, *Las huellas de B'alam* (The Jaguar's
Footprints), which contains newspaper articles he published between 1994

and 1996. These articles discuss, among other topics, indigenous education, Maya cultural affirmation, nationalist discourses, and foreign policy in order to contribute to the interethnic debate in Guatemala. My objective here is to clarify some of the dangers of and limitations to strictly promoting a "politics of difference" that is divorced from other fundamental concerns, especially economic ones.

Along with Luís Enrique Sam Colop,[19] Zapeta is one of the most widely recognized Maya intellectuals in Guatemala. Having done postgraduate work in journalism and anthropology in the United States,[20] Zapeta, a Kaqchikel Maya, writes for the Guatemalan paper *Siglo vientiuno*. He contributes to the opinion section twice a week and also has a weekly radio program. The importance of exploring his texts resides in the fact that Zapeta considers himself to be a postmodern liberal intellectual who seeks to demystify the ideas associated with "an economically and ideologically Left-leaning indigenous person" (Zapeta, *Las huellas* 159), as opposed to Maya intellectuals allied to positions we could identify as being "progressive" or postcolonial (de Lión, Menchú, Pablo Ceto, Sam Colop). Zapeta self-identifies as Maya and relates to the Maya movement. But he feels that the primary objectives of indigenous peoples—multilingual education, political self-determination, the formulation of a new project of the Guatemalan state, national unity on equal economic and cultural conditions—will be gained not through a populist or Leftist ideology, but rather through negotiation with the prevailing neoliberal model in order to create better opportunities for the Maya. According to Zapeta, integration into modernity and economic success depend on building a solid educational project and adopting the "Principle of Liberty" as a philosophical and material basis for a truly "actual" development. Unlike those who begin from a confrontation with the coloniality of power and postulate a political project from below (Luis de Lión and Rigoberta Menchú), Zapeta takes his point of departure from the idea of an established modernity in which current economic differences are more the result of an "underdevelopment" caused by the recently ended civil war than the conditions of subalternity historically imposed upon indigenous peoples. The name and surname of the causes of underdevelopment are the Left and the Guatemalan army. Both caused a psychological damage that continues to hinder the economic development of indigenous peoples and of Guatemala. Zapeta specifies that the current crisis in Guatemala owes to a "stupid *revolution* [that] changed nothing" (443): "On the contrary, the war has left us a poor and divided country" (443).

As for the Left, Zapeta accuses it of promoting a discourse that has imprisoned ethnic and linguistic diversity in a class struggle, interpreting ethnic and linguistic differences according to the assumption that the entire indigenous population consists of poor, illiterate peasants. Zapeta observes that the Left's discourse has become obsolete and does not contribute to indigenous political participation. It only spreads fear and an ethnohysteria that benefits the army and the sectors of power. This discourse "should be eliminated and substituted for one more in line with Guatemalan reality" (*Las huellas* 95). In addition, following David Stoll's argument (*Between Two Armies*), Zapeta suggests that the Left is mostly responsible for the genocide of Mayas in Guatemala and for current economic divisions: it caused "pain, anguish and even death to many Guatemalans who were trapped between two armies" (*Las huellas* 443).

Ironically, Zapeta does not consider himself to be on the Right politically, although in some cases—if not most—his way of thinking coincides with that of the Right. He has no problem with those who label him a "Neoliberal Indian" (*Las huellas* 393). For him, this means trying to do things "in an efficient way": "What I do know is that [the free market] in other places has worked, and it would be good if we at least try it in Guatemala" (160). His ideological motto is, "I am opposed to demagogic populisms as much as state protectionism. Without privileges, I have said; equality before the majesty of the Law, in fact, is the only acceptable equality, is what I have insisted. Competition is what I have dreamed" (12). From these principles, Zapeta proposes to reconceptualize the project of the nation as multicultural and multilingual because it can be "constructed on the foundations of respect for the dignity of the Person, on the basis of a respect for Life, Liberty, and Prosperity, within a State of Justice and a Free Market economy" (13).

With this perspective, Zapeta challenges Demetrio Cojtí, who has criticized his neoliberal stance by stating that "in Guatemala, the principles of liberalism (free competition, equality of opportunity, equality before the law, etc.) are only valid for the Ladino. They do not apply to the Maya, and the Maya *should not* use them" (*El movimiento* 36). Zapeta insists otherwise. He observes that his ideological stand responds to Mayas and non-Mayas who continue constructing the "Indian" as "poor," "barefoot," and "unable to participate in the economy" and as an "authentic" subject incapable of assimilating modernity. He challenges the idea that we Mayas remain "with our gaze fixed on the past" (*Las huellas* 271)—obviously responding to stereotyped constructions of indigeneity like Cojtí's (above). "With the falsity of the *pure* [authentic] culture," Zapeta states, "we are creating communities sealed off at a time when one speaks of an opening up to the world. We have not understood that *pure* does not exist. *Purity* is the continual transformation of our culture. Our cultures are dynamic" (26). The danger of promoting these stereotypes, according to Zapeta, is that they recycle a construction of the Leftist "Indian" influenced by the West, promoting the idea of a "defeated [indigenous] victim, incapable, highly vulnerable, ready to accept any paternalist proposal from nationalists or foreigners" (25). Another danger is that the government continues taking advantage of these discursive constructions to maintain a nation-state that dispenses "crumbs" to the Indians and better opportunities to Ladinos. It is because of this, Zapeta argues, that the nation-state is a "Ladino [state], with a Ladino vision, and for Ladinos" (241). What destabilizes these versions of Maya identity, according to Zapeta, are Mayas' daily use of innovative technologies such as computers, the Internet, and cellular phones, which prove their capacity to compete in the modern world.

In this context, Zapeta outlines an interesting contradiction in regards to the topic of cultural identity. Contrary to Morales and his informants' suspicions about the supposed loss of indigenous cultural specificities through cultural globalization, Zapeta demonstrates a desire to embrace what Morales believes is exterminating Maya identity, in order to reaffirm it. Zapeta represents what Diane Nelson has called a "Maya Hacker": someone who among other things is technologically literate, has studied abroad, "maintains connections in the rural and urban matrix through contact with his small-town home and with many rural-based Mayan organizations, and…frequently contributes to the national press and indigenous publications" (Nelson 252). From this, we can deduce that Zapeta takes advantage of what modernity offers him and uses these technologies and connections between rural and urban systems in order to demonstrate Mayas' capacity "as agents of the future" (Zapeta, *Las huellas* 198).

This "agency" is precisely what Zapeta proposes to emphasize in order to challenge the images of poverty we often find in the mass media and literature about Mayas. Zapeta argues that these representations marginalize Mayas who are in better economic conditions, like those of Quetzaltenango's (the second most important city in Guatemala) Maya bourgeoisie, and who actively participate in the Guatemalan economy.[21] Taking this Maya class as an example, according to his principles of liberalism, Zapeta argues that "undevelopment" is something that is "primarily in our minds" (*Las huellas* 25). He proposes the decentralization of power and resources in order to establish a "base of *symmetrical* (not asymmetrical) relations of power between the peoples involved" (191). In addition, he argues that the Maya movement should promote positive images of indigenous peoples but also a "discourse of liberty and unity as an alternative and a viable path for the development of our children and grandchildren. Mutual respect should be a constant. If we Indians move forward, Guatemala moves forward" (27).

Contrary to those who suggest that his nationalist project is "exclusively" for Mayas—as Morales would argue—the national imaginary Zapeta develops includes Ladinos as well. In fact, for Zapeta, the key to national development relies on the "extent to which we are prepared to include *the other* and not to exclude him (although this may be what *the other* has done to us)" (*Las huellas* 272). And more clearly, he suggests that Mayas should promote a national project that, even while focusing on indigenous cultural and linguistic revitalization, accepts "unity in diversity." He represents this idea metaphorically, describing a Maya textile:

> If we patiently observe how the distinct threads of the textile have been combined little by little, how the colors come together and are intermingled, how each thread is important, how each makes its contribution along with the others, in a unified force, then we see the result: something impressive is woven. Almost by a miracle, there emerges a universe of multiple forms, figures, and colors that finally becomes a magnificent example of harmony and beauty: an indigenous textile, a garment that represents our nationality. (Zapeta, Las huellas 296)

One can see that this project of the nation, symbolized by the "indigenous textile," recognizes "that each thread is important" and the necessity of a "unified force" in realizing a new Guatemalan nation that is finally beautiful and harmonious.

Here we have a discourse that challenges and problematizes the "authenticity" of the Maya subject by placing him within the global village, as well as a national project that promotes a politics of difference that includes the "other." Then what is the problem? Zapeta recognizes that Guatemala is culturally and linguistically diverse, and he supports the movement's efforts to revitalize indigenous languages and cultures (*Las huellas* 22).[22] But is this sufficient to materialize a multicultural, multilingual, multinational nation? We certainly recognize that Zapeta responds to the latent racism in Guatemala in order to recognize a struggle for ethnic affirmation and autonomy.[23] But should this struggle be limited to achieving linguistic, cultural, and political recognition? Are the principles of "liberty" and the "free market" suitable to solving economic disparities and rescue us from "underdevelopment"? Let us explore the idea of "indigenous peoples" promoted by Zapeta. On the one hand, it lets us reflect upon a "politics of difference" that would further the colonialist project of economic inequality. On the other hand, it allows us to examine critically the danger of restricting the goal of the indigenous movement to cultural and linguistic vindication.

Zapeta has a particular class of indigenous person in mind with regards to the construction of a new multicultural and multilingual nation: a "growing group of indigenous entrepreneurs" (*Las huellas* 239) who are in an economic and cultural position to negotiate their future within globalization. At one point, Zapeta declares that his political project advocates for a group that "in practice (and not on paper) values intelligence, honor, knowledge, capability, work, creativity, and human liberty" (142). The emphasis he places on this group's characteristics deserves attention because they are intimately related to the objectives of an enlightened indigenous project. These objectives are manifested more clearly in Zapeta's attitudes toward indigenous peoples in positions of subalternity.

In Zapeta's approach to the Zapatista rebellion, he shows a certain discomfort concerning Chiapanecan indigenous peoples' agency with regard to the media: "Who was going to believe that an indigenous group of Tzotziles, Tzeltales, Tojolabales, *manipulated* by a mestizo with the spirit of Robin Hood, self-proclaimed Subcomandante Marcos, was going to be the first in carrying out a war in cyberspace" (*Las huellas* 329, emphasis added). Note Zapeta's surprise when describing the indigenous Zapatistas who have made use of these modes of representation to bring the attention of the Mexican government and the world to their demands. One finds that, in this false admiration, Zapeta considers them incapable of using the media. For him, a "mestizo" "manipulates" and directs the way, not the indigenous people.

Further, in an analysis that echoes Morales when he discredits Rigoberta Menchú for her use of "cultured" words in her testimonio, Zapeta reproaches Manuela López Alvarado. López Alvarado, a Guatemalan Maya K'iche' woman who in the 1995 elections was a Leftist party candidate for a senate seat, at one point had lectured at a university in the United States. Zapeta, who attended the event, insinuates that her lecture was prepared and influenced by the Leftist party leaders she represented (*Las huellas* 243). Similar to his judgment about the Mayas in Chiapas, here the Leftist leaders occupy a role parallel to that of Marcos: they manipulate indigenous peoples for their own purposes.

On another occasion, the Maya Kaqchikel author also gives himself the authority to discredit the popular mobilizations and protests of indigenous peoples and peasants. Because they have no voice or authority in the mass media (as Zapeta does), their only means of agency are popular protests, land invasions, marches, and roadblocks. These are the only ways they can make themselves heard, pushing people in power to respond to their demands. Considering these means "obsolete" and lacking imagination, Zapeta suggests that the "nation" cannot be built upon these "false columns." On the contrary, this building should follow "an order, a logic that applies to society, we could call *civil rights within the state*" (*Las huellas* 297).

We find worse judgments in Zapeta when he invalidates rumors about the possible uprising of an indigenous guerrilla movement in Guatemala, the Maya Movement of National Liberation. Zapeta refers to them as "vile," "cruel," "liberationist thieves," "a collection of delinquents with an ethnic name who were infected by the syndrome of Marcos the Zapatista" ("Liberación Maya"). They make "unpolluted Indian proposals without access to the daily happenings of the world" and support "an ethnic state that promises vengeance to history" ("Liberación Maya"). He ends by saying that "such Maya liberation movements have to be someone's business; this is how racism is born of antiracism" ("Liberación Maya"). As in his critique of López Alvarado and the indigenous Zapatistas, he suggests that this movement is a product of "manipulation." Instead of exploring the causes that gave life to this uprising, Zapeta states that these "thieves" and "delinquents" represent an obstacle to "the correct path of development" ("Liberación Maya"). They do not represent the aspirations of "all" Mayas.

It is obvious that Zapeta does not seek to represent, nor even less sympathize with, the interests and ideals of indigenous peoples in conditions of subalternity. Protests, as peaceful as they are rebellious, are not appropriate to the "correct path" of Guatemala's development. Zapeta suggests that indigenous peoples in conditions of subalternity are incapable of *speaking for* themselves, are "manipulated" by Leftist intellectuals, by "mestizos" like Marcos or people in power. So who represents the appropriate model to follow in order to materialize a multicultural and multilingual nation, as well as productive economic development in Guatemala? What objectives or aspirations or what sector of the Maya movement does Zapeta represent? He answers these questions by promoting a national project that supports "those Indians who in silence, with intelligence, with their work, with their customs, with their memory, with their reproduction, make daily contributions to the development of the Guatemalan invention" (*Las huellas* 297). This indigenous class is described in more detail in his article "Mercedes Benz *a lá* indigenous" (*Las huellas* 127).

In this article, Zapeta proposes to get rid of the idea that "all Indians are poor" (*Las huellas* 127). He mentions the TV commercials made by Mercedes Benz that praise a "wealthy group [of indigenous people] that has always successfully dedicated itself to commerce and to the production of vegetables, fruit, textiles, construction materials and other goods and services" (127). Zapeta sees these TV commercials as positives because they show these indigenous groups as representing the growth of economic opportunities for Mayas and for Guatemala. Contrary to the Indians who "have made protests and land invasions a way of life" (297), this class of indigenous entrepreneurs, through "hard work, intelligence, and business sense to confront the risks of agriculture" (128) represents *the* model to follow. Their success comes from their capacity and desire to compete in national and international markets and oppose state protectionism.

Zapeta expressed later that in this article he sought to show, above all, how the market and commercial exchange at the national and international levels are not economic processes "foreign" to the Maya communities in the Guatemalan highlands, where there exists a wealthy indigenous class (*Las huellas* 160). Moreover, he clarifies that although he understands the symbolic value of the land, merely to advocate policies of agrarian reform would "condemn us to a subsistence economy" and marginalize other possibilities of development. On the contrary, indigenous peoples "should speak of industry and export" (160). In this way, he justifies the "free market" as a social project based on the privatization of key industries: "If state enterprises are unable to bring their services to those of us living in the countryside, they should let others dedicate themselves to providing the services we lack" (159). He adds: "*If we want to enter and remain in the Information Age, it will be necessary and urgent that GUATEL* [the telecommunications company in Guatemala, which was privatized by a Mexican company] *be privatized*" (118). And later: "The market (understood as relations of exchange between people who honorably and intelligently want to satisfy their needs) is the least bad of the systems that can help us escape this unnecessary poverty" (218).

Zapeta also suggests that the market and indigenous entrepreneurship are not new phenomena. They represent a tradition that stretches back to the pre-Columbian era, when commerce and "free trade" were the norm of indigenous markets:

> Historical evidence shows us that for centuries markets have been vibrant manifestations of indigenous existence and presence. This is why it bothers me so much when, without historical evidence, we are represented as a group (almost as esoteric, cosmological hippies) in which equality and the equative distribution of wealth and land reigned, as these fallacies have no historical basis. In the kingdoms of the Guatemalan highlands there existed (and exist) social differentiation and markets. (Zapeta, Las huellas 129)

As this quotation reveals, Zapeta associates the pre-Columbian markets, with their social inequality, class struggles, and unequal distribution of wealth, as something natural, something that has always "existed." Further, because "markets" have always been the norm of socioeconomic exchange, we have no choice but to accept the logic of the "free" market.

This justification of the neoliberalism and "free trade" raises a problem. Zapeta conceives of indigenous modes of production as being equal to or compatible with capitalism. It is necessary to keep in mind that if the marketplace was a "vibrant manifestation" of pre-Columbian indigenous societies, it cannot be reduced to a market ideology that promotes capitalist ideals. In this sense, Karl Marx's reflections in *Capital: A Critique of Political Economy* about the difference between "use value" and "exchange value" economies are pertinent.

Following Aristotle, Marx describes the fundamental difference between the modes of production in "primitive" societies and capitalist societies with regard to the idea of the market. In "primitive" societies, the driving ideas consist of a commercial exchange based on obtaining C (commodity)–M (money)–C (commodity). The economies of capitalist societies consist of obtaining M (money)–C (commodity)–M (money). M-C-M, for Marx, is the general formula for capital. In this formula, "the circulation of money as capital is an end in itself, for the valorization of value takes place only within this constantly renewed movement. The movement of capital is therefore limitless" (Marx 253). The aim of the capitalist thus becomes "the unceasing movement of profit-making" (254). To put it differently, the market in capitalist societies is based on surplus value or the accumulation of capital, whereas in communal societies the means of production and economic exchange are based on kinship organization. Production is for use and for meeting the needs of the kinship group, rather than for exchange or for personal private gain and profit.

The collision between these two modes of production is evidenced in the literature of the so-called discovery of the New World, in which significant differences about the idea of market exchange emerge. In his diary, Columbus writes:

> *They brought spears and some balls of cotton to barter with and exchanged them with some of the crew for bits of glass, broken cups and pieces of earthenware dishes. Some of them were wearing little pieces of gold hanging from their noses; they were quite willing to exchange these for a sparrowhawk bell of a few glass beads, so insignificant as to be worthless, for, really, however little one gave them, they too were amazed. (106)*

In the exchange of "pieces of gold" for insignificant things like the "sparrowhawk bell of a few glass beads," indigenous peoples evidence an economy of use values, while the Spanish manifest mercantilist ones. Based on these differences, the invaders reduced these conceptions of exchange to "ignorance," "inferiority," or "backwardness" in which the "natives" had no idea of the value of their wealth.

Highlighting these differences does not mean denying Zapeta's claims about romanticizing indigenous societies as a "paradise" where no economic contradictions existed, but rather to recognize that indigenous peoples' division of labor and hierarchy of power were mostly established by religious values and heredity, above economic considerations. According to Alex Dupuy, "the division of labor which does exist in tribal society…is determined from within the units of production—by the skills, the resources and the needs of the household units—with the chief or cacique acting as the mediator between the various households, and not from without the social relations of production by a class which is separated from and controls the process of production" (13).

With this characterization in mind, how, then, can indigenous ideas of exchange and the market be analogous to a capitalist mode of production—the neoliberal one, in Zapeta's case? The conquest clearly shows that there existed profound cultural and economic differences between indigenous peoples and the Spanish. This "encounter," as is known, was defined by the imposition of new rules and economic ideologies based on Marx's premise of mercantilism: MCM. In this context, Zapeta's claim that indigenous markets were replicas of the modern capitalist economic system merely seeks to create a consensus favorable to neoliberalism in indigenous communities.[24] These references to the capitalist indigenous class and to Zapeta's access to globalization (use of the Internet, writing in a national newspaper, having studied abroad, and so forth) display the idea that free trade agreements will create similar opportunities for the Maya in general. However, neoliberalism has proven to be a new phase of advanced capitalism that continues reproducing profound economic inequalities. As a result, we have seen vehement resistance to these models and the privatization of natural resources, as demonstrated by Zapatismo and the Bolivian Movement Toward Socialism (MAS).

It is not difficult to perceive in Zapeta a new class of colonialist indigenous authority that advocates an oppressive mode of production inaugurated by the Spanish. This mode of production was later adopted by criollos and Ladinos, and now it proposes to establish a new "multicultural" nationalism that transfers power to the hands of Maya, Ladino, Xinka, and Garífuna elites. Furthermore, based on the "Principle of Liberty" and the desire that "one day there will exist in Guatemala a political group that in practice (not on paper) *values intelligence, honor, knowledge, ability, work, creativity, and human liberty*" (*Las huellas* 142, emphasis added), Zapeta's discursivity recycles the principles of enlightenment delineated by Emmanuel Kant in his essay "What Is Enlightenment?" (1784).

Kant writes that "enlightenment is the exodus of humanity by its own effort from the state of guilty immaturity" and that "laziness and cowardice are the reasons why the greater part of humanity remains pleasurably in this state of immaturity" (quoted in Dussel, "Eurocentrism and Modernity" 68).

As Partha Chatterjee suggests, according to these statements, Kant believed that being "enlightened" meant becoming "mature," "coming of age," ceasing to depend on the authority of others, arriving at a "free" status, and assuming responsibility for one's actions according to what one learns ("Our Modernity" 9). When a man does not meet these conditions, he does not employ his own judgment; instead, he accepts the custody of those who, having already reached a state of "maturity," can guide him along the appropriate paths. This immature subject does not need to acquire knowledge about the world, for everything is written in sacred books. Nor does he need to exercise his own judgment in regards to what is good or bad. He follows the advice of the "enlightened" beings. This immature subject even lets his shepherd decide what he should eat, wear, and think. Historically, down to the present, these are the conditions that the "guardians of society" have desired.

Zapeta's arguments manifest this Kantian vision through the "Principle of Liberty" he advocates. Those who are in conditions of subalternity are subalterns because they have a "victim" complex, because the idea of "underdevelopment" is "in their minds," because they are being "manipulated" by "mistaken" ideologies. Unlike those who have achieved "maturity" (Zapeta himself and the wealthy Maya class of the Guatemalan highlands), they have not valued "intelligence, honor, knowledge, ability, work, creativity, and human liberty." In other words, subaltern Mayas remain in a state of "immaturity" that has not allowed them to develop these qualities, because this is how they have preferred to be or because they are "lazy." In contrast, the indigenous classes that have achieved maturity are the example to follow—"intelligent" and "hard-working" people who have historically participated in the economy of the "market," exercising scientific reason in the name of the well-being of all humanity. For Zapeta, this is also why it is important to follow the model of economic development "that has worked in other places"; a society that possesses advanced political abilities represents the model to be emulated.

What is missing in Zapeta's perspective is an interpretation that shows how these national and developmental models have acquired their "maturity." As Eduardo Galeano suggests, the prosperity of others has not occurred naturally but rather is the result of relations of domination in which the conquerors have imposed "immaturity" or infantilization on *other* countries (3): "The force of the entire imperialist system rests upon the necessary inequality of the parts which [compose] it, and that inequality assumes ever more dramatic dimensions" (4). Frantz Fanon also reminds us in his passionate postcolonial scream:

> The wealth of the imperial countries is our wealth too.... For in a very

concrete way Europe has stuffed herself inordinately with the gold and raw materials of the colonial countries: Latin America, China, and Africa. From all these continents, under whose eyes Europe today raises up her tower of opulence, there has flowed out for centuries toward that same Europe diamonds and oil, silk and cotton, wood and exotic products. Europe is literally the creation of the Third World. The wealth which smothers her is that which was stolen from the underdeveloped peoples. (The Wretched of the Earth 102)

Despite Zapeta's efforts to endorse a politics of difference that recognizes "unity in diversity" and Maya cultural and linguistic specificities, his ideological stance represents a trap for and a betrayal of Mayas and non-Mayas in conditions of subalternity.[25] The "Maya" national project he advocates does not begin from below but rather departs from those who have already achieved and negotiated a position of power by adopting a capitalist ideology that allows them to compete within the market. One can confidently assert that when Zapeta speaks of realizing a project of difference, he is thinking of a project that is shared by Maya, Ladino, Xinka, and Garífuna elites in Guatemala. It is a national project that recognizes and embraces "difference" only when one accepts the economic capitalist logic espoused by neoliberalism. This position situates him within the context of what Charles Hale and Rosamel Millamán call *Indio permitido* (the permissible Indian); that is, Zapeta "has passed the test of modernity, substituted 'protest' with 'proposal,' and learned to be both authentic and fully conversant with the dominant milieu" (Hale, "Rethinking Indigenous Politics" 19).[26]

Strictly speaking, the "diversity" that is argued for here, contrary to the one represented by de Lión and Menchú, does not consist of the ideals and interests of an indigenous population in conditions of subalternity—the majority, in a country like Guatemala—but rather the ideals and interests of a lettered and wealthy indigenous class. Speaking for elite Mayas means speaking for a "mature" indigenous class that "works hard" (they have sufficient infrastructure—like Mercedes Benz trucks), is "intelligent" (Indios permitidos), with "business-like attitudes" (they are capable of competing in the market). Zapeta clearly proposes a model of "development" that recycles the principles and bases of a capitalist or neoliberal mode of production. In contrast with the previous one—which proposed the integration of the Indian into this mode of production through assimilation or Ladinoization—his model now disseminates the idea that cultural specificities can be accepted and enjoyed only when neoliberalism is embraced. Mayas can be participants in a mode of production that promotes "competition," as well as a system of social classes that continues the economic exploitation of labor (no longer necessarily indigenous) and of natural resources. The politics of difference represented here—the same as that promoted by Morales—does not alter the modes through which political and economic power are reproduced. It perpetuates social segregation. Instead of a multicultural project that emerges from below, Zapeta's perspective leads a project of (neo)liberal multiculturalism that marginalizes the contribution of Guatemalan subaltern classes—both Mayas and non-Mayas—and consequently reproduces coloniality.

For Morales, indigenous peoples' passage into globalization can be carried out through an "intercultural mestizaje" that facilitates a "popular competitiveness" within the global environment. Zapeta's text advocates "unity in diversity," accepting a politics of difference that would go hand in hand with a neoliberal economic politics in the negotiation of a modern "national future." It should be pointed out here that although Zapeta and Morales differ on some points (Zapeta argues for neoliberalism and cultural diversity, measures that make Morales uncomfortable), we find similarities between them. Both Zapeta and Morales, from their respective places of enunciation, argue for a project of the nation that recognizes a "lettered cultural authority" that represents national interests in the political arena. And, to a certain degree, this authority discredits the struggles of indigenous and non-indigenous classes in conditions of subalternity because they threaten the hegemonic ethnic "order" (Morales) or the hegemonic national "order" (Zapeta). These treatments of interculturality parallel those found in North American debates that argue for an idea of the nation that one should respect. Here, I am referring to Richard Rorty's position, which relates to Zapeta's and Morales's.

Rorty's brief essay "The Demonization of Multiculturalism" suggests that the existing partial and ethnic social divisions between blacks and whites in the United States owe more to a lack of jobs and opportunities for ethnic minorities than to racism as such. For Rorty, this is a matter of the "disparities of power rather than differences in culture" (74). Referring to the US black population, he observes that differences entail "the self-fulfilling prediction that [whites] will remain separated from their black contemporaries not just by money and life changes but by a 'difference of culture'" (74). Further, teaching blacks and whites that they "have separate cultural identities does no good at all. Whatever pride such teaching may inspire in black children is offset by the suggestion that their culture is not that of their white schoolmates, that they have no share in the mythic America imagined by the Founding Fathers and by Emerson and Whitman, the America partially realized by Lincoln and King" (74). Rorty suggests that the best way to address differences between the two groups is by "teaching both black and white children what African-American men and women have done for their country." He writes that "mythic America is a great country, and the insecure and divided actual America is a pretty good one. As racist, sexist, and homophobic as the United States is, it is also a 200-year-old functioning democracy—one that has overcome divisions and mitigated inequalities in the past and may still have the capacity to do so" (74–75). Like Rorty, Morales has problems spreading a politics that recognizes the cultural and linguistic differences between Ladinos and Mayas. Doing this would deepen the existing differences in Guatemala and expose the myth of the Ladino nation as a "fraud." He proposes intercultural mestizaje as much to resolve these ethnic divisions as to reaffirm the Ladino nation. Further, Zapeta and Rorty share the idea that racism is not a question of "races" or "ethnicities," but rather a lack of opportunities for "minorities" (or the majority, in our case). Economic and ethnic inequality can disappear if indigenous peoples have opportunities for employment and participation in the nation's economic development. For Zapeta, this is why representations of Mayas who are doing something "positive" economically for their nation and neoliberalism constitute a good way to reaffirm and respond to interethnic questions.

What is at stake for Morales and Zapeta is the creation of a new subject capable of responding to modernization/globalization. From Morales, we get the idea that modernity represents "homogenizing" mechanisms; for Zapeta, modernity represents an opportunity or opening for Indian communities—entering into modernity with cultural and linguistic specificities only when they embrace the conditions of competition it establishes. The dark side of modernity—the coloniality of power (Mignolo, *The Darker Side of the Renaissance*; Quijano "'Raza,' 'etnia' y 'nación'") and its mechanisms of domination, which have been reconfigured in the present—is marginalized in both of these perspectives on modernity. With the cultural authority from which both Morales and Zapeta speak, these perspectives essentially recycle this coloniality of power. Moreover, these authors reaffirm the idea of modernity as a club that imposes certain rules: we cannot enter with our cultural and linguistic particularities intact. Its mechanisms "erase" or "cancel" these particularities (Morales). Or if we can enter with these cultural and linguistic particularities, we should do so while accepting the economic logic based on competition (Zapeta). I would now like to offer some reflections on these two proposals as a means to think about a possible alternative.

Rethinking Interculturality: Some Reflections

In this chapter, I have sought to demonstrate some of the tensions that emerge from the interethnic debate by analyzing texts by two of its most well-known representatives. As already seen, the discussions that govern the debate turn on the ideas of modernity and cultural identity—especially Maya identity. We can discern that the interethnic debate focuses on constructing a compatible cultural identity that permits us "to enter" into modernity or globalization. In these proposals, however, there is not a rigorous questioning of modernity as a colonial project, and this same logic is essentially resignified. Given that the perspectives of Morales and Zapeta represent contradictory political postures to a certain extent, is it possible to elaborate a more viable narrative of interculturality? How can we generate an analysis that can explain the construction of "Maya," "Ladino," "Xinka," or "Garífuna" subjects? Or rather, how can we generate another narrative of modernity that recognizes the struggles for the construction of a non-exclusive interculturality? I now wish to return to the discussion about understanding Ladino identity as "a political signifier that does not have the consensus of all its members but nevertheless seeks to *build* this consensus through the construction of an identity that is historically non-existent" (Morales, *La articulación* 405, emphasis added). We will consider the reflections on how Western power and knowledge have constructed the indigenous subject through an indigenista discursivity.

Morales is correct when he observes that indigenous traditions comprise a cultural mixture. But is hybridity a phenomenon exclusive to indigenous cultures? What about dominant cultures? Are these immune to the influences of subaltern cultures? For me, Morales suffers from the same problem that affected Ángel Rama and his notion of transculturation. Rama advocated modernity and thought that indigenous cultures were incapable of influencing dominant cultures or modernizing processes. Similarly, for example, Morales understands that dominant cultures and globalization, and not indigenous cultures, are what regulate modernizing processes. In his study of globalization, indigenous peoples are sometimes passive entities that receive external influences without questioning them, or they receive these only to bury their traditions and accept the logic of mestizaje or hybridity. But if we constructed pastoral imagery analogous to that elaborated by Morales, we could easily expect that, on visiting tourist sites like Antigua or Panajachel or Tijuana, we would find tourists buying and wearing "traditional" indigenous clothing. Does this mean that the middle or hegemonic classes are "losing" their identity or cultural specificity? For me, this is where we encounter the theoretical limitations of hybridity developed by the Guatemalan critic.

If the theoretical principles Morales develops were applied, let us say, to the people of Calcutta, New York, Singapore, Tokyo, Madrid, or the United Kingdom, we would arrive at conclusions analogous to those that are obtained from places like Guatemala. Because *all* cultures are a battlefield on which they are constantly reconstructed. The "phenomenon of hybridity" is a process in which both subaltern and dominant groups participate, developing through their interaction inevitable contexts of cultural exchange. This exchange involves a necessary "loss," but it also involves regeneration. In any case, it deals with a process that *all* peoples and cultures have survived through cultural borrowings from, exchanges with, and appropriations from other peoples and cultures. What occurs in this series of exchanges, far from "burying" tradition, as Morales suggests, is the creation of a new cultural pact that has as its objective the transformation, adaptation, and affirmation of the continuity of a people, in this case, indigenous peoples.

In light of this reading, then, and as it applies to Morales's study, it should be understood that the Maya diaspora in the metropolis—Guatemala City, México, the United States, Europe—operates through the selective adoption of values and cultural products offered by the West or any other culture with which it has had contact and interaction. Mayas' participation in globalization does not preclude a "loss" of cultural specificities. We can understand this selective adoption, I would argue, as an expansion of knowledge, beyond the regeneration of indigenous values, and the creation of new cultural, epistemological, discursive, and transnational indigenous horizons. It means, strictly, a new and unfinished globocultural space in which metropolitan indigenous subjects situate themselves in order to negotiate their process of ancestral vindication, even to the point of using globalization itself to reactivate their cosmology in the present.

In this context, Morales obligates us to reformulate the category of "culture" in that he makes it clear that no people exists as something "autonomous," "authentic," "essentialized," but rather as an "inevitable" mixture —biological, cultural, ideological. If we agree with this position, though, how can we understand the Maya, the Xinka, the Garífuna, and the Ladino when cultural identity can no longer be conceived of in terms of biology, geography, language, or dress? For me, this means understanding the idea of culture and cultural identity as the field of struggle that, under globalization, necessarily demands a political affiliation. Following this idea, I would suggest that we, whether Maya or non-Maya, approach the problematic of cultural identity not only in biological and cultural terms, but also *from a political affiliation and positioning that, more than being a geographic place or specific language or the way we dress and act, implies a historical experience and a cultural, affective, and political relation from which we think and act.* The idea of a people's cultural identity should be understood, then, not within the sphere of describing biological mixings or cultural exchanges that occur in multiethnic societies, but rather in a political field conditioned by historical struggles that seek to eradicate the oppression of ethnicity, of gender, of class.

As Stefano Varese suggests, following E. P. Thompson and Renato Rosaldo, the field of "culture" should be thought of as

> *a* field of contention, *a* contested domain *in which negotiations between individuals and social sectors of the same ethnic group and between the latter and the external dominant society constantly occur. Therefore, ethnicity, cultural identity, and the struggle to maintain sociopolitical and ethnic autonomy or self-determination can be comprehended more in terms of flexible horizons than of rigid boundaries. A situational phenomenon, Indian ethnicity is socially constructed and reconstructed in a permanent process of dialectical negotiation. ("The Ethnopolitics of Indian Resistance" 64)*

In this context, we recognize that "Maya," "Ladino," "Xinka," and "Garífuna" are identity constructions with flexible horizons, each searching to establish its own place of enunciation.

The "interethnic problem" does not deal with the construction of new identity constructs, such as "Maya," but rather with the resurgence of a historic struggle that modern nation-states have been unable to end: economic and ethnic inequality, especially among Maya populations. It is here—to respond to accusations of a Maya "essentialism" or "fundamentalism"—where we can locate and better understand the postures of Cojtí and Zapeta when they argue for "authenticity" and Maya positionality. Their postures demonstrate what Spivak calls a "strategic essentialism," establishing a political locus of enunciation and legitimacy in order to construct a presence that has been historically marginalized. The use of the category "Maya" by the authors whom Morales studies (above) represents a process of achieving the reaffirmation of a dignity that has been trampled on for more than five centuries. Of course, it is also necessary to distinguish between a "strategic essentialism," which is used merely to establish a politics of difference, and an "essentialism" of those who, beyond arguing for this differentiated presence, take up the causes of anticolonial and antiracist struggles by communities in conditions of subalternity (like those represented by de Lión and Menchú in the first part of this book). For me, this is the moment to emphasize the necessity of the Maya movement finding a place of common national and global struggle through the construction of a place of enunciation and a political affiliation that links indigenous diversity but also, and most important, unites the political struggles of those who endure globalization in conditions of subalternity.[27]

We could argue that "Maya" does not simply mean a new "cultural discursive construction," but rather a political locus of enunciation that, like social movements on the American continent, emerges from conditions of exploitation and marginalization historically shared by those who also have cultural characteristics in common. Moreover, Maya-ness has been constructed as a signifier that requires a political affiliation. Or rather, more than being something biological, Maya-ness is the result of a long historical struggle that, in great measure, has maintained deep cultural and affective ties that have justified and defined resistance to the imposition of colonial politics. If we turn to the Zapatistas' "First Declaration from the Lacandon Jungle," for example, we read: "We are a product of 500 years of struggle.... But today, we say, ENOUGH IS ENOUGH. We are the inheritors of the true builders of our nation. The dispossessed, we are millions, and we thereby call upon our brothers and sisters to join this struggle as the only path." This passage demonstrates the desire to forge a cultural identity derived not from a "purity of blood," but rather from a historical process characterized by resistance to the oppression and political marginalization of Chiapanecan Mayas. The reference to those who "are the inheritors of the true builders of our nation" is indicative of an anticolonial struggle that has maintained the vitality of an affective cultural relation that serves as the foundation for this struggle. The call to the "brothers" indicates that Zapatismo is not about race. It is about solidarity, sympathy, and, most important, political affiliation. This call pushes us in a direction where we find that cultural identity, more than being something "hybrid," "mestizo," or "transcultured," is a political position in the face of neocolonial experiences.

In a similar way, we should understand that the "Maya identity construct" in Guatemala is the product of a very long anticolonial struggle against dictatorship. At present, this struggle has been redefined with the organization of the Maya movement. What remains absent from the discussions of Morales and Zapeta is an understanding of this experience and the historical justification it entails. Because of this, they frequently hurl the rubrics of "essentialism," "fundamentalism," and "vile little thieves" at those who have lived and responded to conditions of marginalization and have fought to change those very conditions. The affiliation that present-day Mayas take with their past should not be understood as a desire to "return" to that past, but to show how the experiences of exploitation, racism, and marginalization lived during the colony have not ended. They are reconfigured in the present. This is the lesson we can derive from the Zapatistas, de Lión, Menchú, and others. It means recognizing that indigenous peoples have been actively involved in processes of historical and cultural transformation that are based on perpetual struggles to eradicate oppression, humiliation, and racism. A discussion of interculturality necessarily implies rethinking the construct "Maya," not in terms of hybridity or as a "biological" identity but as a signifier that can explicate an anticolonial, antiracial consciousness.

For me, thinking of cultural identity in these terms would be more fruitful for our work to organize a true intercultural and multiethnic project and resist a neoliberal globalization that spreads the coloniality of power. "Mayaness," does not represent what is "authentic" or "essentialized." It represents a political affiliation and positionality that, more than a geographic place or specific language or manner of dress or pattern of behavior, imply a historical experience and an affective cultural and political relation from which we think and act. Strictly speaking, "Maya-ness" does not necessarily mean a certain degree of ethnic privilege or purity of blood, but rather a political drive toward the reaffirmation of languages and cultural specificities, as well as—and primarily—a struggle in favor of those who live globalization in conditions of subalternity. If this cultural identity is in some way subject to the "invention of its traditions" (Hobsbawn) or to the invention of an "imagined community" (Anderson), we should recognize the fact that any cultural program or program of political identity will be effective to the extent to which it achieves social transformation and to which it responds to and understands the material conditions of existence and the objective force of history. The case that best illustrates this project is the one presented earlier in this chapter: Marcos, who in his experience in the Lacandon Jungle becomes indigenous and makes the political decision of committing himself to the struggle of Chiapanecan Mayas.

The Maya movement, then, spread the idea that "Maya" does not mean simply a racial or ethnic identity. This is a political affiliation that binds a select group of indigenous and non-indigenous peoples who envision an anti-imperialist, anticolonial, antiassimilationist nationalism in favor of those who survive globalization in conditions of subalternity. Upon developing this position, the movement should not only be working on the reconstruction of a local nationalism based on the notion of interculturality that recognizes difference, but also projecting and aligning itself to the internationalist politicocultural agendas of other social movements—such as Zapatismo, the indigenous movements in the Andes and North America (like the Chicano movement and the American Indian Movement), the Landless Workers Movement in Brazil—which begin from subaltern perspectives in order to reconstruct a new modern club in which everyone has a place. No one expresses this agenda and perspective better than Marcos:

> Marcos is gay in San Francisco, black in South Africa, an Asian in Europe, a Chicano in San Ysidro, an anarchist in Spain, a Palestinian

in Israel, an Indian in the streets of San Cristobal, a gang member in Neza, a rocker in the National University, a Jew in Germany, an ombudsman in the Defense Ministry, a communist in the post–Cold War era, an artist without gallery or portfolio.… A pacifist in Bosnia, a housewife alone on Saturday night in any neighborhood in any city in Mexico, a striker in the CTM, a reporter writing filler stories for the black pages, a single woman on the subway at 10 pm, a peasant without land, an unemployed worker…an unhappy student, a dissident amid free market economics, a writer without books or readers, and, of course, a Zapatista in the mountains of southeast Mexico. So Marcos is a human being, any human being, in this world. Marcos is all the exploited, marginalized and oppressed minorities, resisting and saying, "Enough!" Every intolerated looking for a word, his word, what gives back the majorities the eternal fragments, us. Everything that bothers power and the good consciences, that is Marcos. (Quoted in Bardacke and López, Shadows of Tender Fury *214)*

Marcos elaborates a discourse against every type of intolerance toward the people who, day in and day out, fight to build a noncolonial history. This is nothing less than an invitation to confront and eradicate the tension developed by the coloniality of power.

But if social movements, like the Maya movement, open up the possibility of imagining an inclusive intercultural project, how is this project to be realized in a Guatemalan context? The Maya movement has committed itself to promoting interculturality through educational discourse. What conditions does this field offer for the realization of this project? To what extent does the educational discourse demystify or reproduce a discourse of the "ideal" Guatemalan citizen (for example, one that is linguistically and culturally homogenous)? How has the educational discourse promoted by the Mayas aided in recuperating other identities or consigning them to the margins? These are some of the questions I explore in the following chapter.

5 Toward an Intercultural Education and Citizenship

For those who do not speak our languages, we are invisible.

—Humberto Ak'abal, Raqonchi'aj/Grito

The argument I present throughout this work is that to understand the Maya movement and its struggles, we must place it in dialogue with the non-indigenous counterparts who have given themselves the authority to speak for and about the indigenous world. I suggest that, through this dialogue, we can better grasp the context of the coloniality of power, as well as its constant reproduction from the colonial period to the present. Further, modernity has been the central referent in discussions about the Maya movement. The debates we have discussed, especially in chapter 4, make it clear that unresolved tensions surround the idea of a colonial modernity that excludes the prominence of indigenous peoples. Explicitly or implicitly, there appears to be a discussion about identity politics that seeks to create a space of social coexistence through interculturality. Of course, as we have also seen, the diversity of perspectives on interculturality presents us with contradictions. While some position Maya cosmovision as their central basis of resistance and social-national vindication (de Lión, Menchú, and, to a certain extent, Asturias), others advocate neoliberal politics (Zapeta) or a Latinamericanist intellectual tradition that continues to find the potential vindication of indigenous peoples in mestizaje (Morales).

In sum, these discussions are transposed into the debates on educational discourse in Guatemala. As is known, after the signing of the Peace

Accords, education became the first test of the movement and the Guatemalan nation-state insofar as it translated and materialized a multiethnic, multilingual politics.[1] Keeping in mind the diverse and contradictory intercultural theories, we are obliged to put these questions on the table: What kind of interculturality are we referring to when dealing with education? What are the challenges that this project faces in the context of globalization? To what extent have the new educational reforms and the Maya overcome or recycled the coloniality of power? In this chapter, I explore and problematize these questions in order to expand upon the discussion developed in chapter 4.

The first section focuses on a panoramic, schematic, sociohistorical review of the ideals and objectives of Guatemalan and Latin American non-indigenous intellectual elites in their attempts to establish a modern nation through assimilationist educational projects. I also include some responses of indigenous students to these projects. My approach does not intend to be reductionist in regards to the Guatemalan educational experience but rather seeks to show how education, in its "conservative," "liberal," and even "progressive" dimensions (whether through the Enlightenment, positivism, or Marxism), has recycled the coloniality of power in relation to indigenous peoples. The second part focuses on the actual Diseño de reforma educativa (Educational Reform Design) of 1998 in order to show the similarities and differences between this new educational project and the preceding one, as well as to explore more rigorously this construction of a new intercultural national discourse and its "new" Guatemalan (post)modern citizen.

By studying this educational discourse, we can better understand that the cultural processes we have been studying have not been developed in the abstract, nor in the context of discussions isolated from specific realities. On the contrary, the discursive and epistemological practices of the coloniality of power have had concrete consequences for the populations it has interpreted and constructed. The indigenous subjects spoken about in the discussion of interethnic politics or mestizaje have been shaped in specific social and historical contexts. Moreover, bringing ourselves closer to this discussion lets us explore Maya intellectuals' participation in and impact on the educational discourse, as well as their contributions to establishing the basis for a new national imaginary.

From the beginning, I want to make clear that the educational discourse in Guatemala has not been widely disseminated (the official rate of "illiteracy" attests to this reality).[2] Owing to permanent situations of poverty and violence (like the recently ended civil war) that have not permitted the participation of many communities, education has been characterized by the absence of indigenous students from schools. Luis Enrique López suggests,

"The indigenous population has had the least opportunities of gaining admittance to the educational system, and, given the lack of pertinence and relevance of the model and the fact that this has been planned to be transmitted exclusively in Spanish, the expulsion of indigenous boys and girls from the system occurs fairly early" (53). Although I recognize the immense importance and necessity of carrying out further studies of this topic, in this chapter I do not explore it. My focus is rather on the indigenous students who have received an "education," in order to clarify their academic experiences. Further, I focus on official documents in order to display not only the perception that is held about the indigenous world by those who have elaborated laws and political objectives in the formation of Guatemalan "citizens," but also the impact of Maya intellectuals on this perception.

In Louis Althusser's famous essay "Ideology and Ideological State Apparatuses (Notes toward an Investigation)," the French thinker reflects on how dominant groups ensure the reproduction of relations of power. Althusser affirms that, among the state's ideological apparatuses, the church once occupied the dominant role in carrying out that "reproduction." In capitalist social formation, the church has been replaced by a new ideological apparatus, "although hardly anyone lends an ear to its music: it is so silent! This is the school" (Althusser 155). For me, this Althusserian reflection inspired an entire series of questions and reflections with regard to the duality "education–indigenous peoples." For example, how is it possible that, after more than five hundred years, elements presupposing colonialism continue to be reproduced? How is it possible that racial/ethnic, social, and gender inequalities continue to be common ideas? How is the reproduction of ideologies of domination, which are implemented by the dominant groups and complement the politics of the state, even possible? In each of these questions, we can affirm—following Althusser—that the school has been complicit in the reproduction of relations of power and subordination.[3]

I do not want to suggest that the educational discourse in Guatemala carries the entire weight of the law and therefore bears the greatest responsibility in rearticulating the coloniality of power.[4] As we will see, one paradox is precisely that education has also produced types of critical consciousness that appropriate knowledge spread by the school and use it to contest colonial politics. Before examining these experiences and the class of subjects education has sought to produce, we must first understand, however, that the school has reproduced and justified the existent social order, reinforcing a politics of exclusion that maintains subalternity.[5]

In effect, the liberal discourse regarding the category of "education" in Guatemala has spread ideas of achieving not simply a better standard of living, but the much desired dream of modernity. For example, this category has been associated with affirmations such as "We have to get education to liberate ourselves," "We have to educate to escape backwardness," "We have to educate to become civilized," and "We have to educate to progress." But what do these affirmations mean when we relate them to the historical and material conditions of existence of indigenous peoples? To what extent has education drawn these people out of "backwardness"? Has schooling given them socioeconomic mobility within dominant society? What type of "progress" has education made in regards to Mayas? What civilization is being spoken of in this reference to becoming "civilized"? Or, just as Katherine Iverson asks about indigenous communities in the United States (155), why, despite more than three hundred years of "education," has it so surprisingly failed in its objectives? All these questions reflect an unfinished history of colonization. The educational experiences of indigenous people help us to see what has been at play in hegemonic campaigns that have recycled paradigms of colonial domination. These educational experiences also inspire fresh debates and dialogues in a new process of interethnic relations for modern Latin American nation-states, in this particular case, Guatemala.

From the beginning of the conquest of what today is called the Americas, a systematic imposition of knowledge has attacked the cultural and linguistic specificities of Indian communities. To recall the title of the essay by Simeón Jiménez Turón, education has sought to produce "a cultural death with anesthesia." In effect, the imperial project of transforming the minds of indigenous peoples to secure a cultural identity that can be subjugated or abolished has continued down to the present. This project first operated through military and spiritual campaigns to destroy the memory of indigenous peoples and then to substitute it with the symbols, values, and cultural baggage of the West.[6] In Yucatán, for example, the friar Diego de Landa justified this process: "We found a great number of these books with their letters, and because there was nothing in them that was not the devil's superstitions and falsehoods, we burned them all, which they were amazed at and caused them a lot of grief" (105). To these actions of burning the books and the "falsehoods," we can add other imperial strategies that were no less violent. Pedro de Gante, a figure in the Christianization and literacy campaigns against indigenous peoples during the colonial period, in a letter to Felipe II in 1529 describes another strategy:

> At that time approximately one thousand children were gathered together, and we kept them locked up day and night in our house, and they were forbidden any conversation with their fathers and even less with their mothers, with the only exception of those who served them and brought them food; and the reason for this was so that they might

neglect their excessive idolatries *and their excessive sacrifices, from which the devil had served countless souls. (Mignolo, "Literacy and Colonization" 67, emphasis added)*

These examples illustrate that the primary objective of the dominant group was to make young indigenous peoples "neglect their excessive idolatries" and their own ways of life (read "culture"), depriving them of any contact with their environment and texts and even their parents—especially their mothers—in order to prevent cultural development and diffusion within that environment.[7] It was obviously hoped that, after adopting a Christian epistemology and knowledge allied with the West, these subjects would function as new mediators in the imperial saga of "killing" idolatry and imposing new memories of the world and of life on indigenous peoples.

It has also been claimed that the processes of "independence" and "revolution" constituted "great victories" for Latin American nations in that they ended colonialism and cultural and economic dependence on the West. It has been suggested, for example, that social uprisings, especially those at the beginning of the twentieth century, have opened up spaces for marginalized peoples, establishing them in places of privilege.[8] However, upon considering the educational discourse within these specific sociohistorical contexts, we realize that these uprisings have signified campaigns of plunder and political and epistemological attacks on indigenous cultural and linguistic specificities, reconfiguring the "educational" and "Christianizing" experiences and strategies of the colonial period.

The "educational" practices of the colonial period were not abandoned in either the formation of "independent" nation-states or the revolutions that erupted across the length and breadth of Latin America during the first decade of the twentieth century. On the contrary, the existing educational practices served as a model to continue implementing the coloniality of power. In the case of Guatemala, educational projects no longer necessarily responded to the need of "Christianizing" the Indians but rather legitimated the formation of a culturally and linguistically homogenous nation-state. "Liberation" from Spain and the processes of independence, for example, constituted a new phase of domination and internal colonization directed at indigenous cultural specificities and languages. Clothed in a positivist scientific racism and the age's ideology of Enlightenment,[9] in the name of "civilization" criollo intellectuals established the Law of the Constitutional Congress in 1824, "through the most analogous, prudent, and efficient means, to extinguish the language of the first indigenes" (*Imágenes* 17). This extinction was justified in the following way: "The national language should be one, and as long as those impoverished and poor languages remain so diverse and are still maintained by the first indigenes, the means for enlightening these peoples will neither be equal nor easy, as neither will the path to civilization for this appreciable portion of the State" (17).

Given that the "impoverished" indigenous languages do not serve to enlighten the people or to perfect Guatemalan civilization, they should be eliminated. Clearly, linguistic inferiority is equally associated with racial inferiority and a lack of civilization according to Western ideas of enlightenment. National unity, "the path to civilization," therefore entails cultural violence and ethnocide against Indians. Everything incompatible with "civilization" and "modernity" (read "Europe") should be destroyed.[10]

Parallel to the fate that these languages would suffer, the cultural specificities of indigenous peoples were not protected from assault either. In 1836 the state government, always with regard to the "education" of the indigenous population, established the following: "The Government at present adopts the following laws: no indigenous person will be able to hold the title of Governor, Mayor, trustee, or any other parochial duty, without wearing shoes, ankle boots or boots, a collared shirt, regular pants, dress coat and a hat that cannot be of either straw or palm. They will not be obliged to wear shoes, neither when abroad nor during their work hours" (*Imágenes* 19). Afterwards, Justo Rufino Barrios—the so-called liberator in official texts and the president of the Republic in 1882—decreed that "for legal effects those indigenous peoples of both sexes from the aforementioned town of San Pedro Sacatepéquez *are declared Ladinos*, and beginning next year they will wear the clothing that corresponds to the Ladino class" (Álvarez Medrano and others 21, emphasis added).

These perspectives on the Indian illustrate an evident relationship of power that is inscribed under a certain cannibalistic "universalism." The governing politics separates indigenes socially, economically, politically, linguistically, and culturally in a definitive form as long as they preserve their cultural specificities, which are the objects of prejudice, discrimination, and segregation. These particularities, in whatever form they exist, are even the object of cultural and physical extermination, and there is no possibility of their being incorporated into the national order. In this sense, the formation of the nation and its citizens requires "dressing up" the Indian. Beyond the emphasis on differences, the construction of a nation with strong Eurocentric foundations is sought, imposing a new identity—a Ladino identity—on indigenes. This would seek to hide everything that might disfigure the idea of the "imagined community" (Anderson) shared by the criollo-Ladino nation.

These cultural processes regarding indigenous languages and cultural specificities do not end here. The case of Mexico offers a pertinent example, given that it was the model later followed by the Guatemalan state during the October Revolution (1944–1954). It shows us that not even the "revolutions" of the first half of the twentieth century favored indigenous cultural and linguistic revitalization.

A cultural explosion in search of the Mexican "soul" occurred after the Mexican Revolution (1911–1917), producing cultural capital (Bourdieu, *Capital Cultural*) that disseminated a new mestizo national imaginary. A key area of sociocultural formation and the imposition of such a politics was the educational discourse. To realize this new idea of the mestizo nation, one project created indigenous boarding schools, which shows an obvious kinship with the first "educational" projects established during the colonial period by Bernardino de Sahagun and Diego Durán. Once again, politics sought to isolate indigenous children and young people in order to advocate the values of "civilization."[11] Here, the Casa del estudiante indígena (House of the Indigenous Student) (1926–1932) deserves particular mention. It represents not only a process of internal colonialism but also a psychological project of cultural assimilation for indigenous Mexicans.[12]

During its seven years of existence, the House had as its goal the assimilation of "authentic" indigenous young people into the modern Mexican nation.[13] The students were then supposed to return to their communities of origin and impart the benefits of modern life in their own environment. José Manuel Puig, one of the coordinators of the House, describes its specific role:

> By placing young Indians from all over the country in a situation in which they live together with whites and mestizos from the city, we seek to generate a perfect cohesion of interests and sentiment among the distinct branches of the greater Mexican family. This will ultimately allow us to facilitate the formation of a true national soul.... This institution's [La casa's] goal is to eliminate the evolutionary distance that separates the Indian from the present epoch. By exposing them to a modern, civilized life, we will transform their mentalities, tendencies, and customs, and incorporate them into the Mexican social community. (Quoted in Dawson 334)

Throughout this book, I analyze the reproduction of essentialized categories of "race" that attribute immutable cultural practices to the Indian. Why, then, would these attitudes toward the indigenous world surprise us? As we have seen previously, this quotation implies a separation between Indians and non-Indians through the duality of modernity/tradition, an archaeological gaze that cancels out the indigenous world. The Indian represents something separated from "the present epoch," a cultural entity that is supposedly uncontaminated by or distanced from evolutionary cultural changes. The Indian's way of life does not coincide with the "modern, civilized life" that the House is trying to realize. These ideas, of course, are intimately aligned with the European imaginary of "civilization" and "modernity" and are the referents used to measure the cultural "backwardness" of these subjects.

Further, indigenous peoples are "savages" and "barbarians" because they lack what white people, criollos, and mestizos supposedly possess: civilization. And because the law of historical progress and the doctrine of social evolution guide "civilized" life, the project of the "modernization" or "civilization" of indigenous cultures should be legitimated in the name of eradicating barbarism (Adams, *Education for Extinction* 6). Owing to this "inferior" condition, the mental and moral attitudes, as well as personality, ideas, and abilities, related to the racial "origin" of the Indians represent something "backwards" in comparison with the "advanced" civilization embodied by whites, criollos, and mestizos. Situated at the top of the continent's racial hierarchy, they should lead others on the road to civilization. From the Western perspective, the Indians are subjects that possess neither history nor culture.

Moreover, the passage reveals new processes of colonial violence that compare to the practices of Pedro de Gante, as well as to the Guatemalan criollo and Ladino project referred to earlier. Like de Gante's "Christianization" and literacy campaigns, these processes recruit young indigenous peoples by force (Dawson 337), separating them from their families, this time in the name of national "cohesion" and modernity. But did indigenous boarding schools like the House achieve the "perfect cohesion of interests and sentiment" within the Mexican family? How much did the project eliminate the evolutionary distance separating the Indian from the present? Did this project "transform" the "mentalities, tendencies, and customs" of the Indian?

Far from materializing the "national soul" or social cohesion, this project tried to dominate indigenous peoples through forced mental control. The process stripped indigenous peoples of their own structures of learning, disseminating, and safeguarding memory and tried to implant in them Western forms of seeing and understanding the world,[14] in the name of the "formation" of "Ladino" and "mestizo" citizens, the supposed representatives of the modern nation. This project of cultural and linguistic imposition dislocated the students. The odyssey, voluntary or involuntary, from the community of origin to the school in the city, Europe, or the boarding school is unforgettable for an indigenous student. It tramples on the very dignity of Indian subjectivity, as well as any relationship he or she may have with the indigenous world, to the point of denial and even hatred. Let us turn to testimonies of students who suffered from this cultural violence.

When asked why they refuse to speak in their native languages, some native children respond, "My father says there is no point in it, it is false pride, that Castilian is better" or "Others laugh at our town. They say we are ugly. That we are idiots. That it is because we are poor" (Bello 27). To these, we can also add David Wallace Adams's ("The Federal Indian Boarding School") testimonios of indigenous students "educated" in boarding schools, which also demonstrate some of the psychological consequences of being placed in an unfamiliar space so that the "civilized" world can impose itself. One student recounts:

> I can never forget the confusion and pain I one day underwent in a reading class. The teacher conceived of the idea of trying or testing the strength of the pupils in the class. A paragraph in the reading book was selected for the experiment. A pupil was asked to rise and read the paragraph while the rest listened and corrected any mistakes. Even if no mistakes were made, the teacher, it seems, wanted the pupils to state that they were sure they had made no errors in reading. One after another the pupils read as called upon and each one in turn sat down bewildered and discouraged. My time came and I made no errors. However, upon the teacher's question, "Are you sure that you have made no error?" I, of course, tried again, reading just as I had the first time. But again she said, "Are you sure?" So the third and fourth times I read, receiving no comment from her. For the fifth time I stood and read. Even for the sixth and seventh times I read. I began to tremble and I could not see my words plainly. I was terribly hurt and mystified. But for the eighth and ninth times I read. It was growing more terrible. Still the teacher gave no sign of approval, so I read for the tenth time! I started on the paragraph for the eleventh time, but before I was through, everything before me went black and I sat down thoroughly cowed and humiliated for the first time in my life and in front of the whole class! (Adams 137)

Adams also includes an essay by a student who was "taught" about different races. It shows how he internalized the idea that the white race is the "strongest in the world": "The white people they are civilized…they have everything, and go to school, too. They learn how to read and write so they can read newspaper. The yellow people they half civilized, some of them know to read and write, and some know how to take care of themselves. The red people they big savages; they don't know anything" (Adams 143).

Through the processes of "education," "literacy," and "Christianization" described here, colonialism secures its power, creating conditions in which the colonized can be made into one more colonizer, becoming the oppressor of his own people. Furthermore, more than any other practice, the removal of indigenous children and young people from their homes and communities presents us with concrete evidence of the barbarism and inhumanity perceived in indigenous peoples by the *other*. It is obvious that the other's perception of the Indian is conditioned by a conscious or unconscious discourse of racial, cultural, and linguistic inferiority that legitimates and justifies the theft of lands, material objects, languages, cultural particularities, and so forth, in order to expand ideals with Western foundations. Moreover, "indigenous education" reflects the ideology and theological conviction of "saving" these subjects from paganism and idolatry, of "rescuing" them from their uncivilized state. The suffering these educational processes cause, the crimes against those who do not want to be "saved" or "educated," reveal the violence inherent in constituting the nation-state and its citizens according to Western modernity. That is, these "educational," "nationalist," and "modernizing" initiatives inflict an experience of slavery, including the destruction and fragmentation of indigenous families. The paternalist desire to "integrate" them into the nation and modernity presumes that the organic intellectuals of the nation-state understand the problems affecting these peoples better than the people themselves, that indigenous peoples have nothing to contribute to the educational project or to any other aspect of national life and modernity.

Despite all the assaults on indigenous cultures and languages, despite the efforts of intellectuals and the nation-state to change the hearts and minds of Indians, and despite the conditions created to prevent the development and survival of our peoples, we persevere in transmitting our languages, religions, memory, and other cultural practices from generation to generation. A large sector of the indigenous population has reacted to these assaults in accordance with its own traditions and material conditions of existence. Indigenous peoples continue nourishing their elemental aspects in order to develop and rearticulate their historical memory in the present. In many cases, the effectiveness of civilizing-modernizing the Indians through ethnocentric projects has proven to be limited, even invalid. If we have found subjects who have lived the experience of an "indigenous education" and internalized these colonial perspectives,[15] we also find that these practices have spurred resistance—indigenous families hiding their children under beds, bombarding the agents of "civilization" with rocks (Noriega 378). T. G. Powell reminds us of how the Kickapoo in San Luis Potosí, Mexico, burned a school in 1909 because of the teachers' punishment of indigenous children for learning Spanish "incorrectly" (26). Other peoples have used different means of resistance, such as taking up the same Western educational weapons to destabilize the official educational discourse.

The wars of the Mexican army against the Yaqui of Sonora inspired a patriotic literature and an oral tradition in which the "Mexican" is represented as the enemy. The war gave rise to an organic indigenous intellectual tradition that combined political activism with instruction, self-sufficiency, and the diffusion of a distinct indigenous memory. These intellectuals fostered their own literature and wrote their own history in their native language with the goal of bringing about linguistic and cultural revitalization through the reinvention of their traditions (Vaughan 141). Following these paradigms, Natividad Gutiérrez compiled a series of interviews with indigenous students who were educated in bilingual programs in Mexico during the 1960s.[16] These programs, contrary to what was hoped for by the Ministry of Education, gave rise to a new indigenous intelligentsia that has become one of the most passionate defenders of multiculturalism and self-determination for indigenous peoples. According to Gutiérrez, indigenous intellectuals rejected these assimilationist educational models and the narratives of the "mestizo nation," which were based on a "folkloric" Aztec tradition. They found no identification with "heroes" like Benito Juárez because they saw these as an ideological and material recycling of the material conditions of existence of their own communities of origin. One of them aptly describes the process: "A new consciousness has emerged; the consciousness of being a group of people with their own culture, language, and philosophy. This new consciousness has led us to notice that we live under economic exploitation, racial discrimination, and political manipulation, due to the imposition of a false culture and a superior race, as well as due to [others'] false right of governing our people and deciding for us" (Gutiérrez 167). As with the Yaqui, these intellectuals are working to recuperate and rewrite their own traditions and history in order to propagate the historical memory of their communities from their own perspectives and through their own strategies of learning and disseminating thought. As with Zapatismo, this organic indigenous intelligentsia forges a new model, bilingual intercultural education, which aims to demystify the myth of the mestizo nation by affirming the indigenous world.

Similarly, some Maya intellectuals have developed initiatives (frequently sacrificing their lives) to change the formal educational system.[17] For example, Luis de Lión (see also the second section of chapter 2), was an elementary school teacher in the country's rural areas, where he soon realized the irrelevance of education for indigenous communities. His friend, Luis Alfredo Arango, reminds us that in the 1970s de Lión wrote a document titled "Education as a Form of Ideologization." According to Arango, in this text de Lión concluded that the school system was repressive, classist, discriminatory, and castrating. By teaching "useless data," the objective of Guatemalan education was, according to de Lión, "to provide the national system of production sufficient reserves of cheap and unskilled labor, available to be employed in anything, in exchange for minimum wage" (Arango 20). Arango tells us that de Lión had also realized that the rural school was the ideological apparatus for the "incorporation" of the indigene into "national" life and culture. Paraphrasing some of de Lión's ideas, Arango specifies that the Maya Kaqchikel writer considered the focus of the national educational system to be erroneous not only because it was divorced from the reality and experience of indigenous communities, but also because it imparted teachings that related more to Ladinos in urban areas, people who are "individualist and competitive—they have an idea of success that is diametrically opposed to the indigenous cosmovision, to its integration with nature and the cosmos" (21). Arango's perspective on de Lión's ideas on education reveals de Lión's own revolutionary literary project, which, as we see here, cannot be understood in isolation but rather as being organically rooted in his own experience, political militancy, and writing. His objections to the educational discourse, then, address an entire ideological and political program that recycles colonialism.

In effect, the assaults on indigenous linguistic and cultural specificities are occurring before our very eyes in a "globalized" present that supposedly embraces difference. The experiences of racism in distinct national and international contexts provide evidence of its ongoing metamorphosis, its varied contents, forms, and degrees of intensity. These function equally as mechanisms to legitimate power over groups based on an interminable dichotomy of superiority/inferiority. Further, education has not given students sufficient tools to become fully realized political subjects in the future, nor has it achieved "the creation of unified consciousness that pertains to a collective, above all because the students do not recognize the socially selected referents (traditional practices, common history, political borders and territories, and the like). They do not develop spaces of solidarity; in sum, they do not internalize a series of principles that define the nation as the most important fact and where those who live in a given territory are an active part of it" (*Imágenes* 136).

We can, without a doubt, affirm that the formal educational discourse has reproduced an exclusionary and ethnocentric hegemonic order. That is, instead of achieving national "cohesion," eradicating "backwardness," teaching to ensure "progress," and bettering the lives of indigenous peoples, education has been a state ideological apparatus for colonialization. The school, for the most part, has imposed Western rules, values, and norms instead of promoting a cultural and national unity or intercultural exchanges, thus deepening relations of inequality between the diverse peoples of Guatemala. Moreover, instead of promoting linguistic and cultural revitalization and the self-sufficiency of indigenous communities, it has sought to erase these. The school has been the place to obliterate indigenous knowledge and superimpose other forms of seeing and understanding the world. Paradoxically, those who have lived these assaults have created alternatives of resistance out of them. They have proposed to empower their cultures by using the very tools of oppression, as demonstrated by de Lión, the Yaqui, and indigenous Mexican intellectuals. Even though the Maya movement has come to question and defy the entire epistemological "educational" corpus, what do indigenous Guatemalans propose in order to overcome this cultural/colonial violence? How can interculturality be realized through education? What class of interculturality does the new national "educational reform" propose? I focus on these questions in the second section of this chapter.

The New Education Reform and Bilingual Intercultural Education: Challenges for the National and Intercultural Citizenship

One of the most important documents in Guatemala's recent history is El Diseño de reforma educativa (The Educational Reform Design)/Runuk'ik jun K'ak'a Tijonik (1998). This text is significant in that it challenges the formal educational discourse: it proposes the epistemological and practical restoration of interethnic relations by implementing pedagogical practices that guide the student to the materialization of a multicultural, multilingual, and multinational subjectivity.[18] It is important to point out that these ideals have their origins in the struggles and sacrifices of thousands of indigenous peoples in their quest to realize a place for their descendents in the country's present and future. Ruth Moya, for example, reminds us (152, n. 16) that during the 1980s those who advocated for bilingual educational projects that defied the educational status quo were murdered, accused of being "communists" for their ideas. Moreover, according to Demetrio Cojtí, the construction of the project and the document itself entailed transcending a series of barriers imposed by government functionaries determined to continue furthering the interests of the hegemonic classes ("Educational Reform" 118–22). In many cases, the ideals of the intercultural nation conceived from the indigenous perspective have filtered in clandestinely, or from abroad, or through international organizations that support initiatives favoring the interests of indigenous peoples. In this sense, the Educational

Reform displays a context of power and struggle for the control and diffusion of knowledge and meaning that are not unrelated to the discussion here and will guide our reflection in this second part.

Given this context, it must be mentioned that the document's most innovating aspect is the steadfast desire to recognize and fortify the cultural and linguistic diversity of the indigenous peoples of Guatemalan society. Despite the fact that many of its initiatives and institutions are at an impasse, even to the point of disappearing, the document's proposals still find relevance within governmental initiatives focused on cultural diversity. It should also be recognized that this was the state's first attempt to implement an educational project that fortifies Maya cultural and linguistic identity.[19] Although I share the euphoria of these efforts, I also feel that we must include critical observations that stimulate the specialists and teachers engaged in this undertaking to reflect on their own sociocultural and sociolinguistic condition within the project of cultural/national vindication. I realize that some will see my entrance into this field as "dangerous," given that many already consider the Educational Reform to be "radical" in its efforts to realize the multiculturalism it espouses. I cannot, however, simply turn the page on some of its limitations. This is why I feel that discussion and debate about the educational project are important in order to consider more carefully the challenges that come with both Maya cultural and linguistic revitalization and intercultural national and subjective formation.

With this in mind, I propose a critical approach to the educational project, not with the goal of discrediting these efforts or their historical precedents but rather to identify and fill in a few of its gaps. My reflections and observations come out of the studies and fieldwork I have carried out on bilingual intercultural education in Guatemala, as well as workshops on popular education and self-sufficiency in which I have participated in Chiapas, Mexico. As I have suggested, education has, for the most part, served to legitimate the coloniality of power, so the questions that guide my reflections are, To what extent does the Educational Reform overcome the errors of the preceding models? How are the limited representations of cultural identity in the educational discourse to be remedied? Related to chapter 4, I again insist that the Maya movement should revise its discussion on cultural identity in the educational discourse. I argue that cultures are a dynamic process, that they accommodate and respond to changing historical circumstances every day. Further, I insist that the movement, instead of spreading the idea of a biological cultural identity, should emphasize Mayaness as a political affiliation and positioning that implies, more than a geographic place or a specific language or how one dresses or acts, a historical experience and an affective and political cultural relationship from which we think and act (see the final section of chapter 4). Finally, I argue that interculturality in the educational discourse should confront the coloniality of power.

The Educational Reform is the result of indigenous peoples' demands for the recognition of cultural and linguistic diversity, culminating in the Accord on Identity and the Rights of Indigenous Peoples in March 1995, as well as the Peace Accords signed by the government and the guerrillas in 1996. Out of these advances emerged institutional changes of which the Educational Reform is one significant example. The fundamental priority of education today is the creation of an educational model appropriate for the country's cultural and linguistic diversity, by revising the formal educational curriculum and school textbooks. The Educational Reform emphasizes that "this does not mean dividing the country and the State, but accomplishing a new social pact that takes into account the [country's] diverse realities, recognizes and respects their expressions, rights and necessities, without the mediation of violence and polarizing confrontations" (Diseño 26).

The delegation in charge of developing this plan situates the project in the context of globalization: "How can the country insert itself in the global order with possibilities for self-determination and development?" (Diseño 23). This situation, they tell us, gives impetus to a new search for "socioeconomic alternatives that grant all Guatemalans a better quality of life" (55). If it was previously thought that these opportunities could be realized through the construction of a culturally and linguistically homogenous nation-state, the new strategy consists of strengthening the nation through the recognition of cultural and linguistic diversity. The reform seeks an educational system with better coverage of and increased cultural and linguistic relevance to the diverse ethnic populations that compose Guatemala (26). As well, it should prepare children, young people, and adults for the job market. In this way, the document tells us, education can contribute to the construction of a new multiethnic, multicultural, and multilingual nation (79).

This project is realized through ten institutional areas: politics, jurisprudence, the economy, culture, pedagogical techniques, linguistics, the development of resources, social communication, scholastic infrastructure, and productivity. In each of these areas, the Educational Reform emphasizes the importance of practicing the concepts of a democracy in which the "citizens assume human rights, social and political coexistence, and a culture of peace as a philosophy of education in the family, the school, and the community" (Diseño 34). Moreover, education has the goal of imparting a broad understanding of the constitutional principles of the democratic, multiethnic, multicultural, and multilingual state (35) and eradicating the well-defined interethnic relationships that have normalized certain negative stereotypes and a relative devalorization of indigenous cultures in everyday life.

With these goals, the reform seeks to better the quality of life, consolidate peace, and transform the state and society. This requires the formation of citizens who respect and value their own culture, as well as those of the nation's other peoples, such that all are proud of the nation's diversity and contribute to the strengthening of its unity (Diseño 13). The reform's goals and objectives with regard to this "new" citizen and the Guatemalan nation point toward the following:

- The refinement and comprehensive development of the person and of the Maya, Ladino, Garífuna, and Xinka peoples

- The valorization of the family as the basic social nucleus and as the first and permanent educational authority

- The knowledge, valorization, and development of the nation's cultures and universal culture

- A contribution to the critical analysis of reality for the solution of problems, the impetus of comprehensive, sustainable development, the abatement of poverty, and the betterment of the quality of life for the entire population

- The fortification of the self-esteem and identity of people, each of their peoples, and the nation

- The establishment of peaceful and harmonious coexistence among the people, founded on inclusion, tolerance, solidarity, respect, equality, equity, and mutual enrichment that eliminates all manifestations of discrimination

- Political, civic, and citizen training for the participation in and democratic exercise of a culture of peace, respect, and the defense of human rights

- The internalization and practice of values, attitudes, and ethical practices responsible for and committed to the defense and development of the national and cultural patrimony

- Reflection on and response to the characteristics, needs, and aspirations of a multicultural, multilingual, and multiethnic country, respecting, fortifying, and enriching its personal identity and that of its peoples, as the nourishment of unity in diversity (Diseño 37–38)

If prior educational proposals on national identity referenced a single language and culture, uniformity of customs, and a common "universal" tradition, the reform challenges and seeks to demystify the myth of the modern Ladino or mestizo nation. The passages cited here are notable for ideas that place emphasis on the "development" and the "fortification" of self-esteem, the implementation of a "peaceful" and "harmonious" coexistence, the formation of citizens who value and respect these differences and at the same time have a civic sense of what it means to be "multicultural," "multilingual," and "multiethnic." Obviously, the hope is that these goals and objectives will forge a new cultural identity that, instead of denying or shaming cultural and linguistic "differences," considers these to be fundamental attributes for strengthening the country socially and economically.

In practice, the reform has tried to realize these objectives on diverse fronts. With the participation of the Academy of Maya Languages (ALMG), it sought to standardize indigenous languages through the production of texts in indigenous languages, such as dictionaries, pedagogical materials, and books that compile myths and legends, and the like. The purpose of producing these materials was the revitalization of these languages at the elementary school level.[20] Further, the Ministry of Education implemented the so-called Professional Development of Human Resources. In 2002 this program sought to improve the professional profile of preschool and elementary school teachers, granting them an advanced high school degree based on their participation in a two-year professionalization program that improved their pedagogical competence. The process included political, sociocultural, and linguistic training through instruction in five areas: "Culture and Languages of Guatemala," "The Socio-cultural Context of Guatemala and Educational Reality," "Reading to Learn," "Reading and the Production of Texts in L1," and "Mathematics and Logical Thinking." Moreover, according to the Ministry of Education, this project responded to the country's educational needs, as well as its multiethnic and multilingual characteristics.[21]

Hand in hand with the reform and the professionalization of educators, the Guatemalan Ministry of Education created the General Directorate of Bilingual Intercultural Education (DIGEBI).[22] This institution has precedents in the education ministry's previous attempts to respond to Guatemala's linguistic diversity. The first of these was "bilingualism" as a method of assimilation through the Project of Bilingual Education in 1980, which later became the Program of Bilingual Bicultural Education (PRONEBI) in 1984. Thanks mostly to the Accord on Identity and the Rights of Indigenous Peoples, in 1995 PRONEBI became DIGEBI with the goal of developing a supposedly more balanced and efficient bilingualism for the project

Bilingual Intercultural Education.[23] Perhaps one of the institution's most significant accomplishments was a certain degree of autonomy from the state in its implementation of the BIE project in eleven of the country's states. For the most part, these states were demographically indigenous.

In *Curricular Guidelines for Elementary Bilingual Intercultural Education* (1998), DIGEBI describes its priority as "structuring the curriculum of the bilingual bicultural pre- and elementary school for six years of study in all the territorial and communal languages" (i). Beyond producing adequate school materials for boys and girls, the institution's strategies include teaching indigenous language speakers how to read and write their languages and training them in the pedagogy of bilingual intercultural education; institutionalizing Maya languages; developing a curriculum centered on the student and not on the teacher; raising public awareness of the benefits of bilingual intercultural education; tying the educational project to the needs of the community; and, finally, constantly monitoring the project. Moreover, the curriculum's intersecting dots seek to reinforce aspects of cultural identity, interculturality, and bilingualism, guaranteeing peace, democracy, the rights of indigenous peoples, and greater gender equality (5). All these proposals also center on the "recovery" of Maya cosmovision to shape the future citizen of the multicultural and multilingual nation through a new balance between economic and social development and nature.

There is no doubt, then, that in comparison with the previous educational experiences dealt with in the first section of this chapter, the Educational Reform is an appropriate alternative. It recognizes and seeks to respond to the country's cultural and linguistic diversity, as well as other conditions of inequality in Guatemala. Without a doubt, the project demonstrates the prominence achieved by indigenous peoples in their demands for political recognition, as well as their impact on state politics. Beginning with the Maya cosmovision and the recognition of diversity, their proposals and objectives aspire to a quantitative and qualitative education that betters their opportunities and quality of life and to peace and to the transformation of the state so that its institutions are "multiculturalist, supportive, egalitarian and respectful, above all in a multicultural, multiethnic, and multilingual country" (Diseño 52). Further, the reform is also commendable in that it establishes a context for "the formation of citizens who respect and value their own culture and those of the other peoples that make up the nation, so that they take pride in their diversity and contribute to the strengthening of unity" (*Lineamientos* 13). However, if these proposals respond to an educational politics that looked down upon the coexistence of difference, it is also important to recognize that more careful analysis of the reform reveals some limitations, especially in regards to its idea of interculturality.

Although the reform advocates the recognition and epistemological resignification of Guatemala as a "multilingual," "multicultural," and "multinational" country, it is not too far removed from the reproduction of the coloniality of power, especially the idea of cultural identity. For all intents and purposes, its idea of "interculturality" is similar to the (neo)liberal multiculturalism advocated by Estuardo Zapeta (see the second section of chapter 4).

To begin, the reform claims that it seeks equal recognition and value of the country's diverse cultural expressions and that part of this is the recognition that "cultures are not static and that change is essential to their vitality and the continuity of time" (Diseño 78). Despite these affirmations, the approach to "culture" that the reform proposes is one that privileges ethnocentric elements. In the first chapter of Diseño, emphasis is placed on the "cultural diversity" of the Guatemalan nation. It provides brief summaries and descriptions of the country's communities—the Maya, Ladinos, Xinkas, and Garífunas. With regards to the Ladino population—based on Claudia Dary's study of mestizaje, "Historia del mestizaje [History of Mestizaje]"—we are told that Ladino identity is expressed through the use of "Spanish as the maternal language, which possesses certain determinate cultural characteristics of Hispanic origin with indigenous cultural loan-words (foods, tools, and so on) and that [the Ladino] dresses in what is commonly called Western fashion" (Diseño 19). It is then added that in the southwestern region of the country, Ladino culture "is influenced by its economic activities, among which cattle farming, rubber production, and other forestry activities stand out" (19).

I have already spoken about some of the consequences of constructing subjects from perspectives with these colonial dimensions.[24] Here, it is enough to add that, following the contributions of Edward Said (Orientalism), these stereotyped constructions of (Ladino) colonial identity still proceed from a notion of "culture" that betrays its own principles of understanding cultures as capable of changing for the sake of their "vitality and continuity in time." Also, this notion ignores the exploitative dimension of such constructions. Once again, we find a discourse of identity constructed from a certain "authenticity" that imprisons identity, in this case, Ladino, in a membership that excludes certain subjects. For example, it excludes those Ladinos not involved in economic activities such as cattle raising, rubber production, and forestry. This description of Ladino culture inscribes notions that are equally applicable to indigenous subjects for whom Spanish is a maternal language, who have cultural characteristics of "Hispanic origin," and who likewise count cattle farming, rubber production, and forestry activities among their principal economic activities. As an exercise to counteract this perspective, I can reference a study that expounds upon how, owing to situations of internal colonialism and a politics of Hispanization, there have emerged generations of Mayas whose mother tongue is Spanish.[25] Ruth Moya also makes reference to the K'iche' Maya of Quetzaltenango, who are assumed to have lost their language around fifty to one hundred years ago because of schooling in Spanish, "the only possible language [in which schooling was available] at that time" (151, n. 10). For the most part, the discursive grammar of the coloniality of power is recycled and resignified in order to inscribe a cultural "authenticity" that marks "difference" and ethnicity based on particular cultural characteristics. In this sense, the educational project in the reform argues for an "intercultural democracy" in which what is "multilingual, multicultural, and multinational" equals a culturalist project of cultural relativism,[26] projecting "differences" according to an essentialist regime. In Cathryn McConaghy's book *Rethinking Indigenous Education: Culturalism, Colonialism, and the Politics of Knowing*, she alerts us to the danger of constructing an educational discourse based on these principles. Despite her work's different sociocultural context (Australia), her conclusions can be used to reflect upon and interpret the situation in Guatemala.

Among the essential characteristics of the cultural relativism in the Australian educational discourse that McConaghy outlines, one finds claims that all cultures and beliefs are equal, that racism is the product of ignorance, that the objective of antiracist and anticolonial education is to make individuals more sensitive to the cultural differences of indigenous peoples, that indigenous cultures are "different" and not deficient, that the object of education is the "salvation" of indigenous cultures and languages, and that education is necessary in order to break cycles of poverty and dependence (216–17). McConaghy adds that the cultural relativism in the Australian educational discourse about aborigines, in spite of its reaction to assimilationist politics, represents another facet of liberal virtues in the sense that its strategic affirmations "disguise the inability of cultural relativism to disrupt the hierarchical social structures that remain a feature of contemporary Australian colonialism" (217). In other words, the aspects of "difference" are recognized, but not the role that capitalist economic politics has played in creating those "differences."

In addition, McConaghy observes that cultural relativism is organized through concepts that are nurtured on liberal notions of "equality." These notions of "equality" seek to eliminate a critical consciousness and, instead, to institutionalize cultural and social notions of "partiality" and "disinterestedness." The danger of an educational focus stemming from cultural relativism is that it deflects attention from critical matters like material depravation and the subaltern experiences of economic exploitation and racism. McConaghy concludes that this particular celebration of "difference" obscures the presence of power and control, inequality and injustice: "Just as the promotion of tolerance and recognition does not mean the end of racism and material injustices, it is important to consider whether we can expect the same results from the current wave of programs that promote an 'uncritical' recognition of Indigenous cultures, histories and achievements" (218).

Following this line of reflection, McConaghy's concerns about the institutionalization of difference through cultural relativism should arouse a critical consciousness. This does not mean denying the existence of cultural and linguistic differences, nor the need to revitalize and fortify cultural and linguistic identities, especially indigenous identity. Rather, the educational discourse should also be accompanied by projects that expose and elucidate new and historical forms of oppression. The growth of new technologies has made forms of exclusion and mystification ever more sophisticated. To return to a suggestion from Luis Enrique López's study, when constructing an indigenous education that reaffirms languages and cultural specificities, "it is necessary to transcend the merely idiomatic plane to span the political, social, cultural, and pedagogical planes as well" (65). Furthermore, this means that the educational project, especially BIE, should not only valorize indigenous languages and cultures but also consider these "as a pedagogical resource and as the repositories of wisdom, knowledge, attitudes and values capable of enriching the education of *all students*" (55, emphasis added). In effect, the use of indigenous languages in school should contribute to the restitution of fluid, communicative ties between students and community elders, as well as ties to the content of local cultures (wisdom, knowledge, technology, oral tradition, ethics, and epistemology in general). In addition, these principles should not be presented only to Maya populations but should primarily be a bridge to non-indigenous communities.

This brings me to another problem arising from the Educational Reform, especially the BIE project and the idea of interculturality. Regarding languages, the current educational commission, as well as Maya and Ladino intellectuals, demands that indigenous peoples learn Spanish and adopt "universal values," completely absolving Ladinos from having to learn indigenous languages and explore indigenous wisdom. The section about "students" in the chapter "Guatemalan Educational System" from Diseño, for example, postulates that indigenous students need to "*learn* to read *and* write in their own language, within their cultural context and in Spanish" (Diseño 46, emphasis added). But the Ladino students should merely "have the *opportunity* and *access* to learn indigenous languages" (46, emphasis added). These principles are again emphasized in DIGEBI's guidelines, which speak of the necessity of "developing intercultural education for the entire population, *and bilingual intercultural education for indigenous girls and boys*" (1, emphasis added). As these passages indicate, the Educational Reform promotes two "intercultural" projects. One seeks to raise Ladinos' awareness of the country's cultural and linguistic diversity, that is, that Guatemala is "multicultural, multilingual, and multinational." The other interculturality calls upon indigenous peoples not only to understand this diversity but also to integrate into modernity and the Guatemalan nation through learning to read and write in their native language and the adoption of the Spanish language.

All of this would seem to indicate that when one speaks of "developing more socially and culturally pertinent programs in order to respond to the needs and characteristics of the *country's indigenous population*" (Diseño 27, emphasis added), or of a "quest for broad coverage of high quality and with cultural relevance," or of "guaranteeing the promotion of development that the country needs" (14), one is trying to turn these populations into subjects who are competitive within globalization. In other words, the "new" educational discourse for indigenous peoples seeks the construction of subjects who will have better possibilities and technical and industrial skills to compete in today's globalization if they revitalize their native languages, their cultural identity, and Maya cosmovision—and adopt Spanish, "universal" wisdom, and modern technology. This view is also shared by some Maya intellectuals, such as Otilia Lux de Cotí.[27]

In Lux de Cotí's essay "Educación Maya, perspectiva para Guatemala [Maya Education, A Perspective for Guatemala]," she describes the "profile of the Maya student": among other things, the Maya student should be "capable of living in harmony with people similar [to himself or herself] and nature's other beings," "capable of living in a multicultural and multilingual society," "as a Maya prudent and critical before their reality" (111). Once again, Mayaness is the principal referent for change that should take place in Guatemalan society. Indigenous peoples, but not Ladinos, should "live harmoniously with people similar [to themselves]" and should be "capable" of coexisting with difference or preparing themselves for the demands of globalization. It is appropriate to ask ourselves, How do these perspectives differ from the "intercultural" politics endorsed by Ladinos? To what extent do these "educational" initiatives recycle the "indigenous problem" viewed by non-indigenous intellectuals ever since the colonial period? In fact, if we compare the postulates of the Educational Reform and Lux de Cotí with those of some Ladino intellectuals, we notice an incredible ideological similarity.

At an indigenista congress on indigenous education in Mexico during the 1940s, then-president Lazaro Cárdenas declared that "we should give recognition to the Indio, but we do not want to Indianize Mexico, but rather make our Indians Mexican" (Peña 24). Cárdenas's attitude has echoes in Guatemala, largely reaffirmed by Ladino intellectuals like Mario Roberto Morales and Mario Alberto Carrera. Morales, in his article "Sujetos interétnicos y moda posmo en xela [Interethnic Subjects and Postmo Fashion in Xela]," refers to a workshop on interculturality in Quetzaltenango, "Xela," and how a Maya Mam woman responded to the question "How do you understand interculturality?" She said, "Well, I understand that interculturality is when, for example, I am speaking in Mam with a person from my community and, if a Ladino comes by, I speak to him in Spanish, but then continue in Mam with the other person." These words exemplify the idea of interculturality Morales postulates and endorses in regards to language, and he suggests extending this idea to other aspects of culture, such as food, dress, and religion. Morales adds that this woman articulates the differences between the Ladino and indigenous codes. We can see that, beyond Maya cultural specificities, she desires to adopt aspects of "Ladino" culture, such as the Spanish language.

An attitude similar to that of Morales is found in Mario Alberto Carrera's article "La inmutabilidad de la palabra *indio* y ahora su sustitución [The Immutability of the Word *Indian* and Its Present Substitution]." Carrera also celebrates those indigenous people who dress "after the Western fashion without losing their culture" and who learn Spanish in order to communicate interculturally. Carrera presents these indigenous people as an example of the subaltern subject's reaction to globalization, and he urges all Mayas not only to know "their vernacular culture, but also be informed of global culture…so that the great indigenous masses do not remain isolated in a romantic ostracism of a Maya past that was extinguished one thousand years ago." Here, it is also worth mentioning that Carrera's perspective on the importance of "being informed of global culture" is reaffirmed in an editorial in *Prensa Libre*—one of the most popular newspapers in the country. Titled "En el día de los pueblos indígenas [On the Day of the Indigenous Peoples]," the editorial discusses whether "in practice" Guatemala could have two or more official languages. According to the *Prensa Libre* editors, Spanish enables indigenous peoples to relate to and integrate with the globalized world, given that it is unrealistic "even to dream that technology would employ one of these Maya languages" ("En el día" 14).[28] Ironically, these declarations claim to be responding to the need of "eradicating" discrimination: "This work should include the identification of racist or discriminatory attitudes, thoughts, and sentiments that are often considered almost natural as much by those who discriminate as by those who suffer discrimination" (14).

Through a rhetorical question, Stefano Varese condemns these attitudes toward indigenous languages: "Must one point out the grave problems of schizoid incapacitation that confront members of ethno-linguistic minorities when their mother tongue and their cultural code are discriminated against and suppressed. Any cognitive act is a linguistic act…so all discrimination against a language is political aggression against the possibility of a people's self-realization" (*Proyectos étnicos* 22). Aggression against Maya linguistic agency is part of a politics that aims to recycle old paradigms of domination and neutralize the creation of linguistic systems that give us new ways of interpreting the world through epistemological alternatives. In the exaltations of Spanish by *Prensa Libre*, Carrera, and Morales, in the reform, and in the suggestions of Lux de Cotí, we find the recodification of a certain desire that the Maya "modernize," adopting Spanish as a first step in the process of "not being isolated in global culture." These attitudes toward language suggest that indigenous cultures still remain in a state of backwardness and their first step toward eradicating this backwardness is to learn Spanish, for it is "unthinkable" to use indigenous languages to move within modernity. As we can see, the referent continues to be an idea of Western modernity, embodied here by "Spanish." The reaffirmation or "revitalization" of Maya languages acquires a degree of empowerment only to the degree that these languages serve indigenous peoples as a means to communicate among themselves, not in the sense that the other or the nation would adopt a bi(multi)lingual democratic norm. In the intercultural model proposed, indigenous peoples should adopt the dominant culture in order to move within the environments of the nation and modernity; the other is not required to learn from indigenous peoples. This interculturality continues a relationship of power that assigns indigenous peoples—their languages, cultural specificities, cosmovision—to a position of subalternity in relation to Ladinos.

By saying this, I am in no way suggesting that the Maya should resist Western modernity or close themselves off from other knowledges, other technologies, or other languages, such as English or Spanish. To reiterate, by reflecting on these "intercultural" perspectives, we discover that both Mayas and Ladinos continue recycling the so-called Indian problem. That is, the Maya should "modernize," should adapt to modernity, should make use of modern Western "technologies." Ladinos, however, do not have to learn from us. They do not have to adapt themselves to our modernity or learn Maya languages or cosmovision. We remain obligated to assimilate *their* modernity. For me, this is a more sophisticated form of recycling the problem and of continuously reaffirming the status quo. Instead of creating a true intercultural project in which there is an equal cultural exchange between Maya, Ladino, Xinka, and Garífuna populations, this project insists that we Maya should come closer to the other, should understand their world, and the other need make no effort to learn from us.

Regarding languages, we could ask Morales and Carrera, for example, ¿lal tat Morales, xukuje lal tat Carrera, kakowin la katzijon pa ri qach'ab'al? ¿lal tajin katijoj ib la che ri na'oj b'anikil ri uk'iya'lil kiwach ri mayab' tinamit? ¿Jampa' chiri le kaxlantaj winaq kakik'am xukuje kakichakub'ej ri na'oj b'anikil, ri k'iya'lil kiwach ri mayab' tinamit? ¿Jampa' chir' kaketamaj ri echab'al qech ri oj mayab' winaq? The Maya already practice interculturality by learning Spanish and moving within "hybrid" spaces, as Morales and Carrera recommend. But where is the Ladino desire to learn the languages of the Maya, the Garífuna, or the Xinka and to move in modern indigenous spaces? Is it hoped that only indigenous peoples will practice interculturality? Would studying an indigenous language or learning about Maya cosmovision not be a first and fruitful step toward realizing a democratic and equitable intercultural project? In any case, these attitudes toward Maya languages reveal how the very project of interculturality recycles elements of colonialism, characterized by conflict and a struggle for power and knowledge, the objective of which is to maintain the subaltern status of the indigenous world.

Further, it has been shown that the intercultural subjects par excellence are the indigenous. For example, through violence or other colonial mechanisms, those who dominate have constituted their institutions by imposing their values, memories, and lifeways on the "dominated." From the very moment the state and its ideological apparatuses were established in the lands of Abya Yala, these institutions made or sought to make indigenous populations intercultural communities—whether or not through conflict. Although indigenous communities at times have resisted, they have opened their minds to other linguistic-cultural horizons, other knowledges. For the most part, they have already been constituted—in the sense of the word espoused by Morales and Carrera—as intercultural subjects. The educational "reform" and the Bilingual Intercultural Education project only reinforce what has been constituted since the conquest, except that now these practices are being institutionalized. Everything indicates that the real challenge confronted by the Educational Reform and BIE is not so much the task of making Maya populations "interculturally bilingual" or "sensitive to difference," but rather finding a way of turning Ladinos into intercultural and bi(multi)lingual subjects. Moreover, the Educational Reform should be examined for the impact on globalization that indigenous languages and cultural specificities should have, as well as among Guatemala's Ladino population. The project of the intercultural nation and intercultural citizenship should mean—to reverse Cárdenas's position—Mayanizing the Ladino nation and Western modernity.

In reality, there is a "Ladino problem." The "Indian problem" in Guatemala is nothing less than an equivocation.[29] The group that has closed its doors to Maya epistemology is the Ladino population. It has accepted an "archaic" vision of Maya civilizations, the cultural aspects of everything that textbooks celebrate as being exotic. Ladinos have problems accepting and appreciating the historic connection between their civilization and the philosophical and political contributions of the Maya, past and present. For example, as made clear at the beginning of this chapter, there remain both a political anxiety about difference and a desire to exercise a more sophisticated cultural and epistemic violence against everything considered different from or inferior to Ladino culture. There is still a pervasive disrespect for indigenous cultures that prevents intercultural coexistence, perpetuating relations of power that distance Ladinos from the continent's first inhabitants. For the most part, Ladinos cling to Eurocentric perspectives that reaffirm the coloniality of power, refusing to build the foundations of equal intercultural exchange. In sum, Ladinos, like the Maya, must practice the two interculturalities that the reform seeks to materialize.

This does not mean the institutionalization of a politics demanding that Ladinos learn Maya, Garífuna, or Xinka languages. Speaking a Maya language does not necessarily end racism or economic, linguistic, and gender inequality. After all, the colonizers used indigenous languages in their imperial saga, learning the secrets and beliefs of our peoples in order to turn them against themselves. Rather, it means constructing a critical subaltern perspective along with a linguistic pedagogy and Maya cosmovision. We can state without any danger that the Educational Reform, the project of BIE, and the perspectives on interculturality examined here begin with a harmonious notion of interethnic relations, thus marginalizing their conflictive nature. The reform critiques formal education and its homogenizing emphasis and proposes instead the construction of a citizenship that recognizes "cultural and linguistic diversity" as the cornerstone of the Guatemalan nation. The ideas of "multiculturalism" and "interculturality" that it promotes, however, lack specific historical content and a critical perspective.

For example, the current project of interculturality does not account for the tension and conflict in past and present interethnic relations. The categories of "racism" and "discrimination" are the result of historical processes producing relations of power that enforce inequalities. But the current project seems to regard them as the result of a "lack of understanding" and a failure to appreciate the other's cultural differences; "ignorance" of cultural differences is the principal cause of ethnic and linguistic prejudice. As an answer to this ignorance, the new educational project promotes "tolerance" of all cultures and the "recognition" that, beyond Ladinos, there exist the Maya, Xinka, and Garífuna peoples and that, beyond Spanish, there are twenty-three indigenous languages in the country. The idea of "intercultural democracy" rests on being "better informed" about cultural differences through the educational discourse. In this approach to interculturality, however, there is no focus on the historical problems of colonialism and the coloniality of power, the system of stratification based on social, ethnic, economic, and cultural hierarchies that fuel ongoing mechanisms of exclusion and oppression of otherness.

John Willinsky's book *Learning to Divide the World: Education at Empire's End* gets to the heart of the diversity or multiculturalism problem. How have the categories of "race," "diversity," "ethnicity," and the like acquired their current authority? Willinsky suggests that, in order to understand education's complicity in elaborating and reproducing a system of knowledge that divides the world into an "us" and a "them," multicultural education should begin by interrogating how the ethnic and racial divisions of the world have occurred (5). He also explains how education, from this "us" and "them," has justified (and justifies) the hierarchical privilege of the West as a civilization superior to others. Multiculturalism should not be understood as being isolated from the problem of the coloniality of power. The divisions of "race" and "ethnicity" have been instituted via colonialism. Let us look at a concrete example. In a talk I had with a teacher who trains Maya elementary school teachers as part of the BIE project, the teacher recounted how he once decided to share with his students an excerpt from Eduardo Galeano's book *The Open Veins of Latin America.* After reading the text aloud, he noticed that two of the students were crying. Others began to tell how they, their parents, their relatives, or their friends had lived experiences of racism and exploitation like those described in the reading. Tensions arose as his students expressed "hatred" not only of the system but also of "Ladinos," accusing them of being racist and exploitative. Not knowing what to do, the teacher subsequently declared the discussion closed and changed the topic. He also decided not to include any more readings from Galeano.

This anecdote illustrates that the tensions of an unfinished history of colonialism and the coloniality of power are present in the daily lives of indigenous peoples. Should we pretend to eradicate these tensions by turning the page on the discussion in order to make a fresh start? What happens to these students outside school? How does the reform respond to these tensions? How can this educational model "develop more socially and culturally appropriate programs in order to address the needs and characteristics of the [Guatemalan] population" (Diseño 27) when it ignores the reality of these conflicts? One of Gerald Graff's suggestions is precisely "to teach these conflicts" (64) and to explain that interculturality is also a struggle for power that reflects and articulates tensions on multiple levels. This pedagogical practice should not be interpreted as a desire for confrontation, but rather as a desire to deal with reality. If this painful reality is ignored, education will continue reducing interethnic relations to a discourse and will never achieve its aim of being a truly transformative pedagogical practice.

Centering a debate on these conflicts, especially those that include the categories of "racism," "discrimination," "coloniality," or "cultural identity," is indispensable because it permits the construction of a social and historical context. This enables the elaboration of a truly intercultural educational program appropriate for diversity. Further, from these conflicts the project of interculturality can acquire more relevance: it can teach that disagreement can be discussed in order to produce a critical consciousness. Only in this way can the Educational Reform accomplish its role of social transformation on the national, regional, local, and even global levels.

Following this line of argumentation, a Guatemalan intercultural education should depart from Willinsky's premise in regard to the division of the world into "races" and "ethnicities." By not filling the terms *multilingual*, *multicultural*, and *multinational* with a critical content and not referring to their historical precedents, intercultural education is in danger of perpetuating this division of the world. That is, without explaining why the world has been divided in the first place, education cannot engender respect for "cultural, ideological, political, and religious pluralism" (Diseño 38), nor even less will "diverse" populations be able to enjoy the harmonic relations of "equality and respect" (38). Moreover, the educational discourse should strive to shape antiracist and anticolonial citizens instead of merely spouting jargon in the name of honoring cultural and linguistic differences. Economic inequality and racial, ethnic, and linguistic discrimination persist in Guatemalan society today. These are the lessons that de Lión and Menchú have taught us. In their respective criticisms of colonialism and globalism, both construct a Maya epistemology that serves to create a new modernity.

In effect, both de Lión and Menchú want to make us understand the historic and actual importance of indigenous cultures as viable alternatives in the construction of an intercultural nation and citizenship. In their narratives, these two intellectuals and activists demonstrate how, despite the weight of colonial assaults, our cultures hold the key to the survival of the Guatemalan nation. This key is not simply found in the objects of material prosperity, but principally in the strength, will, and communal interdependence that have sustained our communities. We have endured, even in the most extreme conditions of physical and material deprivation. As a survivor of this shameful history of "modern" Guatemala, Menchú leaves us this message, pushing us to confront and assume responsibility for that history. In a similarly argumentative vein, Edward Said observes that "history cannot be swept clean like a blackboard, clean so that 'we' might inscribe our own future there and impose our own forms of life for these lesser people to follow" ("Preface").

To this we can equally add the words of John Edgar Wideman describing the struggles of black movements to overcome adversity (xxiii). He observes that, for the other, remembering the horrors that indigenous peoples have lived, accepting the challenges and responsibilities that this history places on all of us, is like facing an unpleasant difficulty, a disagreeable obligation or debt that has hung around our necks for a long time. We know in our hearts that we must address the crimes and consequences of this history, but we have evaded this, as if our indecision will make this burden disappear one day. Strictly speaking, we cannot turn the page on history and impose new memories that erase the horrors of war and a traumatic colonial experience. But we can begin again by learning from the experiences of those subalterns who have survived the experiences of exclusion and colonialism.

By showing the limitations and problems inherent in the current project of "intercultural" education, I am not suggesting that this project should be thrown away. Rather, I want to make it known that interculturality cannot operate or be expressed independently from the material conditions of existence of a population. On the contrary, intercultural education must respond to the necessities of indigenous peoples in regards to their historical memory, resolve the existing tensions, and make non-Mayas part of indigenous modernity. We cannot speak of an intercultural citizenship or nation of the future without first confronting the coloniality of power. The educational model, especially as it refers to indigenous peoples, should be reconstructed on Maya historical memory. The past must be understood not as something static or retrospective, but rather as a process linked to the present and to the future we want to construct. Our historical memory should be the political and epistemological source for rearticulating a Maya cosmovision that is not isolated from the adversities we endure at present, but linked to those experiences in their cultural, political, and epistemological dimensions.

In a society like that of Guatemala—with a history of plunder, genocide, foreign capitalist intervention, and four decades of state-sponsored terrorism—retrieving unofficial history and rescuing historical memory should form *the* curricular axis, not only for the project of intercultural education but for the national project as well. The Educational Reform presents us with the opportunity of a new dialogue and the opportunity for social renovation so that we can rethink the categories of "citizenship," "nation," and "modernity" in a democratic manner.

6 Conclusion
Final Thoughts

We resist the repression, the huge massacres, the bombings, the hunger, and the illnesses. And here we will continue resisting, resisting the violence, the persecution, and the intimidation. We will continue fighting to be acknowledged as a people and for the legalization of our lands. Ours is a difficult struggle.

—*María, Comunidades de Poblaciones en Resistencia–Sierra,*
Our Culture Is Our Resistance

In this work, I have shown the diverse discursive sites in which the coloniality of power operates, as well as how some representatives of the Maya movement have contested or reaffirmed this experience. Additionally, by exploring the prominent role that interculturality plays in both Maya and non-Maya discourses, I have demonstrated and problematized new and diverse political alternatives in order to rethink the nation and intercultural citizenship in Guatemala. As we have seen, from a vision of Guatemala that is culturally and linguistically homogenous, we have moved toward a vision of the Guatemalan nation that is multicultural, multilingual, and multinational. Upon entering this new imaginary, we have realized that tensions emerge between those who seek to manifest these cultural differences and specificities in recognition of cultural and linguistic diversity (de Lión, Menchú, Zapeta) and those who seek to defend the current hegemonic policies of mestizaje and hybridity (Morales).

Having brought these debates and tensions to the fore, my goal is to create a discussion that pushes us to confront these tensions and the coloniality of power. I feel that a process of Maya cultural and linguistic revitalization and the creation of a new nation and modern intercultural citizenship must take into account the conflicts that have historically defined interethnic relations. However, I also recognize that this book's greatest shortcoming lies in that it does not centralize the role and importance of the Xinka and Garífuna. A discussion of the interculturality and future of the Guatemalan nation is incomplete without their participation. Although the Maya movement has garnered a large amount of critical attention, it remains to be seen what the Xinka and Garífuna say about and propose for the future of the intercultural Guatemalan nation. I hope that this project, at the very least, opens up the possibility of dialogue with them.

I have suggested (especially in the second part of this book) that, by not confronting the coloniality of power, some members of the indigenous movement run the risk of trumpeting a culturist project that, beyond channeling and specifying their objectives and demands, will ultimately open up their knowledge and cultural specificity to the market such that these may be reappropriated by the dominant groups. As made clear in the last section of chapter 4, the movement's greatest challenge is that of creating both an intercultural subaltern epistemology and a political program inscribed in the agenda of other social movements challenging a neoliberal globalization that is determined to rearticulate the status quo.

In this context, we continually insist that the Maya movement, hand in hand with the politics of cultural revitalization, should articulate a critical perspective that organically ties its situation to the historical processes that have produced the conditions of inequality we have been confronted with historically. As we saw in the first part of this book, the Maya cosmovision that Asturias, de León, and Menchú rearticulate points in this direction and can serve as a cornerstone in the construction of an anticolonial, antiracist, and anticapitalist critical locus of enunciation. Despite their limitations, I believe that the proposals of de León and Menchú, in particular, open up the possibility of conceiving an intercultural subaltern epistemology from Maya cosmovision. This is an epistemology that both critiques capitalist and neoliberal modes of production and reaffirms indigenous cultural, linguistic, and religious values, an epistemology based on an ancestral imaginary and an entire history of resistance and survival in the face of colonialism and the coloniality of power. Moreover, the cultural identity constructed by de León and Menchú projects an indigenous agency that obliges us to rethink the narrative of modernity as one in which ancestral values have the capacity to influence political and structural change. In opposition to those who have imagined that Maya-ness is anti-modern, we present another type of modernity, one that, beyond individuality and competition, insists upon the collective and on articulating a cultural space for the exchange of knowledge and for intercultural coexistence.

Intellectuals like Zapeta and those who participated in the construction of the Educational Reform commit themselves to difference—the reaffirmation of Maya culture and language—but promote it in order to fortify, perhaps unconsciously, a neoliberal economic model based on diversity. What they end up endorsing is the idea that globalization is like a battlefield where indigenous people have the ability to "compete" and achieve a type of "American Dream." Of course, the perspectives of Mayas and non-Mayas in conditions of subalternity, the "delinquents" to whom Zapeta refers in chapter 4, remain excluded from this battlefield. The new educational model, while condemning previous educational models for being assimilationist and complicit in the modern colonial project, operates under a logic that constructs indigenous subjects as having the capacity to adopt a neoliberal mode of production, that is, subjects who will operate as "Indios permitidos" (Hale and Millamán) in the global arena. Despite this model's recognition of and argument for a politics of difference, the educational project it espouses does not seek to have dominant cultures learn anything from an indigenous modernity. The idea of a capitalist modernity remains unquestioned and continues to be the path to achieving unity and an intercultural democracy.

If we focus on the idea of the nation and its relationship to indigenous peoples since the nineteenth century, we find that capitalism has always been the preferred mode of production.[1] Are we not, once again, reproducing the coloniality of power? Unfortunately, so-called free trade agreements would seem to confirm this.

In newspaper articles that reference the meeting of Central American presidents with George W. Bush in 2003 in order to discuss the Central American Free Trade Agreement (CAFTA), we find the following declarations made by these presidents.[2] Francisco Flores of El Salvador observed that the treaty "will be a mechanism for development...and the reduction of poverty in the isthmus." Ricardo Maduro from Honduras likewise states, "[CAFTA] will aid us in reducing poverty" and will further "the development of Central America." Costa Rica's Abel Pacheco added, "In President Bush we find a willingness to help Central America. For us, the agreement will be a way out of underdevelopment." And finally, the ex-president of Guatemala, Alfonso Portillo, maintained, "President Bush told us that he is not interested in a free trade agreement that would benefit those who are doing well, but in one that will benefit those who are doing poorly." In regards to all these statements, it is appropriate to ask, To what extent do these treaties "benefit" the region? How do they promote a "way out of underdevelopment," as well as "reducing poverty"?

In the Guatemalan context, beyond the slight information we have received through the media, there have been no public meetings to discuss the "benefits" of these agreements. The discussions approving them have taken place behind closed doors.[3] At this point, I want to show what is at stake for the region of Mesoamerica and its diverse populations through a brief critical discussion of the Puebla–Panamá Plan (PPP), which is a branch of CAFTA and of the ambitious project known as the Free Trade Agreement of the Americas (FTAA). From the outset, it should be stated that, despite the significant recession produced by these treaties in recent years,[4] Central American officials are still pressured to continue implementing these agreements. During a visit to Guatemala in 2003, the now ex-president of Mexico Vicente Fox reaffirmed that the PPP was "cruising along" (Luisa Rodríguez). Upon exploring and expanding this discussion, we find that, far from being advantageous, these "free" trade agreements evidence an extremely sophisticated form of colonialism and rearticulate a new exclusionary economic modernity that continues to spread the coloniality of power.

The Plan Puebla–Panamá: Por el desarrollo sustentable y socialmente incluyente (Puebla–Panamá Plan: For Sustainable and Socially Inclusive Development) (2000) tells us that it represents a "strategy of regional development" put forth by the Mexican president Vicente Fox and officials from Central America in the year 2000. The plan seeks to build infrastructure (highways, airports, trains) in the region from Puebla to Panama in order to take advantage of each country's economic situation. According to the leaders involved, the PPP's intention is "to reduce poverty, to facilitate access to basic social services for vulnerable populations, and to contribute to the full development of Mesoamerican peoples" (5). Further, it seeks "to promote the conservation and sustainable use of natural resources and participatory mechanisms in environmental management, especially for local communities" (5).

In regards to infrastructure, the plan has as its central axis the construction or modernization of approximately 3,000 kilometers of highway from Puebla to Panama, the restoration or expansion of the region's marine ports, the construction or improvement of airports, the improvement of railways, the construction of dams and hydroelectric plants to promote private investment in electricity, the construction of hospitals and schools in marginalized regions, the construction of hotels and restaurants in key areas to promote tourism and ecotourism, and the promotion of the creation of maquiladoras (sweatshops) and factories to produce jobs (PPP 6–12). According to Vicente Fox, this project would open up the possibility of at least three hundred thousand jobs just within Mexico, thereby reducing the rate of migration to the United States, as well as taking a step toward the "eradication" of poverty. For the PPP's initial cost of $4,017,170,000, the leaders of Central America and Mexico have applied to institutions like the World Bank, the Inter-American Development Bank (IDB), and the International Monetary Fund (IMF), among others, for loans.

The PPP and CAFTA are the most recent initiatives to "modernize" Mesoamerica and insert the region into the capitalist system in order to achieve a certain degree of competitiveness in the global arena.[5] However, upon analyzing these modernizing proposals more closely, we find that, far from being "a way out of underdevelopment" and a response to the needs of the "poor," these projects reaffirm a more sophisticated colonialist order. As with each previous "modernization" project in Latin America, leaders and authorities have sought neither the opinions nor the decisions of the peoples whom these projects impact. Once again, government officials who pretend to know what is best for the people do not even ask permission to use the natural resources they intend to exploit. For the most part, these resources are located in territories occupied by the people whom the projects claim to benefit. In regards to southern Mexico—Chiapas, for example—the PPP initiative maintains that

> the south–southeastern region offers vast economic potential. Land, forests, biodiversity, and climate; water in rivers and lakes in the interior; coasts with beaches of extraordinary beauty; a strategic position, opening onto both the Pacific and Atlantic Oceans; potential for agriculture, livestock, forestry, fruit cultivation, and fishing, as well as abundant labor force. (PPP 1, emphasis added)

Who are the readers this text is addressing? Obviously, they are not the "abundant labor force" in the south–southeast of Mexico. Furthermore, the "vast economic potential" and the "strategic position" suggest a scene prepared for exploitation and fails to consider the diverse populations that inhabit these territories. At every turn, the passage appeals to the transnational corporations that possess the financial resources and the necessary infrastructure to exploit the region of Mesoamerica. This perspective, not surprisingly, echoes an entire discursive colonial tradition in which foreign economic interests have always been sought to help realize the dream of a Western-based modernity. We can recall two distinct instances, separated in space and time but nonetheless ideologically related.

Seeking to legitimate the conquest of Tenochtitlán, in 1520 Hernán Cortés wrote Emperor Charles V with the hope of obtaining more soldiers and financing for his expansionist enterprise. To achieve his objectives, Cortés seduced his readers, painting pictures of a terrestrial paradise in which a "New Spain" could be materialized. In his famous second letter, in which he refers to Tenochtitlán, he writes:

There is in this city a market where each and every day upward of thirty thousand people come to buy and sell, without counting the other trade which goes on elsewhere in the city. In this market there is everything they might need or wish to trade, provisions as well as clothing and footwear. There is jewelry of gold and silver and precious stones and other ornaments of featherwork and all as well laid out as in any square or marketplace in the world. There is much pottery of many sorts and as good as the best in Spain. They sell a great deal of firewood and charcoal and medicinal and cooking herbs. There are establishments like barbers, where they have their hair washed and are shaved, and there are baths. Lastly there is amongst them every consequence of good order and courtesy, and they are such an orderly and intelligent people that the best in Africa cannot equal them. (Cortés 67–68)

The phrases "there is" and "there are" in this quotation are key. They create the illusion of riches and an established order, to motivate readers on the Iberian Peninsula to immigrate to the "New World." This newly "discovered" territory offers the conditions of possibility for a new existence, for enjoying new resources, given that "there is" everything necessary to create a new civilization, a "New Spain." Beatriz Pastor Bodmer has suggested that this is one of the important differences between Cortés's discourse and that of the other conquistadores. The familiar model of "plunder" is now replaced by the "development" of the colony's resources. "Centers are to be created and organized for the development of agriculture, handicrafts, and trade...exploration will henceforth be oriented toward the mining of copper, tin, and iron for weapons and tools, so that New Spain may become independent from her current suppliers" (Pastor Bodmer 94).

Three centuries later, in 1845 Domingo Faustino Sarmiento echoes this ideology in his book, *Facundo: Civilization and Barbarism*, which is nothing less than an ideological and political program to establish "civilization" (that is, European civilization) in Argentina. According to Sarmiento, this project can be achieved by attracting Europeans to Argentinean soil so that they build a new "Paris" in America. Referencing the country's physiognomy, Sarmiento writes:

As a notable feature of the physiognomy of this country, one could indicate the agglomeration of navigable rivers that meet in the east, from all points on the horizon, to unite in the Plata and gravely present their stupendous tribute to the ocean, which takes it on the flank, not with-

out visible signs of turbulence and respect. But these immense canals,
excavated by the solicitous hand of nature, do not bring about any
changes at all in national customs. The son of the Spanish adventurers
that colonized the country detests navigation, and feels himself impris-
oned within the narrow confines of a boat or launch. When a large
river cuts off his path, he calmly undresses, prepares his horse, and
directs it to swim toward some barren island out in the distance; arriv-
ing there, horse and horseman rest, and from island to island, the
crossing is finally completed. (46–47, emphasis added)

This passage, like that of Cortés, clearly demonstrates tactical objectives. Once again, we find the desire to capture the reader's interest through the description of a vast panorama apparently ready to be exploited. The "agglomeration of navigable rivers," "immense canals" carved by the "solic-itous hand of nature," are indicative that national resources are not being exploited by the land's inhabitants, who instead detest what nature has cre-ated for interrupting their daily routine. Sarmiento implicitly suggests that "nature" is participating in the civilizing project and what it needs is the guidance of Europe (France, in this particular case). The space described is ready for those Europeans who can and want to take advantage of it.

Obviously, these three perspectives on the Latin American landscape show not only a clear similarity but also the continuity of a project with objectives and ideological elements that reflect the coloniality of power. Through these environmental descriptions of Mexico and Argentina, such perspectives elucidate economic programs that seek to plunder and exploit resources and labor in these respective territories. With regard to free trade agreements, for the most part, these projects are profiled as a new cultural and civilizing process that continues to measure "development" or "under-development" based on the "success" of "advanced" countries. The eco-nomic model to be followed remains a Western one, which, according to its advocates, will lead the peoples of the Americas "out of underdevelopment" and toward the "eradication" of poverty. Whether or not the peoples of the Americas are capable or mature enough to create a noncapitalist form of development is never considered.

Moreover, even if these treaties do offer some employment opportuni-ties, indigenous people in a subaltern condition are not the beneficiaries of these megaprojects in the long run. On the contrary, "free" trade agreements, like previous modernizing traditions, contribute to the obliteration of forms of social cohesion and relations among communities in order to substitute these for the values of competition, individuality, and disrespect for nature and land. Like Asturias's character in *Men of Maize*, Gaspar Illom, and his interpretation of a similar situation, we are dealing with an utter destruction of natural resources that benefits commercial agriculture, the ones who knock the trees down with axes in Asturias's novel. Even when we adopt the principles disseminated by these projects, we realize that transnational companies become the beneficiaries. Their principal attraction to the so-called Third World lies in paying its labor force significantly lower wages than in nations of the "First World." Along these lines, we can also see that most of the capital accumulated by these companies, instead of remaining in the countries where these companies have established themselves, returns to their country of origin. Osvaldo Martínez makes an appropriate characterization of this economic logic. He suggests that deposits of foreign capital that enter these markets are attractive for the neoliberal propaganda they spread. But these programs of "free" trade lose "much of their appeal when we realize that, at the very least, a third of these investments are composed of migratory capital and short-term reserves that come and go with great speed, constituting the key factors of destabilization in the financial crises suffered by the region in the 1990's" (Osvaldo Martínez 11–12).

Few Latin American businesses have the capacity and freedom of movement possessed by European and American companies. In most cases, Latin American companies lack the economic resources to establish themselves in regions of the so-called First World and thus compete equally with their counterparts. All of this brings us to the conclusion that when we speak of "free trade," far from making a reference to the commercial enterprises of countries like Guatemala, El Salvador, or even Mexico, we are referring to transnational corporations' freedom to move into new spaces and territories. We are referring to their ability to install themselves in any part of the "Third World" in order to extract resources and exploit labor in such a way that these mostly benefit their own capitalist economic programs. Strictly speaking, "free" trade agreements come to be a renovated and subtler manifestation of contemporary capitalism. As Carlos Fazio suggests, this forms part "of a project of continental geostrategic and Western imperialist scope in which the sectors of financial capital, the multinational consortiums, and the oligarchies of the countries of the Mexico–Central America region all participate" ("El juego del poder" 60).

We can thus understand why indigenous movements, whose members have historically, personally lived through this plunder and exploitation, have defined the foundations of their struggles as a resistance to "free trade." It is no coincidence that the Zapatistas rebelled precisely on the day that the North American Free Trade Agreement (NAFTA) went into effect. It is no coincidence that the popular movements in Bolivia said no to the privatization of gas and water by a Spanish company. And, finally, it is no coincidence that, upon Vicente Fox's arrival in Guatemala in 2003, thousands of indigenous and non-indigenous peasants made their voices heard in a protest against free trade agreements, screaming "Fox go home!" and "No to the TLC and the PPP!"[6]

We should also understand that these treaties did not begin in 1994. They have historical precedents in the colonial and post-independence periods as demonstrated above with Cortés and Sarmiento. As in those earlier programs, contemporary neoliberal logic comes accompanied by political, economic, and military intervention. We can likewise affirm that the expansion of free trade agreements like the PPP and CAFTA is part of a global strategy to exploit an abundant supply of raw materials at lower costs of production and with guaranteed access to emerging markets. Although these programs create new jobs, these gains are rarely enough to offset the massive displacement of traditional industries and rural farmwork.

Since the expansion of neoliberal economic logics, represented here by free trade agreements, the greatest challenge we face is that of disarticulating a new recycling of economic-cultural paradigms that do not recognize the economic forms at capitalism's margins. I do not believe that this is a denial of "development" but rather that new proposals of neoliberal modernization represent a new consequence of the plundering and exploitation of our communities' resources. We need to create a plan of development that includes the voices and proposals of those who historically have suffered the experience of conquest and now collectively seek a more viable economic path for all people. Taking into account the actions of social movements like Zapatismo in Mexico and the Movement Toward Socialism in Bolivia, the Maya movement must bear in mind that the fight for the recognition of "difference" takes place in a world in which the "market" has made cultural diversity a myth. Although it celebrates difference, the submission of difference to the market's logic of expansion seeks to establish strict limits on the very possibility of the preservation and creation of other ways of life. Silvia Rivera Cusicanqui alerts us to this when she observes that even if the elites

> have learned the rhetoric of the "pluri-multi"...they still have not abandoned their noble disdain for manual labor and for the languages, the forms of society, the productive and political contributions of indigenous societies, putting into evidence their merely ornamental rhetorical management of cultural diversity. They likewise have not abandoned their closed control over public decision making—however legitimate it may be—nor the racist, misogynist, and exclusionary structure that organizes its daily conduct. ("Oprimidos pero no vencidos" 13)

Any celebration of difference and particularity that ignores the transnational structures of geopolitics and of capitalist accumulation cannot but be implicated in the global dynamics of this world system as it continues legitimating the coloniality of power in the field of economic exploitation.

Despite the liberalization of the economic system and its continued diffusion of these "democracies," we cannot overlook the fact that the market disseminates an idea of economic progress and stability that possesses a Western referent. Contemporary social movements face the challenge of demystifying the idea of the "market" as representing a possible "democratic opening" for the subaltern. The Maya movement must keep in mind that multinational corporations are continuing their quest to establish control over the diverse populations of the "Third World," recycling and reinforcing old structures of economic and cultural inequality at the national and global levels. Moreover, even diversity is being sublimated in the name of these transnational corporations' interests in order to incorporate those who are "different" (indigenous, blacks) into processes that reaffirm corporative neoliberal objectives.

In my view, the Maya movement and its political projects should begin from the material conditions of our existence and from an analysis of the relations of power—because these experiences are ongoing. Colonialism and the coloniality of power are realities that we encounter every day. Moreover, capital is a category that currently exercises even more force in structuring our lives at the global and local levels. In other words, the conditions of economic inequality under which we live structure other inequalities, furthering the coloniality of power on every level—ethnicity, gender, language, memory, imaginaries. As demonstrated in the last section of chapter 4, the Maya movement must inscribe a politics and an epistemology that challenge the coloniality of power. A struggle for the recognition of difference will not make "free" trade agreements disappear. We need to recognize that the best lessons in resisting these threats are those we can learn from people who have survived the colonial experience and modernity in conditions of subalternity. I reiterate that the struggle for the recognition of difference should be organically attached to a new form of resistance to the neoliberal capitalist mode of production. Interculturality, as made clear in regard to Menchú in chapter 3, should involve an epistemology and a politics that argue—to recall the Zapatista neologism—for "humanity and against neoliberalism." The Maya movement and other indigenous movements throughout Latin America offer us not only a chance to dream but also the opportunity to create a noncolonial history and experience.

Guatemala, Chiapas, Pittsburgh, 2001–2006

Notes

Chapter 1
Introduction: Globalization, Coloniality, and Social Movements

1. See Seijo.

2. In Guatemala, *Ladino* is a synonym for *mestizo*. According to Mario Roberto Morales, "*Ladino* refers to those who, accepting or not an evident biological and cultural miscegenation, identify with the values of the so-called 'Western culture,' follow their models and accommodate them to the reality of their countries, usually scorning what they perceive as autochthonous, indigenous, and different from those models, unless the differences are viewed as an archaeological trace of a mythic, splendorous past" ("A fuego lento" 1). *Criollo* commonly refers to direct descendents of Europeans born on American soil. They do not consider a "blood" mixture with indigenous or blacks as characteristic of their cultural identity.

3. Besides Cojtí, see also Falla ("El movimiento indígena").

4. The Peace Accords comprise the following: (1) Comprehensive Agreement on Human Rights, (2) Agreement on the Resettlement of Population Groups Uprooted by the Armed Conflict, (3) Agreement for the Establishment of the Commission to Clarify Past Human Rights Violations and Acts of Violence That Have Caused the Guatemalan Population to Suffer, (4) Agreement on the Identity and Rights of Indigenous Peoples, (5) Agreement on Socio-economic Aspects and the Agrarian Situation, (6) Agreement on the Strengthening of Civilian Power and the Role of the Armed Forces in a Democratic Society, (7) Agreement on a Definitive Ceasefire, (8) Agreement on Constitutional Reforms and the Electoral Regime, (9) Agreement on the Basis for the Legal Integration of the URNG, (10) Agreement on the Implementation, Compliance, and Verification Timetable for the Peace, and (11) Agreement on a Firm and Lasting Peace (December 1996). For more detail on the content of these accords, see the United Nations and Costello.

5. Besides Cojtí, another Maya intellectual who became part of the FRG was Otilia Lux de Cotí, who had condemned the racism and genocide perpetrated against the Maya population. She actively participated in the Recovery of the Historical Memory (REMHI) project, which compiled testimonies from the survivors of Guatemala's civil war.

6. Estuardo Zapeta echoes this perspective when he talks about the Maya movement:

In the indigenous movement, fortunately, there exists a variety of thought. From radical Leftists, who are few but…make a lot of noise, to the ones who believe that unity is possible within diversity. There are also cosmogonist esoterics, intellectuals, populists, peasants, radical feminists, neoliberal merchants, the culturales, historicists, those who believe that issues of identity and rights come from the North, and those who are ashamed of being indigenous, just to mention a part of the diversity of *being* and *existing* indigenous presence within the Guatemalan plurality. (*Las huellas* 143)

A similar discussion on the different faces of the Maya movement is developed by Victor Montejo when he talks about leadership (Maya Intellectual Renaissance, especially 124–31).

7. Among other studies about the Maya movement, Bastos and Camus (*Abriendo caminos* and *Quebrando el silencio*); Falla; Fischer and Brown; Gálvez Borrell and Dary; Grandin; Nelson; Smith ("Maya Nationalism"); Warren (*Indigenous Movements and Their Critics*); Warren and Jackson; Wilson. More recently, Arias (*Taking Their Word*, especially his chapter on the Maya movement); Hale (*Más que un Indio*); Montejo (*Maya Intellectual Renaissance*).

8. See Amin; Dussel ("Eurocentrism and Modernity"); Hinton (*Annihilating Difference* 1–40, *Genocide*); Lander ("Modernidad, colonialidad y posmodernidad."); Mignolo (*The Darker Side*, *Local Histories*); Quijano ("Coloniality and Modernity/Rationality," "Coloniality of Power, Eurocentrism, and Latin America," and "'Raza,' 'etnia' y 'nación'"); Rivera Cusicanqui (*Oprimidos pero no vencidos*).

9. The concept of "Third World" has the disadvantage of obscuring fundamental topics related to the racial, ethnic, class, cultural, and gender inequalities occurring within a particular third world. The discussion of the Maya movement developed in this book shows this. Nevertheless, even though this category has its limitations, I use it here to point out not only a neocolonial and ambivalent fallacy but also a radical anti-colonial and anti-racist collective critique. For a better informed discussion about the so-called Third World and its ambivalences, see Shohat and Stam (25–27).

10. In a letter to the Catholic kings, Christopher Columbus indicates that the writings of Nicolas and Marco Polo informed his knowledge about the travels to the Orient. Columbus writes the following to the kings: "on the information which I had given Your Majesties about the *lands of India* and a ruler known as the Great Khan" (81, emphasis added). As we can see here, Columbus interpreted and imagined the lands of the Indies—and therefore "Indians." For a study about Columbus's discourse, see Pastor Bodmer.

11. In this book, I use the category of subalternity coined by Ranajit Guha (*Elementary Aspects* vii): the general attribute of subjects or collectives marginalized in terms of class, caste, gender, and age or in any other manner.

12. This is the beginning of processes like Quijano's and Mignolo's "coloniality of power," Dussel's "Western modernity" ("Eurocentrism and Modernity"), Gruzinki's "colonization of the imaginary" (*La colonización*), Lienhard's "fetishism of writing" (*La voz*), and O'Gorman's (*La invención, Cuatro historiadores*) and Rabasa's (*Inventing America*) "invention of America."

13. For the debates about postcolonial studies, see Ashcroft, Griffiths, and Tiffin; Gandhi; Loomba; McClintock, Mufti, and Shohat; Williams and Chrisman. For discussion on the debates about postcolonialism in Latin America, see Adorno; Klor de Alva; Mallon; Mignolo ("Are the Subaltern Studies Postmodern or Postcolonial?" and "Colonial and Postcolonial Discourse"); Seed ("Colonial and Postcolonial Discourses," and "More Colonial and Postcolonial Discourses").

See also Beverley ("Subalternity and Representation"); Castro Gómez and Mendieta; Rabasa, Sanjinés, and Carr; Rivera Cusicanqui and Barragán.

14. I am making reference to the words of Arturo Arias when he writes about indigenous cosmovision: "This phrase has become something of a myth. Indigenous peoples themselves employ it constantly without explaining its content. Therefore, this notion operates like a trope that can mean almost anything" ("La literatura").

15. The concept of interculturality in Latin America emerged at the end of the 1970s with the expansion of globalization. It is conditioned by, among other things, the weakening of the nation-state and its homogenizing tendencies—for example, indigenismo (in Latin America, the literature about the indigenous world written by non-indigenous intellectuals) and Hispanization, terms that were challenged by ethnic movements demanding recognition of their cultural, religious, and linguistic differences. Anthropologist Edward T. Hall coined the concept to respond to discussions about cultural diversity, such as "multiculturalism" and "cultural pluralism," in Canada, Australia, the United States, and Europe, including England, Spain, and France. These concepts spread from the nation-state to promote tolerance toward the migrant populations from the "Third World." In Latin America, the term *intercultural* was first used at the Congress on Indigenous Education that took place in Oaxaca, Mexico, in 1983 when the "intercultural approach" in education was proposed to defend the culture of indigenous people (Lozano Vallejo, Meentzen, and Aguilar 34). In Guatemala, the concept became official—especially for education—in 1995 with the signing of the Agreement on Identity and the Rights of Indigenous Peoples.

16. The idea of US multiculturalism has been defined around liberalism. It basically entails certain recognition of diversity as long as the "other" (Black, Asian, Native American) embraces the economic capitalist logic. For a discussion about the debates on multiculturalism in the United States, see Appleton; West.

17. For a contribution that could be considered an introduction to the literary texts from these writers, see Ament. For a study that includes a panoramic view of Guatemalan literature, see Zimmerman (*Literature and Resistance*). In addition, see Arias's chapter on the emergence of a "new Maya literature" in *Taking Their Word*.

18. In 2004 Ak'abal did not accept the national Miguel Ángel Asturias literary prize. In an interview with Juan Carlos Lemus, he gave the reasons why he rejected the prize:

> For me, it is a simple thing. The prize has two names: it is called "National Prize," and that is already a name. And then, the other one is "Miguel Ángel Asturias." I have to tell you the truth. When I became familiar with Miguel Ángel Asturias's *The Social Problem of the Indian*, it hurt me very much. With that work, he offended indigenous people of Guatemala, and I am a part of those people. Therefore, I do not feel honored to receive a prize with the name of the Nobel Prize's name, even though it has a lot of merit.

The next year, the prize was awarded to Rodrigo Rey Rosa. In response to Ak'abal, he used the prize money to create B'atz: The Literary Prize in Indigenous Languages.

19. For other studies that complement and extend this discussion about the Maya movement and racism in Guatemala, see note 7 and the studies by Adams and Bastos; Casaús Arzú; González Ponciano; Taracena. (All are listed in the bibliography.)

20. The Xinkas are indigenous people who trace their origins to the Maya Post-classic period (1200–1524). Displaced by the Aztecs, they migrated south, settling in what are today

Guatemala and El Salvador. In the present, the Xinka population lives, according to official records, in the eastern Guatemalan districts of Santa Rosa, Jutiapa, and Jalapa. The official records, based on the population that speaks the native language, estimate that their population ranges from three hundred to one thousand people.

The Garífunas, or Garinagus, have African origins and live on the Atlantic coast of what are today Belize, Guatemala, Honduras, and Nicaragua. In Guatemala, they live in Puerto Barrios and Livingston. Their history can be traced back to the seventeenth century, when much of the slave trafficking and migration took place in Central America. Currently, according to official records, the Garífunas represent between 3 and 5 percent of Guatemala's total population. See Diseño (19–21).

Chapter 2
From the "Indian" as a Problem to the Indian as a Political and Social Agent

1. In regards to indigenismo, I think especially of Gonzalo Aguirre Beltrán's 1992 statement about this discursivity in Latin America, particularly Mexico: "The organic base of such an ideology [indigenismo] is represented, not certainly by the Indian, but rather by the mestizo. Indigenismo and mestizaje are polar processes that complement each other to a point where it is impossible to think of their existence as separate. Indigenismo requires as a condition sine qua non of its existence, the human substratum that mestizaje supplies" (113). Besides Aguirre Beltrán, see the studies by Luis Villoro, Henry Favre, and Antonio Cornejo Polar that also analyze the relationship between indigenismo and mestizaje.

2. For a study that analyzes the relationship between historiography and indigenous peoples, see Attwood.

3. In the past few decades, a debate has emerged concerning the racism in Asturias's master's thesis. We have already mentioned how Humberto Ak'abal rejected the national Asturias literary prize. For the Maya perspective on Asturias's thesis, see Cojtí (El movimiento Maya 38); González ("Una interpretación de Hombres de maíz"); Zapeta (Las huellas 218). For the Ladino perspective, see Liano ("Vida nueva, nación nueva" 55); Morales (La articulación 248); Prera Flores and Méndez de Penedo (21).

4. For discussion of social policies based on the ideology of indigenismo during the nineteenth and twentieth centuries, see Jesús Amurrio González's El positivismo en Guatemala and Artemis Torres Valenzuela's El pensamiento positivista en la historia de Guatemala, 1871–1900.

5. Among the critics who began challenging indigenismo in Latin America are Guillermo Bonfill Batalla in México profundo and José Alcina Franch in Indianismo e indigenismo en América (addressing the tendencies related to nativism).

6. De Lión used this name as a writer. His original name was José Luis de León Díaz.

7. We owe the observation of El tiempo being the "first Maya novel" to Arturo Arias, who wrote the prologue to the second edition of the book. According to Arias, the novel is Maya because, contrary to other books, it shows the influence of the Popol Wuj (a cyclic narrative with direct references to the Maya K'iche' book of history and creation). Also, it emphasizes the notion of community and collectivity above individuality. For Arias, the most salient Maya characteristic of the novel is its narrative voice, which, for the first time, speaks from an indigenous point of view, something that is absent from indigenista discourse ("Asomos de la narrativa indígena Maya" i–vii).

8. De Lión is not the only Maya writer in Guatemala. The reading I propose here of his text as a response to indigenismo through the self-affirmation of Maya-ness can also be applied to writers such as Humberto Ak'abal, Gaspar Pedro González (*La otra cara, El retorno de los Mayas*), Rigoberta Menchú (*Crossing Borders, Rigoberta Menchú: La nieta de los Mayas*), and Victor Montejo (*El Q'anil, Testimony*).

9. It is important to note that the discipline of anthropology in the past decade has tried to demystify these types of representations in order to formulate close relationships with the objects of study. In the case of Mesoamerica, see *Pluralizing Ethnography*, edited by John Watanabe and Edward Fischer, which explores these particular topics. In chapter 2, I offer some reflections about the role of anthropology and its relationship to indigenous peoples in Guatemala when I address the Menchú–Stoll debate.

10. Gerald Martin tells us that "the solutions offered by Asturias to the Indian 'problem' were the conventional remedies of 'Ladinoization' and 'integration'—measures that were officially adopted by the Guatemalan Indigenista Institute three decades later—and, above all, immigration" (487).

11. The first attempts by Ortiz to define his famous concept can be traced back to his work analyzing Afro-Cuban poetry during the forties and fifties. Ortiz interpreted that textual production not as authentically African, but rather as "mulata" or "mestiza," because it is written in Spanish and combines African and Spanish cultural elements. Miguel Arnedo has an interesting study about Ortiz's analysis of and conclusions on Afro-Cuban poetry. He suggests that the Cuban ethnographer attributes a mulata cultural identity to the poetry with the purpose of making "acceptable" the textual production with African origins. This attitude, for Arnedo, reveals Ortiz's implicit racism toward blacks.

12. Vanguardia and costumbrismo are two literary trends that took place toward the end of the nineteenth century (costumbrismo) and the beginning of the twentieth century (vanguardia) in Latin America. Representative of the vanguardia style is the poetry of Vicente Huidobro, Cesar Vallejo, and Pablo Neruda. These authors experimented with the most innovative literary styles coming from France at the time, especially surrealism. Costumbrismo literature evokes images of everyday, local—especially rural—life, mannerisms, and customs. It primarily incorporates indigenous elements and is characterized by social realism and romanticism. One of the most well-known examples of this genre is *Tradiciones peruanas* by Peruvian Ricardo Palma.

13. John Beverley proposes an interesting rereading of transculturation in his analysis of the Quechua play *Ollantay* (in *Subalternity and Representation*). Contrary to what Ortiz and Rama suggest, Beverley gives priority to subaltern agency and influence on the hegemonic Spanish cultural production. The use of the Quechua language, as well as other cultural forms, filters some of the Quechua ideologies directed to a specific Quechua audience. For Beverley, this subaltern influence represents a "transculturation from below" (*Subalternity* 54). For additional discussions of transculturation, see Schmidt and Sobrevilla.

14. In the first section of chapter 4, I offer a reading of cultural globalization in which I emphasize the agency of indigenous subjects by using Beverley's notion of "transculturation from below" (*Subalternity* 54). I exemplify this notion in the experiences of Subcomandante Marcos and José María Arguedas and how they model the assimilation of indigenous cultures.

15. See Prieto (618).

16. The argument about Asturias's nationalist project is developed by Arturo Arias (*La identidad de la palabra*, especially the fourth chapter) and Dante Liano ("Vida nueva, nación nueva").

17. I discuss "free" trade agreements in the final chapter.

18. Perhaps the best example on this topic would be Asturias's *The Eyes of the Interred*. In this novel, Asturias narrates the "success" of a nonviolent revolution that ends with a dictatorship and with class exploitation by the United Fruit Company. The central character, Octavio Sansur, after adopting the pseudonym of Juan Pablo Mondragon, raises the political consciousness of the people, who later form a strong popular movement that includes peasants and elites and ends US imperialism.

19. Chapter 4 contains an analysis of the relationship between the school and indigenous peoples.

20. We need to remember that Asturias won the Nobel literary prize in 1967. The award, obviously, had a major impact in Guatemala and the rest of Latin America.

21. Because de León moved in Ladino literary circles and did not speak a Maya language, some critics have concluded that he was a "Ladinoized" or assimilated intellectual. Others have concluded that he was in "limbo." That is, he wanted to be a Ladino but was rejected by the Ladino world; at the same time, his desire to be part of that Ladino world distanced him from the Indian world. Nevertheless, these perspectives about the Maya author avoid contemplating what his closest friends say about how de León perceived himself. Francisco Morales Santos, for instance, says that "Luis de León did not see himself as Ladino" (Morales Santos, *Introducción*, pg. 2). This perspective is also evidenced in de León's works. He was very conscious of his cultural and colonized condition as an indigenous intellectual. He wanted to understand and analyze the Ladino world not to become assimilated, but rather to criticize and destabilize that Ladino world. From this, we can conclude that he deemed it necessary to criticize Asturias and his version of the indigenous world because Asturias was the Ladino author par excellence in Guatemala.

22. See de León's short story collections, *Los zopilotes*, *Su segunda muerte*, *Pájaro en mano*, and *La puerta del cielo*, and his poetry collections, *Poemas del Volcán de Agua* and *Poemas del Volcán de Fuego*.

23. For a summary of Guatemala's civil war, see Comisión para el Esclarecimiento Histórico. For studies that contextualize the armed struggle and the civil war, see Fried and others; Jonas; Porpora (71, 83); Sanford (*Buried Secrets*); Schirmer (*The Guatemalan Military Project*); Schlesinger and Kinzer.

24. This information is available online, for instance, at http://www.gwu.edu/~nsarchiv/NSAEBB/NSAEBB15/01-41.html. See also Montenegro (9). I thank Mayari de León for providing additional details about the disappearance of her father.

25. The Committed Generation in Guatemala emerged in the 1950s after the CIA's intervention in Arbenz Guzmán's coup d'etat. Later, this generation of intellectuals saw in the Cuban Revolution a certain hope for an alternative political model based on socialism. Besides de León, this generation includes Otto René Castillo, Roberto Obregón, and Huberto Alvarado. Alvarado wrote the first important text (*Por un arte nacional, democrático y realista*) that sought to define a more militant role for the writer and artist in constructing a new nationalism in Guatemala.

26. Perhaps the literary text that best defines Dalton's ideas and those of Central America's Committed Generation would be his poem "Song to Our Position [Canto a nuestra posición]," which he dedicated to the memory of Otto René Castillo after his death. To access this poem, see http://www.literatura.us/roque/otros.html.

27. It is obvious that Dalton was unfamiliar with Asturias's relationship with some of the mili-

tants in the Guatemalan Workers Party (PGT) and the Revolutionary Armed Forces (FAR). As we know now, Asturias had consulted the PGT and the FAR before making his decision. The latter said that its struggles in Guatemala could find a voice through Asturias in Europe. For this particular information, see Asturias's own comments (*1899/1999: Vida, obra* 416–20) and the discussion developed by Julio César Macías in *La guerrilla fue mi camino: Epitafio para César Montes*. Furthermore, see Rodrigo Asturias's (son of Asturias) text "Dos puntualizaciones y una reflexión retrospectiva" (*1899/1999* 422–24).

28. Among other texts, see *Los zopilotes* and *Pájaro en mano*.

29. In 1954 Jacobo Arbenz Guzmán was removed from office after a military intervention supported by the CIA and led by General Castillo Armas. For a study that analyzes this particular event, see Schlesinger and Kinzer (*Bitter Fruit: The Story of the American Coup in Guatemala*).

30. Although *El tiempo* was published in 1985, it was actually written between 1970 and 1972. The Maya author did not live to see the publication of his only novel. Francisco Morales Santos says that he received the manuscript from Maria Tula, de Lión's widow. Tula says that de Lión had told her that if something happened to him, she should hand his writings to Morales Santos. The first edition of *El tiempo* was published in 1985 by Serviprensa Centroamericana, a year after de Lión's "disappearance." The second edition was published in 1996 by Artemis y Edinter. I use the second edition in this book's references.

31. See the studies of Arias ("Asomos de la narrativa indígena Maya"), Bubnova, Liano (*Visión crítica*), and Morales ("Luis de Lión, el indio por un indio").

32. See also Castellanos (23–28), who, despite a more rigorous reading of *El tiempo*, draws similar conclusions to those of Rodas.

33. The rape of the wooden Virgin of Concepción shows a striking similarity to a scene in Salvador Carrasco's film, *The Other Conquest*. The film begins with Motecuhzoma II's fictitious son, Topiltzin, being captured and punished by the Spanish conquistadores after they find him writing a codex to record the memory of the Nahuas and the brutality of the Spanish conquest. The Spanish let him live after his sister, who is having an affair with Hernán Cortés, intervenes. Topiltzin is later sent to a monastery in order to be Christianized. The film concludes with Topiltzin's conspiracy to steal the image of a Virgin that has been offered as a gift to Cortés. After contemplating it, Topiltzin takes the image to his room, and the next day, they find him dead on top of her.

34. This, obviously, would be the posture of a writer like Mario Vargas Llosa, who makes it explicit in his book, *La utopía arcaica: José María Arguedas y las ficciones del indigenismo*. José María Arguedas's books, Llosa writes, represented "a desperate nostalgia for a lost world that is ending, for the most part already destroyed" (*La utopía arcaica* 273).

35. In a conversation with de Lión's daughter, Mayarí de León, she told me that her father's personal library included Fanon's *The Wretched of the Earth* (alongside Asturias's *Men of Maize* and the *Popol Wuj*), with underlining of the text and annotations in the margins.

36. Francisco Morales Santos refers to this particular point. He writes that de Lión was conscious that "a writer who came from the countryside, like himself, writes a literature that will not be for the people about whom he writes," and, quoting de Lión, Morales Santos adds, "but for those who actually read it, that is, the bourgeois to whom literature relates" ("Luís de Lión" 32).

37. Juan León, a leader from the CUC and Defensoría Maya, capitalizes on this idea when he

talks about how the Accord on the Identity and Rights of Indigenous Peoples is the result of efforts by Mayas who participated in both the armed struggle and the popular movement: "Indigenous peoples have taken advantage of the spaces they occupied in the guerrilla army and the popular movement. They have been able to gain experience and reinforce their vindication because the majority of people in the popular movement now occupy the central roles of the indigenous movement today" (quoted in Heckt 55–56). Later he adds: "The fact that the guerrilla army fought for this accord is the most important step that we have taken...and the fact that the government that represents the State has recognized for the first time that there exists systematic discrimination against indigenous peoples and the cultural differences among peoples...is a great step forward, and it has set a precedent" (57).

Chapter 3
New Colonial and Anticolonial Histories

1. Stoll's book was originally published in 1999. For this chapter, the quotations I use come from the new edition (2008), which also includes a foreword by Elizabeth Burgos and an afterword by Stoll.

2. For the reader unfamiliar with Guatemala's recent history and the civil war that officially took place between 1960 and 1996, the conflict has its origins in the Cold War. It began with the overthrow of the democratically elected president Jacobo Arbenz Guzmán in 1954, orchestrated by General Castillo Armas and supported by the Central Intelligence Agency (CIA). After six years of "anti-communist" persecutions against those who had supported Arbenz, a group of nationalist officers declared war on the dictatorship of General Miguel Ydígoras Fuentes and "US imperialism" on November 13, 1960 (Schirmer, *The Guatemalan Military Project*). A long period of excessive violence, repression, impunity, and violations of human rights carried out by the Guatemalan army began, affecting several sectors of civil society, including intellectuals, students, peasant leaders, and indigenous activists. The state became militarized, and Guatemala did not see democratic elections again until 1986. In terms of the rebel groups, after the first uprising in November, in 1962 there emerged the Revolutionary Armed Forces (FAR), a coalition of ex-military officers, intellectuals, students, and peasants who concentrated their fight in the Peten region in northern Guatemala. In the 1970s other rebel groups became public, including the Guerrilla Army of the Poor (EGP), whose popular base was located in Huehuetenango, and the Organization of the People in Arms (ORPA), located in the western region of the country, especially in San Marcos. In 1982 these organizations received the public support of the Guatemala's Workers Party (PGT), which later led to their unification under the banner of the Guatemalan National Revolutionary Unity (URNG). Nevertheless, by 1982 these organizations had been hit hard by the Guatemalan army, to the point that they had to leave unprotected large sectors of the population that lent them support. Thousands of peasants were assassinated, especially in 1982–1983. Under General Ríos Montt's military strategy "Bullets and Beans," the army attacked rural peoples, especially Maya, who were considered "subversive." For many, this short period is remembered as the "Maya Holocaust." The bibliography about the civil war in Guatemala is extensive, but the *must read* studies are *Guatemala, memoria del silencio* (Guatemala, Memory of Silence) and *Guatemala, Never Again* (Proyecto Interdiocesano Recuperación de la Memoria Histórica).

3. From now on, I will refer to this organization as *EGP*.

4. Menchú's narrative has been considered a testimonio, which is, according to John Beverley's definition, "a novel- or novella-length narrative in book or pamphlet...told in the first person by a narrator who is also a real protagonist or witness of the event he or she recounts, and whose unit of narration is usually a 'life' or a significant life experience" (*Against Literature* 70). Testimonio as a genre has ignited a long range of discussions and debates in its own right. See Beverley (*Against Literature, Subalternity and Representation, Testimonio*); Beverley and Achugar; Carey-Webb and Benz; Gugelberger (*The Real Thing*); Jara and Vidal.

5. For the Menchú–Stoll controversy, see Arias (*The Rigoberta Menchú Controversy*); Forster; Morales (*Stoll–Menchú*); Rus; Sanford ("From *I, Rigoberta*," "The Silencing"); Schirmer ("Whose Testimony?").

6. By *Guevarismo*, he means narratives that promote guerrilla insurgency based on the *foco* ideology. "Foquismo," as we know it, was developed by Ernesto "Che" Guevara. It is based on a "vanguard" movement that is to lead the people in their struggle for liberation. Their rebellion, according to Guevara, springs from the basic needs of peasants and is supposed to raise a collective political consciousness that will later strengthen support for socialism. Stoll interprets Menchú's narrative as articulating Guevara's ideology and endorsing the EGP (*Story of All Poor Guatemalans* 9).

7. For studies that focus on Guatemala's Maya movement, see note 6 in the introduction.

8. One of the reports published by the Guatemalan Commission for Historical Clarification (CEH) states that during the war, 626 villages were destroyed; more than 200,000 people were executed or "disappeared"; about 1.5 million people were displaced by the violence; and more than 150,000 people went into exile in Mexico (Sanford, "From *I, Rigoberta*" 29). The CEH confirmed its conclusions based on the work of Monsignor Juan José Gerardi, who started a collective project called Recovery of the Historical Memory (REMHI). The project collected six thousand testimonios of war survivors in Guatemala and found that, during the civil war, the Guatemalan army committed 90 percent of the killings and the guerrillas, 6 percent. This was later confirmed by the CEH, which added four thousand more accounts of survivors. This commission, authorized by the Peace Accords committee, corroborated REMHI's statistics about the killings. Significantly, these works also concluded that such killings were "acts of genocide" against the Maya population. See *Comisión para el Esclarecimiento Histórico*.

9. From now on, I will use *CUC* to refer to this organization.

10. The book was awarded the prestigious Cuban literary prize Casa de las Américas in 1983.

11. *I, Rigoberta Menchú* also generated a series of debates and controversies about multiculturalism and the so-called cultural wars in the United States. For instance, in the book *Illiberal Education: The Politics of Race and Sex on Campus*, Dinesh D'Souza dedicates an entire chapter ("Travels with Rigoberta") to Menchú's testimonio. For a discussion on these debates, see Bell-Villada; Beverley (*Against Literature*, especially his first chapter); Pratt.

12. See the response to Stoll's book by the editors of Verso (the publisher of *I, Rigoberta Menchú*), "The Attack on Rigoberta Menchú," available at http://www.versobooks.com/verso_info/menchu.shtml.

13. For example, Menchú participated in a presidential forum with Guatemala ex-presidents Jorge Serrano Elías and Ramiro de León Carpio. She demanded that they not only recognize Mayas' participation and prominence in Guatemala's history but also admit the state's historic violation of indigenous peoples' human rights. See Zimmerman's "Rigoberta Menchú after the Nobel" (114–17).

14. See Menchú's "Rigoberta Menchú's Open Letter to George W. Bush" and also her texts on the Elían González incident ("Por Elían, por la justicia" 154) and her *Rebelión* discussion of Algeria's Saharaui refugees.

15. One of the most significant contributions of *I, Rigoberta Menchú* has been its enrichment of the discussions on testimonio in the US academy. See the bibliography in note 11.

16. Stoll reaffirms this point when he says, "Rigoberta's story is not a fabrication. A substantial portion of her family and village was in fact murdered" (*Story of All Poor Guatemalans* 300).

17. See Stoll's earlier work *Between Two Armies*.

18. Among the authors who discuss these issues are John Beverley, Carol Smith, George Lovell and Christopher Lutz, and Kay B. Warren. See their contributions in Arias's *The Rigoberta Menchú Controversy*.

19. From now on, I will use *INTA* to refer to this institution.

20. For a study that examines this particular incident in Stoll's book, see Arias's chapter "The Burning of the Spanish Embassy: Máximo Cajal vs. David Stoll" (*Taking Their Word*).

21. See Smith's "Why Write" and Warren's "Telling Truths" in Arias's *The Rigoberta Menchú Controversy*.

22. Although Said describes an East/West paradigm, his theoretical framework and conclusions may also be applied to a colonialist context in the North/South of the Americas.

23. The ideological tendencies expressed in the works of Child and Cooper are not limited to Stoll; they can also be related to some of the textual production in Latin America. In literature, for instance, Cooper's legacy is evidenced in Argentinian Domingo Faustino Sarmiento's *Facundo: Civilization and Barbarism*, in which blacks and Indians represent "barbarism." Sarmiento later put into practice his ideas about eliminating barbarism, when he became president (1869–1874). During that time, he carried out policies of removal and genocide against indigenous and black peoples in order to civilize Argentina and catch up with the United States: "Let's be America, like the sea is the ocean. Let's be the United States. [Seamos la América, como el mar es el Océano. Seamos Estados Unidos]" (Sarmiento, *Conflicto y armonía* 18). Cooper's and Child's ideologies also echo in the words of Peruvian novelist Mario Vargas Llosa, who writes of indigenous peoples in Peru: "If forced to choose between the preservation of Indian cultures and their complete assimilation, with great sadness I would choose modernization of the Indian population…modernization is possible only with the sacrifice of the Indian cultures" ("Questions of Conquest" 52–53).

24. This agenda is illustrated in Stoll's desire to reduce the authority of Menchú's narrative as a text that denounces colonialist and genocidal policies in Guatemala. Victor Montejo observes that, in a conference, Stoll was asked by a participant how, because Menchú's text has "problems of narration," can we use the text now? According to Montejo,

> Stoll said that he heard someone propose that the best way to teach it is to treat Menchú's biography as an epic novel. It is the truth, but mythologized, or call it a myth-history; we may treat the book as a collection of stories falling into the category of what Miguel Ángel Asturias called magical realism. I think this is a postmodern trick that will push back in time and make unreal the pain and suffering of the Mayans. Thus, it will be easy to forget that the reparation recommended by the truth commission has not yet been carried out. According to the epic approach, we can now read the Menchú book like *El poema de Mío Cid*, *Roldán*, or even the *Adventures of Don Quixote*. To imagine the recent Guatemalan holocaust as an epic is to remove ourselves from the reality of this genocide

that has left two hundred thousand deaths. (Montejo, Victor. "Truth, Human Rights, and Representation: The Case of Rigoberta Menchú." *The Rigoberta Menchú Controversy*. Arias 372–91)

Stoll's response evidences not a desire to confront the horrors of the war, but rather to reduce the force and agency of Menchú's testimonio regarding these issues.

25. For studies that focus on the relations between Guatemala and the United States, see Dunkerley; Fried; Porpora (71, 83); Schirmer (*The Guatemalan Military Project*); Schlesinger, Kinzer, and Coatsworth.

26. See Broder's "Clinton Offers His Apologies to Guatemala."

27. See Attwood; Attwood and Arnold; Castro-Gómez; Hinton (*Annihilating Difference: The Anthropology of Genocide* and *Genocide: An Anthropological Reader*); Lander (*La Colonialidad del saber*, especially the introduction); Mignolo (*Local Histories/Global Designs*); Said (*Culture and Imperialism, Orientalism*).

28. Besides Fabian, we can include revisionist approaches to the discourses of history and anthropology by Attwood; Attwood and Arnold; and Hinton.

29. See Stoll (*Rigoberta Menchú and the Story of All Poor Guatemalans* 138).

30. Two of the most important studies about this particular debate are Carlos Guzmán Böckler and Jean-Loup Herbert's *Guatemala: Una interpretación histórico-social* and Severo Martínez Peláez's *La patria del criollo*.

31. For a discussion about these debates, see Smith's "Introducción" to *Guatemalan Indians and the State* and Zimmerman's *Literature and Resistance in Guatemala*, Vol. I, especially 60–82.

32. See chapters 20, 21, 22, 24, and 31 of *I, Rigoberta Menchú*, in which she discusses these organizations and her formation as an activist.

33. The interview between Atxaga and Menchú in the first part of the book does not include page numbers. I therefore include my own numbering, which goes from 1 to 15. Menchú's poem "Patria abnegada [Denied Country]" would be page 1.

34. Even though *Rigoberta Menchú, la nieta de los mayas* has been published in English as *Crossing Borders*, I provide my own translations from the Spanish text because there are gaps in the English translation.

35. Feminism in Guatemala and the role of Maya women within this movement have been debated in the past decade. Such debates include perspectives different from those espoused here by Menchú. For these discussions, see "Los desafíos de la diversidad. Relaciones interétnicas: Identidad, género y justicia" and "Mujeres mayas abriendo caminos."

36. Friedan, or Friedman, was a well-known feminist who wrote, among other books, *The Feminine Mystique* and *It Changed My Life: Writings on the Women's Movement*.

37. Gramsci differentiated between "traditional" and "organic" intellectuals. The latter are those who have cultivated strong ties and political relations in their communities and combine political activism with their writings. Sometimes, "organic intellectual" also means one who does not know how to read or write but nonetheless participates in changing history through his or her struggle or protest. See Gramsci's first chapter, "Intellectuals."

38. Mario Roberto Morales (*La articulación*) provides a reading of *I, Rigoberta Menchú* as a text that represents what he calls "intercultural mestizaje": "Both Burgos' text and the collaborators, like Menchú's narrative, and its consequent synthesis are transcultured discourses. I insist in adding: mestizo discourses" (141). The intent of Morales's reading, however, can be interpreted

as a desire to establish his narrative in favor of transculturation and hybridity about Maya discourses. Contrary to this perspective, I would say that the first testimonio, just like the second one, is the result of intercultural relations, that is, the desire to show the coexistence of diverse people within a similar social context. For a discussion of the idea of "intercultural mestizaje" developed by Morales, see chapter 4.

39. Galeano, Beltran, and Ak'abal appear in the Spanish edition of the book, but not in the English one.

40. This tragedy is one of the most moving episodes in the text (*La nieta* 94–98). The massacre occurred in October 1995 after a group of Maya refugees returned to Guatemala in light of the peace dialogues. When they established themselves in Guatemalan territory, they were harassed by Guatemalan soldiers who interrupted a communal celebration. The army opened fire on them, killing ten people and injuring twenty-five.

41. Besides referring to the fax machine, on another occasion Menchú recommended that indigenous peoples appropriate technology and science to express their ideas and to spread their cultures:

> I believe that indigenous peoples should take advantage of and capture all the great values and discoveries of science and technology. There are great achievements reached by science and technology, and we cannot say, we indigenous peoples will not participate in these achievements. Because we cannot remain like isolated insects, immune to 500 years of history. No, we have been protagonists of history. We have also participated in these achievements. (Quoted in Brittin and Dworkin 212)

42. It should be mentioned that these approaches to "difference" are similar to those endorsed by the Zapatistas in southern Mexico in their struggle for a "world where many worlds fit." I analyze some of these ideas in chapter 4.

43. Let us remember her words:

> That is my cause. As I've already said, it wasn't born out of something good, it was born out of wretchedness and bitterness. It has been radicalized by the poverty in which my people live. It has been radicalized by the malnutrition which I, as an Indian, have seen and experienced. And by the exploitation and discrimination which I've felt in the flesh. And by the oppression which prevents us from performing our ceremonies and shows no respect for our way of life, the way we are…therefore, my commitment to our struggle knows no boundaries nor limits. This is why I've traveled to many places where I've had the opportunity to talk about my people. (Menchú and Burgos 246–47)

Chapter 4
Rethinking Modernity and Identity Politics in the Interethnic Debate in Guatemala

1. What is known as "neoliberalism" in Latin America has its origins in the "Washington Consensus" toward the end of the eighties. The economic discussions during this time dealt with finding ways to spread a new capitalist mode of production on a global scale. Modeled after the liberalism of the nineteenth century, institutions like the International Monetary Fund (IMF) and the World Bank (WB) in the United States spread the economic philosophy of development based on the "free" expansion of the markets, businesses, and capital by canceling governmental intervention and economic protections. This move gave way to competition between companies that proposed to offer basic services such as medicine, education, and electricity to the popula-

tions in the countries of the Third World, where their economic policies were approved by local governments. This model, then, is endorsed by transnational companies that hold large sums of capital and embrace economic policies based on "free" trade agreements such as the North American Free Trade Agreement, the Free Trade Agreement of the Americas, and, most recently, the Central American and Dominican Republic Free Trade Agreement. In my final reflections, I offer a brief analysis of the challenge that the Maya movement faces regarding these "free" trade agreements. In this chapter, I limit myself to addressing the cultural logics spread by globalization. For a study that discusses neoliberalism, see George, and for a discussion about globalization and neoliberalism in Central America, see Robinson, especially the section on "Transnational Elite Agenda" (50–54).

2. Neoliberalism, represented in free trade agreements, has encountered a resistance in Guatemala led by the National Coordinator of Peasant Organizations (CONIC). For a history of this organization's origins, see http://www.cnoc.org.gt/.

3. Perhaps the most representative text on this ideological tendency would be Severo Martínez Peláez's *La patria del criollo*, which argues that the existence of the "Indian" was a Spanish feudal legacy reinforced through a criollo agrarian economy. The differences between Indians and Ladinos were understood in ideological and economic terms.

4. The book that provided a new orientation was Carlos Guzmán Böckler and Jean-Loup Herbert's *Guatemala: Una interpretación histórico-social*. These authors questioned the articulatory limits of mestizaje in encompassing cultural and linguistic differences between Ladinos and indigenous peoples. They suggested that the Left needed to recognize those cultural and linguistic differences if it wanted to integrate indigenous peoples into its struggle. Also important is the crucial role Catholic Action played in this process by developing grassroots projects within indigenous communities, allowing them also to develop projects to revitalize indigenous cultural specificities and a political consciousness based on Liberation Theology. For studies that analyze these issues, see Arias (*Taking Their Word*, especially his chapter "Forever Menchú"); Beverley and Zimmerman; Falla; Smith (*Guatemalan Indians and the State*, "Maya Nationalism"); Zimmerman (*Literature and Resistance*).

5. Two Internet sites where one can find several articles by the authors involved in the interethnic debate in Guatemala are Carlos Mendoza's blog, "Democracia Multicultural," at http://democraciamulticultural.blogspot.com/ and *Alberdio: Revista electrónica de discusión y propuesta social* at http://www.albedrio.org/. To access the electronic sites of the Guatemalan newspapers, follow their respective links: *Prensa Libre* at http://www.prensalibre.com, *Siglo veintiuno* at http://www.sigloxxi.com, *El periódico* at http://www.elperiodico.com.gt, and *La hora* at http://www.lahora.com.gt/.

6. A concept that is analogous to that of Canclini's and Morales's hybridity has been developed by one of the most well-known critics of postcolonial studies, Homi Bhabha. His idea of hybridity recognizes a "third space" that helps to transcend the "exoticism of cultural diversity" or "multi-culturalism" in the formation of an internationalist culture. Bhabha points out:

> It is significant that the productive capacities of this Third Space have a colonial or post-colonial provenance. For a willingness to descend into that alien territory— where I have led you—may reveal that the theoretical recognition of the split-space of enunciation may open the way to conceptualizing an *inter*-national culture, based not on the exoticism or multi-culturalism of the *diversity* of cultures, but on the inscription and articulation of culture's *hybridity*" (38).

7. For the Peace Accords, see note 4 in the introduction.

8. In a different register, historian Greg Grandin develops a similar questioning of Maya intellectuals as elitist. See Grandin, especially his conclusion.

9. Morales deepens this argument, with the same conclusions discussed here, in his essay "El neomacartismo estalinista (o la cacería de brujas en la academia 'posmo')."

10. The ballet-drama *Rabinal Achi* (Maya K'iche' for *Man of Rabinal*) is a text that traces its origins to the pre-Columbian Maya world. The ballet-drama presents the conflict in the K'iche' city of Rabinal between Rabinal Achi and the town leader's son, Cawek, a rebel who has brought much pain to the village. Cawek challenges Rabinal to a battle and loses. He accepts his defeat with pride and dies decapitated. This ballet-drama is performed annually in various highland towns of Guatemala.

11. Cojtí uses a similar logic of authenticity when he defines the "Maya People" through their languages. He writes: "By *Maya People* it is understood the ethnic collective members of the *Maya linguistic family*, a concept that not only wants to include Mayas that live in Guatemala but also those who were ceded or remained under the jurisdiction of other states" (*El movimiento Maya* 15, emphasis added). This understanding, however, does not include Mayas who have lost their native language because of assimilative educational policies but nevertheless identify themselves as Maya.

12. We find a similar position to that of Cojtí in the Maya *qa'anjob'al* writer Gaspar Pedro González. When talking about oral Maya tradition, he says that it has

> been defended and preserved carefully in the minds of the members of society, preserved against all danger, knowing that dominant culture has tried to cancel it. But for more than twenty-five katuns, it has survived in practice, within the intimacy of the community, when surrounded by a bonfire. *There, in the faraway village with no electricity and with no mass media social communication*, the family or young people gather together to listen to the guardians of the popular wisdom narrate their ancestral stories, tales, myths, and fables, which will soon be carried out to other corners of the community by these skillful narrators responsible for perpetuating the literature of their elders. (*Kotz'ib', Nuestra literatura* 103, emphasis added)

As can be seen, González, like Cojtí, defines an authenticity that remains alive in the rural areas in which "electricity" and "mass media social communication" are absent.

13. For a critique of *Hybrid Cultures* and other texts by Canclini, see Beverley (*Subalternity and Representation*), especially chapter 5; Joshua Lund, especially his introduction. For a critique about the "cult of mestizaje," see Millar.

14. I borrow the notion of "transculturation from below" from Beverley (*Subalternity and Representation*). See note 13 in chapter 2.

15. Recently, and in some way similar to Morales's critique, Ak'abal was attacked by the novelist Marco Antonio Flores, who suggested that Ak'abal's rejection of the 2004 national literary prize (Miguel Ángel Asturias) was a conscious, indigenous, anti-Ladino conspiracy. See Flores's "El montaje del farsante [The Staging of the Deceiver]," I–IV.

16. I analyze the education discourse in Guatemala in chapter 5.

17. Marilyn G. Millar has a very interesting study about "the cult of Mestizaje" in Latin America. She offers a rigorous analysis of the origin and history of the term, its discursive variations, and how it continues to be recycled as a rhetoric tool in the present. The study by Morales, in its effort to propose mestizaje as the only way to vindicate a cultural and national identity, enters in the discussion elaborated by Millar. See her epilogue.

18. For a discussion about these debates between Maya culturales and populares, see Bastos and Camus (*Abriendo caminos*); Cojtí (*El movimiento Maya*); Fischer and Brown; Hale (*Más que un Indio*); Montejo (*Maya Intellectual Renaissance*); Nelson; Warren (*Indigenous Movements and Their Critics*).

19. Sam Colop is Maya K'iche' and writes an opinion column titled "Ucha'xik" (the word derives from the K'iche' verb *cha'*, which means "to say"; *Ucha'xik* is the passive form of the verb and literally means "his saying") for the newspaper *Prensa Libre*, one of the most popular in Guatemala. His opinion column criticizes what he considers racist perspectives and colonialist policies against Mayas.

20. Zapeta was a student of Robert Carmack at the University of Albany, New York. Carmack has done extensive studies about Maya K'iche' people. Among his books we can mention *Rebels of Highland Guatemala: The Quiché-Mayas of Momostenango* and *The Quiché Mayas of Utatlán: The Evolution of a Highland Guatemala Kingdom*.

21. For a study that talks about this bourgeois Maya class in Quetzaltenango, see Grandin; Velásquez Nimatuj.

22. For Zapeta, this cultural and linguistic reaffirmation should be materialized through an educational project that "takes into account the language and culture of indigenous communities at all levels and as an initial instrument of the educational process. This model does not deny the Spanish dialect, but rather it incorporates it as a second language in order to avoid the semi-linguistic limitations in which we have fallen in Guatemala" (*Las huellas* 179). Zapeta then adds that, with "this model, the mother language would not be just a *transitional* instrument, but rather it would represent a medium for the positive self-esteem of the student, who, in turn, would make the educational experience effective, efficient and in accordance with the social context" (179).

23. Kay B. Warren has justified the movement's effort to focus on racism rather than on class. She suggests that Mayas aim to "radically reconfigure who is to blame for a social critique. For them [Mayas], Ladino peasants, urban migrants and working classes are implicated with the elites in reproducing a prejudice that has had a destructive effect in daily life. A large number of 'public' institutions are also implicated" (*Indigenous Movements* 50). In this sense, according to Warren, for all Mayas it is about bringing into light the latent racism in order to open a debate about indigenous rights and participation in discussions about the nation.

24. In terms of this discussion, we can also turn to Michael Taussig's *The Devil and Commodity Fetishism*. In this study, he focuses on the consequences of introducing a capitalist mode of production in societies that still hold indigenous exchange values. The relevance of Taussig's study in regards to Zapeta is that the former is interested in interrogating those who interpret precapitalist social formations as being similar to, or copies of, a modern capitalist economic system. See especially Taussig's chapters 3 and 4.

25. Zapeta has been criticized by other Mayas in Guatemala, not only for embracing neoliberalism but also for not endorsing the adoption of Convention 169 of the International Labor Organization, concerning indigenous and tribal peoples in independent countries. In his article "El derecho a una respuesta [The Right to a Response]," Zapeta includes Máximo Abraham Ba Tul's opinion of this decision. Ba Tul wrote the following to him: "Much sadness is felt...when we get to know that there are Maya brothers who lend themselves to these games, and continue serving the interests of a hegemonic class that has the political and economic power in our country, at the price of the suffering and sweat of the poor and oppressed people" (Zapeta, *Las huellas* 65).

26. For a discussion about the category of "Indio permitido" (permitted Indian), see Hale and Millamán (284–88).

27. I have in mind anti-globalization movements like the one in Seattle in 1999, indigenous movements in the Andes, Zapatismo, and the Landless Workers Movement in Brazil. In the academic terrain, it is important to note the contributions made by the Subaltern Studies Group in Asia and Latin America, postcolonial studies, and the textual critical production of intellectuals such as Edward Said, V. Y. Mudimbe, and Mahmood Mamdani. In Latin America, I can also mention the works of Enrique Dussel ("Eurocentrism and Modernity"), Aníbal Quijano ("'Raza,' 'etnia' y 'nación'"; "Coloniality and Modernity/Rationality"; "Coloniality of Power"), Silvia Rivera Cusicanqui and Rossana Barragán, and Edgardo Lander ("Modernidad, colonialidad y posmodernidad").

Chapter 5
Toward an Intercultural Education and Citizenship

1. For a discussion about the Educational Reform and the Peace Accords in Guatemala, see Cojtí ("Educational Reform") and Heckt.

2. The illiteracy rate in the past decade in Guatemala is, according to official records, 35 percent (Programa 32). I put the word *illiteracy* in quotation marks in order to reference the definition used by Denise Arnold and Juan de Dios Yapita in their book about textual struggles in Bolivia (20). According to these authors, the characteristic of "illiteracy" has been ascribed to a person who has not attended school and has not acquired the Western system of reading and writing. However, this does not mean that the person lacks knowledge, nor ways of exchanging it with others, but rather his system of knowledge has not been recognized within the dominant society.

3. The studies of Michel Foucault about how power is reproduced have been the cornerstone of postmodern and postcolonial schools. His studies have been adopted by Edward Said, who has made valuable contributions concerning the reproduction of Eurocentric ideologies that construct knowledge about an "other" in order to domesticate and dominate him. See Foucault; Foucault and Gordon; Said (*Orientalism*). See also John Beverley (*Subalternity*), who argues that higher education is an institution that continues recycling an epistemology that maintains subalternity. See especially his first chapter.

4. The study by Serge Gruzinski, *Images at War*, describes other mechanisms the West has used to colonize indigenous peoples. Gruzinski explores the role that image played in the campaigns to Christianize, assimilate, and nationalize indigenous peoples in Mexico from the colonial period up to the twentieth century. For a discussion of the colonialist role of the "image" in Gruzinski, see the second section of chapter 2 and my discussion of de Lión's *El tiempo principia en Xibalbá*.

5. Some studies that I consider significant about the discourse of education and its intimate relationship to the status quo are Paulo Freire's *Pedagogía del oprimido* (Pedagogy of the Oppressed), Martin Carnoy's *Education as Cultural Imperialism*, Adriana Puiggrós's *Imperialismo y educación en América Latina*, and John Willinsky's *Learning to Divide the World*. In addition, we can include the theoretical discussion developed by Pierre Bourdieu in *The Logic of Practice*, which coins the category of "cultural capital" in the development of a nationalist educational curriculum. See especially his chapter "Modes of Domination." In Guatemala, some important contributions include the studies published by the Association for the Advancement of the Social Sciences in Guatemala (AVANCSO). Also, see *Imágenes homogéneas en un país de rostros diversos* and Maike Heckt's *Guatemala: Pluralidad, educación y relaciones de poder*.

6. On this topic, see Gruzinski (*La colonización de lo imaginario* and *Images at War*). These experiences have been presented in films also. Salvador Carrasco's *The Other Conquest*, for instance, begins with the violent aggression by Spanish soldiers against Topiltzin, the son of Motecuhzoma II. Topiltzin denounces the Spaniards' brutality in a codex and attempts to preserve the Nahuas' memory. After being captured by the Spaniards, Topiltzin is spared execution, thanks to his sister, who is Hernán Cortés's lover. His "salvation," though, consists of being "educated" by the Spanish priests, who try to eradicate the idolatry and barbarism of the Indians.

7. What de Gante narrates resembles other colonizing practices in the hemisphere. The English, for instance, sent children and youths to Europe to be educated and, upon their return, made them participate in the colonizing processes. See Noriega (380–81).

8. See, for instance, Arze Quintanilla (19–25) and Klor de Alva.

9. Carlos Newland writes that education served to "illuminate and civilize populations" and was "offered to women because, without her improvement, their kids would not be improved. In general, civilization was a synonym of diligence and political stability, and barbarism of laziness and anarchy. From here education would serve to better the economic productivity and the adaptation of the individual to society" (337).

10. The Guatemalan government during this period even proposed the following: "It will be awarded by the Government a gold medal of merit to any individual or foreigner that during this year of 1836 presents the best system or method to civilize and provide elementary education, and with it, the knowledge of the Spanish language, to indigenous peoples" (*Imágenes* 19).

11. These violent civilizing practices through boarding schools have also been exposed in films. We can mention two that were based on concrete experiences. *The Education of Little Tree*, based on the novel with the same title, was written by Forrest Carter and published in 1976. The film and the novel tell the story of a Native American child who is separated from his family to be "educated" and "civilized" in a boarding school. Another film is *Rabbit-Proof Fence*, which is based on the testimonial narrative of Molly Craig, an aboriginal woman from Australia. The film narrates the story of three aboriginal children who escape a governmental camp that "domesticates" and "educates" aboriginal workers in order to integrate them into the dominant society. In literature, these experiences have also been represented by indigenous writers such as José María Arguedas in *Deep Rivers* and Gaspar Pedro González in *A Mayan Life*.

12. The category of "internal colonialism" in Latin America has its origins in the 1970s with Pablo Gonzalez Casanova's "Sociedad plural, colonialismo interno y desarrollo" and Rodolfo Stavenhagen's "La dinámica de las relaciones interétnicas: Clases, colonialismo y aculturación." According to Gonzalez Casanova, internal colonialism "corresponds to a social structure based on domination and exploitation between internally heterogeneous and distinct groups...it is the cultural heterogeneity that historically produces the conquest of people by other people, and that allows us to speak not only of cultural differences (that exist between urban and rural populations and in social classes), but also of the differences of civilization" (Cardoso and Weffort 176). Gail Kelly and Philip G. Altbach describe internal colonialism as the control of an independent group over another independent group within a nation (3). In our case, we can say that we are talking about the hegemonic control of mestizos or Ladinos over indigenous peoples.

13. For the directors of this project, an "authentic Indian" was a person who did not speak Spanish, wore sandals and "traditional" clothes, and lived in rural areas.

14. The case of Mexico is very interesting because it allows us to extract important lessons. Besides internal colonialism of the indigenous people, there exists an imperialist educational

project. In 1924 Robert Lansing, secretary of state under US president Woodrow Wilson, made reference to the educational project needed to "dominate" Mexico:

> Mexico is an extraordinarily easy country to dominate, as it is necessary to control only one man: the President. We must abandon the idea of installing an American citizen in the Mexican presidency, as that would only lead us, once again, to war. The solution requires more time: we must open the doors of our universities to young, ambitious Mexicans and make the effort to educate them in the American way of life, in our values, and in respect for the leadership of the United States. Mexico will need competent administrators, and over time, these young people will come to occupy important positions and will eventually take possession of the presidency itself. And without the United States having to spend a single cent or fire a single shot, they will do what we want, and do it better and more radically than we ourselves would have done. (*Construyendo alternativas* 49–50)

These words seem to be inspired by Thomas B. Macaulay's 1835 text "Minute on Indian Education." He maintained that the English, after colonizing India, should do the following:

> We must at present do our best to form a class who may be interpreters between us and the millions whom we govern; a class of persons, Indian in blood and colour, but English in taste, in opinions, in morals, and in intellect. To that class we may leave it to refine the vernacular dialects of the country, to enrich those dialects with terms of science borrowed from the Western nomenclature, and to render them by degrees fit vehicles for conveying knowledge to the great mass of the population. (Macaulay 430)

15. There are many indigenous parents who encourage their children to learn Spanish or English instead of their native language so that their kids can have better job opportunities in the labor market. For a discussion about this topic and "ambivalent subjects" who bet on education as a mechanism for cultural affirmation, see *Imágenes homogéneas*.

16. Ernesto Barnach-Calbó Martínez makes reference to bilingual education programs in Mexico, Guatemala, and Bolivia. These programs use "indigenous languages as a bridge for faster, effective and less traumatic learning of Spanish and assigned courses. The knowledge of the official language is obtained, definitely, sacrificing the mother language since its final goal is neither bilingualism nor the acceptance of linguistic and cultural pluralism, but rather the cultural homogenization through other means, just like the projects in that field operated in the US" (Barnach-Calbó Martínez 23–24).

17. For studies that discuss these experiences, see Fischer and Brown (especially the introduction and the chapter by Warren, 89–106); Heckt (35–81); Moya (152, n. 16).

18. The Educational Reform is the collective work of the Parity Commission for Educational Reform (COPARE), formed in April 1997. From its beginnings, COPARE was composed of ten members: five delegates from the government and five members from indigenous organizations. Eventually, COPARE became the Consultative Commission for Educational Reform (CCRE). The CCRE included diverse members who represented civil society. Its responsibility, among others, was to fix the guidelines for the realization of the Educational Reform at a national level, advise the Ministry of Education in the process, and establish mechanisms of educational procedures. This institution was made official in 1997 with a legal validation that was based on the Accord on Identity and the Rights of Indigenous Peoples (1995).

19. For a discussion about these challenges and the context in which the Educational Reform emerges, see Cojtí's "Educational Reform in Guatemala."

20. After the Peace Accords, the production of texts in indigenous languages, such as grammars and dictionaries, ignited debates about the standardization of Maya languages. Much of the textual production from the Academy of Maya Languages of Guatemala was challenged by the Linguistic Project Francisco Marroquín (PLFM), which began to develop its own books to revitalize indigenous languages.

21. This project failed after one year. According to some teachers, the government did not offer enough incentives for them to participate. Others spoke of disorganization in the program to prepare teachers. In a strike led by the Guatemalan Teachers Union that lasted a little more than three months in 2003, the cancellation of this project was one of the teachers' demands.

22. From now on, I will use *DIGEBI* to make reference to this institution.

23. Bilingual Intercultural Education came into existence because of the necessity of providing leading spaces for indigenous peoples. Indigenous movements in the Andean and Mesoamerican regions have occupied a central role in these policies. See Arnold and Yapita; Heckt; López; Moya.

24. See the first section of this chapter and the chapters that focus on Asturias (2), Stoll (3), and Morales (4).

25. See Álvarez Medrano and others, especially pages 7–9 and 21–24.

26. The definition of cultural relativism is provided by Anne-Katrin Eckermann, who writes: "A culture cannot be better than another one, a culture cannot be superior to another one" (3).

27. Otilia Lux de Cotí is a recognized Maya activist and leader who participated in the Commission for Historical Clarification (CEH) in Guatemala, an institution that investigated and identified human rights violations during the civil war. Similar to Cojtí, her legitimacy as a representative of the Maya movement crumbled when she accepted the job of minister of culture and sports with the government of Alfonso Portillo (2000–2004), one of whose leaders was General Efraín Ríos Montt. See note 2 in chapter 3 for additional information on Ríos Montt.

28. We find similar attitudes in *Prensa Libre*'s 2004 discussions about opening a "Maya University" ("Universidad Maya, idea controversial" and "Universidad Maya, una universidad para todos"). It is suggested, for instance, that teaching classes in Maya languages "complicates the enrollment of teachers" and "can be interpreted as a way to separate Maya students from Ladinos." To these charges, the Association of University Students responded that the Maya University should be for everyone, not just indigenous peoples.

29. Demetrio Cojtí talks about this Ladino problem in his discussion of the Educational Reform and the limits of the Peace Accords ("Educational Reform in Guatemala"). He says that government officials in Alvaro Arzú's administration resisted the project of national bilingual intercultural education. According to Cojtí, they said that only indigenous peoples themselves could deal with their own problems, which were local, not national (109). On another occasion, Cojtí writes that non-Mayas "are in need of interculturality because they turn their back on everything that is indigenous. They do not want to accept it. They reject it and disqualify it" (Heckt 129). In addition, see Heckt's discussion of intercultural education, pages 127–44.

Chapter 6
Conclusion: Final Thoughts

1. See Velásquez Nimatuj for a study that talks about the socioeconomic differences between Maya people and the "Maya bourgeoisie" in Quetzaltenango as the result of a stratification created by the implementation of capitalist policies at the end of the nineteenth century.

2. For these quotations, see "TLC para los más pobres. Promesa: Presidentes centroamericanos pidieron protección de sectores a EE.UU." (2003).

3. The incident about the approval of the free trade agreement between the United States and Costa Rica is a good example of this. According to the media, a secret memo made its way into the public sphere indicating the ways certain official authorities should be "persuaded" to approve the treaty. The scandal forced Minister of Exterior Relations Kevin Casas Zamora, who wrote the memo, to resign. For additional information about CAFTA and this particular incident, see http://www.nocafta.org.

4. Here, I am making reference to the World Trade Organization's (WTO) meetings in September 2003 in Cancún, Mexico, where several countries involved in the talks about the implementation of ALCA decided not to approve the agreement. Caribbean countries, such as the Dominican Republic, declared that the way ALCA was structured would cause catastrophic consequences for the Third World. For these discussions, see González Amador and Rosa Elvira Vargas.

5. As William I. Robinson suggests, the integration of Central America in the capitalist system has its origins in the colonial period. The capitalist logic was again adopted during the independence through liberalism, and now it continues with the free trade agreements. Robinson writes: "The region's insertion [in the capitalist system] was further deepened and transformed in the twentieth century, and particularly in the post–World War II period, with the expansion of agro-exports and Import-Substitution Industrialization (ISI), through the Central American Common Market (CACM). Since the 1970s what has transpired is a transition to a qualitatively different mode of insertion corresponding to globalization" (64).

6. See Ramírez, Sandoval, and Rodríguez. The popular protests during Vicente Fox's visit to Guatemala were led by the National Coordinator of Peasant Organizations (CONIC). For a history of this organization's origins, see http://www.cnoc.org.gt/.

References

1899/1999: Vida, obra y herencia de Miguel Angel Asturias. Madrid; Nanterre: ALLCA XX; Université Paris, UNESCO Editions, 1999.

Adams, David Wallace. *Education for Extinction: American Indians and the Boarding School Experience, 1875–1928.* Lawrence: UP of Kansas, 1995.

———. "The Federal Indian Boarding School: A Study of Environment and Response, 1879–1918." Diss. Indiana U, 1975.

Adams, Richard, and Santiago Bastos. *Las relaciones étnicas en Guatemala, 1944–2000.* Guatemala: CIRMA, 2003.

Adorno, Rolena. "Reconsidering Colonial Discourse for Sixteenth- and Seventeenth-Century Spanish America." *Latin American Research Review* 26.3 (1991): 135–45.

Aguirre Beltrán, Gonzalo. *Obra antropológica X: Teoría y practica de la educación indígena.* 1973. México: Fondo de Cultura Económica, 1992.

Ak'abal, Humberto. *Guardían de la caída del agua.* Guatemala: Artemis y Edinter, 1996.

———. *Raqonchi'aj/Grito.* Guatemala: Cholsamaj, 2004.

Althusser, Louis. *Lenin and Philosophy, and Other Essays.* New York: Monthly Review, 1971.

Alvarado, Huberto. *Por un arte nacional, democrático y realista.* Guatemala: Ediciones Saker-ti, 1953.

Álvarez Medrano, Flor de Maria, Pedro Guoron Ajquijay, and David Tirado Romero. *Del pensamiento a la palabra: De la palabra al desarrollo: Idiomas Mayas y desarrollo social.* Guatemala: ESEDIR and Mayab' Saqarib'al; Editorial Saqil Tzij, 1996.

Ament, Gail R. "The Postcolonial Mayan Scribe: Contemporary Indigenous Writers of Guatemala." Diss. U of Washington, 1998.

Amin, Samir. "¿Globalización o apartheid a escala global?" World Conference on Racism. Durban. 28 Aug.–1 Sept. 2001. Lecture. 15 July 2002. <http://www.nodo50.org/csca>.

Amurrio González, Jesús Julián. *El positivismo en Guatemala.* Guatemala: U de San Carlos de Guatemala, 1970.

Anderson, Benedict R. *Imagined Communities: Reflections on the Origin and Spread of Nationalism.* London; New York: Verso, 1991.

Appleton, Nicholas. *Cultural Pluralism in Education: Theoretical Foundations.* New York: Longman, 1983.

Arango, Luis Alfredo. "Jose Luis de Leon Diaz: El maestro." *Conversatorio: Homenaje imaginario a la obra literaria de Luis de Lión.* 19–22.

Arguedas, Alcides. *Pueblo enfermo: Contribución a la psicología de los pueblos Hispano-Americanos.* Barcelona: Vda. de Luis Tasso, 1910.

———. *Raza de bronce.* La Paz: Gonzalez y Medina, 1919.

Arguedas, José María. *Deep Rivers.* Trans. Frances Horning Barraclough. Austin: U of Texas P, 1978.

———. *Tupac Amaru kamaq taytanchisman; Haylli-Taki. Canto a nuestro padre creador Tupac Amaru; Himno-Canción.* Lima: Ediciones Salqantay, 1962.

Arias, Arturo. "Asomos de la narrativa indígena Maya." *El tiempo principia en Xibalbá.* By Luis de Lión. Guatemala: Artemis y Edinter, 1996. i–vii.

———. "Descolonizando el conocimiento, reformulando la textualidad: Repensando el papel de la narrativa centroamericana." *Revista de Crítica Literaria Latinoamericana* 21.42 (1995): 73–86.

———. *La identidad de la palabra: Narrativa guatemalteca del siglo veinte.* Guatemala: Artemis y Edinter, 1998.

———. "La literatura, la problemática étnica y la articulación de discursos nacionales en Centroamérica." *Istmo* 8 (enero–junio 2004). 15 de junio de 2004. <http://www.denison.edu/collaborations/istmo/articulos/literariedad.html>.

———, ed. *The Rigoberta Menchú Controversy.* Minneapolis: U of Minnesota P, 2001.

———. *Taking Their Word: Literatura and the Signs of Central America.* Minneapolis; London: U of Minnesota P, 2007.

Arnedo, Miguel. "Arte Blanco con Motivos Negros: Fernando Ortiz's Concept of Cuban National Culture and Identity." *Bulletin of Latin American Research* 20.1 (2001): 88–101.

Arnold, Denise, and Juan de Dios Yapita. *The Metamorphosis of Heads: Textual Struggles, Education, and Land in the Andes.* Pittsburgh: Pittsburgh UP, 2006.

Arze Quintanilla, Oscar. "Del indigenismo a la indianidad: Cincuenta años de indigenismo continental." *Indianismo e indigenismo en América.* Comp. José Alcina Franch. Madrid: Alianza Editorial, 1990. 18–33.

Ashcroft, Bill, Gareth Griffiths, and Helen Tiffin. *Post-colonial Studies: Key Concepts.* London; New York: Routledge, 2000.

———. *The Post-colonial Studies Reader.* London; New York: Routledge, 1994.

Asturias, Miguel Ángel. *The Eyes of the Interred.* New York: Delacorte, 1973.

———. *The Green Pope.* New York: Delacorte, 1971.

———. *Guatemalan Sociology: The Social Problem of the Indian.* 1923. Trans. Maureen Ahren. Introd. Richard J. Callan. Tempe: Arizona State UP, 1977.

———. *Hombres de maíz (edición crítica).* Ed. Gerald Martin. Nanterre: ALLCA XX; Université Paris X Centre de recherches Latino-Américaines, 1992.

———. *Men of Maize, Critical Edition.* 1949. Trans. Gerald Martin. Pittsburgh: U of Pittsburgh P, 1994.

———. *El Señor Presidente.* Coord. Gerald Martin. Barcelona; Nanterre: Galaxia Gutenberg; ALLCA XX, 2000.

———. *Strong Wind.* New York: Delacorte, 1968.

———. "La tesis." *1899/1999: Vida, obra y herencia de Miguel Ángel Asturias.* Madrid; Nanterre: ALLCA XX; Université Paris, UNESCO Editions, 1999. 136–39.

Attwood, Bain, ed. *In the Age of Mabo: History, Aborigines, and Australia.* St Leonards: Allen and Unwin, 1996.

Attwood, Bain, and John Arnold, eds. *Power, Knowledge, and Aborigines.* Bundoora: La Trobe UP; National Centre for Australian Studies, Monash U, 1992.

Bardacke, Frank, and Leslie López, eds. *Shadows of Tender Fury: The Letters and Communiques of Subcomandante Marcos and the Zapatista National Liberation Army.* New York: Monthly Review Press, 1995.

Barnach-Calbó Martínez, Ernesto. "La nueva educación indígena en Iberoamérica." *Revista Iberoamericana de Educación* 13 (1997): 13–33.

Barrios de Chungara, Domitila, and Moema Viezzer. *Let Me Speak! Testimony of Domitila, A Woman of the Bolivian Mines.* 1977. Trans. Victoria Ortíz. New York; London: Monthly Review, 1978.

Bartra, Armando. "Mitos en la aldea global." *La Guillotina* 38 (verano 1998): 38–41.

Bastos, Santiago, and Manuela Camus. *Abriendo caminos: Las organizaciones Mayas desde el Nobel hasta el Acuerdo de Derechos Indígenas.* Guatemala: FLACSO, 1995.

———. *Quebrando el silencio: Organizaciones del pueblo Maya y sus demandas (1986–1992).* Guatemala: FLACSO, 1993.

Beckett, Jeremy, ed. *Past and Present: The Construction of Aboriginality.* Canberra: Aboriginal Studies, 1988.

Bell-Villada, Gene H. "Why Dinesh D'Souza Has It In for Rigoberta Menchú." *Teaching and Testimony: Rigoberta Menchú and the North American Classroom.* Carey-Webb and Benz 50–51.

Bello, Vicente. "Entre 'castilla' y popolca, la escuela indígena atrapada." *Educación 2001* 7 (diciembre 1995): 27–31.

Beverley, John. *Against Literature.* Minneapolis: U of Minnesota P, 1993.

———. "Prólogo." *La articulación.* Morales 9–20.

———. *Subalternity and Representation: Arguments in Cultural Theory.* Durham: Duke UP, 1999.

———. *Testimonio: On the Politics of Truth.* Minneapolis: U of Minnesota P, 2004.

———. "What Happens When the Subaltern Speaks: Rigoberta Menchú, Multiculturalism, and the Presumption of Equal Worth." *The Rigoberta Menchú Controversy.* Arias 219–36.

Beverley, John, and Hugo Achugar, eds. *La voz del otro: Testimonio, subalternidad y verdad narrativa.* 2nd ed. Guatemala: U Rafael Landívar, 2002.

Beverly, John, Michael Aronna, and José Oviedo, eds. *The Postmodernism Debate in Latin America.* Durham-London: Duke University Press, 1995.

Beverley, John, and Marc Zimmerman. *Literature and Politics in the Central American Revolutions.* Austin: U of Texas P, 1990. New Interpretations of Latin America.

Bhabha, Homi K. *The Location of Culture.* London; New York: Routledge, 1994.

Blackburn, Robin, and Heraclio Bonilla. *Los conquistados: 1492 y la población indígena de las Américas.* Santafé de Bogotá: Tercer Mundo Editores; Quito: FLACSO; Libri Mundi, 1992.

Bonfil Batalla, Guillermo. *México profundo: Una civilización negada.* 1st ed. México: Secretaría de Educación Pública; CIESAS, 1987.

Bourdieu, Pierre. *Capital cultural, escuela y espacio social.* 1997. México: Siglo Veintiuno Editores, 2000.

———. *The Logic of Practice.* Cambridge: Polity, 1990.

Brittin, Alice, and Kenny C. Dworkin. "Rigoberta Menchú: 'Los indígenas no nos quedamos como bichos aislados, inmunes, desde hace 500 años. No, nosotros hemos sido protagonistas de la historia.'" *Nuevo Texto Crítico* 4.11 (1993): 207–22.

Broder, John M. "Clinton Offers His Apologies to Guatemala." *New York Times* 11 Mar. 1999. 12 Mar. 1999. <http://query.nytimes.com/gst/fullpage.html?res=9D05EFD7163EF932 A25750C0A96F958260>.

Bubnova, Tatiana. "The Indian Identity, the Existential Anguish and the Eternal Return (*El tiempo principia en Xibalbá,* by Luis de Lión)." Durán-Cogan and Gómez-Moriana 178–200.

Burgos, Elizabeth. "The Story of a Testimonio." *Latin American Perspectives* 26.6 (Nov. 1999): 53–63.

Cabezas, Omar. *Fire from the Mountain: The Making of a Sandinista.* 1st ed. New York: Crown, 1985.

Callan, Richard. *Miguel Ángel Asturias.* New York: Twayne, 1970.

Cardoso, Fernando H., and Francisco Weffort, eds. *América Latina: Ensayos de interpretación sociológico-política*. Santiago: Editorial Universitaria, 1970.

Carey-Webb, Allen, and Stephen Benz, eds. *Teaching and Testimony: Rigoberta Menchú and the North American Classroom*. Albany: State U of New York P, 1996.

Carnoy, Martin. *Education as Cultural Imperialism*. New York: McKay, 1974.

Carrera, Mario Alberto. "La inmutabilidad de la palabra indio y ahora su sustitución." *Siglo veintiuno* [Guatemala] 6 Apr. 2000, opinion sec. 6 Apr. 2000. <http://www.sigloxxi.com>.

Carter, Forrest. *The Education of Little Tree*. Albuquerque: U of New Mexico P, 1976.

Casaús Arzú, Marta Elena. *Guatemala: Linaje y racismo*. Guatemala: F y G Editores, 2007.

Castellanos, Sagrario. "Mujeres, antagonismo y Xibalbá." *Conversatorio: Homenaje imaginario a la obra literaria de Luis de Lión*. 23–28.

Castillo, Otto René. *Informe de una injusticia*. 1979. Guatemala: Ministerio de Cultura y Deportes, 1993.

Castro-Gómez, Santiago. "Ciencias sociales, violencia epistémica y el problema de la 'invención' del otro." *La colonialidad del saber*. Lander 145–62.

Castro-Gómez, Santiago, and Eduardo Mendieta, eds. *Teorías sin disciplina: Latinoamericanismo, postcolonialidad y globalización en debate*. México: Editorial Porrua, 1998.

Chakrabarty, Dipesh. *Provincializing Europe: Postcolonial Thought and Historical Difference*. Princeton: Princeton UP, 2000. Princeton Studies in Culture/Power/History.

Chatterjee, Partha. *Nationalist Thought and the Colonial World: A Derivative Discourse*. Minneapolis: U of Minnesota P, 1986.

———. "Our Modernity." SEPHIS and CODESRIA. Rotterdam–Dakar, 1997. Lecture.

Child, Lydia Maria Francis. *Hobomok and Other Writings on Indians*. Ed. Carolyn L. Karcher. New Brunswick: Rutgers UP, 1986. American Women Writers.

Cojtí Cuxil, Demetrio. *Configuración del pensamiento político del pueblo Maya*. Guatemala; Quetzaltenango: Asociación de Escritores Mayances de Guatemala, 1991.

———. "Educational Reform in Guatemala: Lessons from Negotiations between Indigenous Civil Society and the State." *Multiculturalism in Latin America: Indigenous Rights, Diversity, and Democracy*. Ed. Rachel Sieder. London: Palgrave Macmillan, 2002. 103–28.

———. *El movimiento Maya (en Guatemala)* = *Ri Maya' Moloj Pa Iximulew*. Guatemala: Editorial Cholsamaj, 1997.

———. *Políticas para la reivindicación de los Mayas de hoy: Fundamento de los derechos específicos del pueblo Maya*. Guatemala: Editorial Cholsamaj; SPEM, 1994.

Columbus, Christopher. *The Voyage of Christopher Columbus. Columbus' Own Journal of Discovery*. Trans. and introd. John Cummins. New York: Saint Martin's, 1992.

Comisión para el Esclarecimiento Histórico. *Guatemala, memoria del silencio, Resumen del informe de la Comisión para el Esclarecimiento Histórico*. Guatemala: Programa de Derechos Humanos y Reconciliación USAID, 2001.

Construyendo alternativas 181–82 (diciembre 2001–enero 2002).

Conversatorio: Homenaje imaginario a la obra literaria de Luis de Lión. Guatemala; Antigua: Galería Imaginaria, 1991.

Cook-Lynn, Elizabeth. "How Scholarship Defames the Native Voice…And Why." *Wicazo Sa Review* (fall 2000): 79–92.

Cooper, James Fenimore. *The Last of the Mohicans*. New York: Signet Classic Printing, New American Library, 1962.

Cornejo Polar, Antonio. *Escribir en el aire: Ensayo sobre la heterogeneidad socio-cultural en las literaturas Andinas*. Lima: Editorial Horizonte, 1994.

———. *La novela peruana*. 2nd ed. Lima: Editorial Horizonte, 1989.

Cortés, Hernán. *Hernan Cortes: Letters from Mexico*. Trans. and ed. Anthony Pagden. Introd. J. H. Elliot. New Haven; London: Yale UP, 1986.

Costello, Patrick. "Historical Background." *Accords, An International Review of Peace Initiatives: Negotiating Rights, The Guatemalan Peace Process* 2 (1997). 15 Apr. 2000. <http://www.c-r.org/accord/guat/accord2/index.shtml>.

Dalton, Roque. "Otto René Castillo: Su ejemplo y nuestra responsabilidad." *Informe de una injusticia.* By Otto René Castillo. 1979. Guatemala: Ministerio de Cultura y Deportes, 1993. xix–xxxiv.

Dary, Claudia. "Historia del mestizaje." *Identidad: Colección, conozcamos Guatemala.* Numero 17. *Prensa Libre* [Guatemala] 2 de septiembre 1995: 6–10.

Dawson, Alexander. "'Wild Indians,' 'Mexican Gentlemen,' and the Lessons Learned in the Casa del Estudiante Indígena, 1926–1932." *The Americas* 57.3 (Jan. 2001): 320–61.

"Los desafíos de la diversidad. Relaciones interétnicas: Identidad, género y justicia." Spec. issue of *Revista de Estudios Interétnicos* 18.11 (noviembre 2004).

de Lión, Luis. *Pájaro en mano.* Certamen Permanente Centroamericano "15 de septiembre." Guatemala: Serviprensa Centroamericana, 1986.

———. *Poemas del Volcán de Agua (Los poemas míos).* Guatemala: Serviprensa Centroamericana, 1994.

———. *Poemas del Volcán de Fuego.* Guatemala: Bancafe, 1998.

———. La puerta del cielo y otras puertas. Guatemala: Fundación Guatemalteca para las Letras; Editorial Artemis y Edinter, 1995.

———. *Su segunda muerte.* Guatemala: Nuevo Siglo Ediciones, 1970.

———. *El tiempo principia en Xibalbá.* 1985. Guatemala: Artemis y Edinter, 1996.

———. *Los zopilotes.* Guatemala: Editorial Landívar, 1966.

Diamond, Stanley. "A Revolutionary Discipline." *Current Anthropology* 5 (1964): 432–37.

El diseño de reforma educativa/Runuk'ik jun K'ak'a Tijonik. Guatemala: Comisión Paritaria de Reforma Educativa, 1998.

D'Souza, Dinesh. *Illiberal Education: The Politics of Race and Sex on Campus.* New York: Free Press; Toronto: Collier Macmillan Canada; Maxwell Macmillan International, 1991.

Dunkerley, James. *Power in the Isthmus: A Political History of Modern Central America.* London; New York: Verso, 1988.

Dupuy, Alex. "Spanish Colonialism and the Origin of Underdevelopment in Haiti." *Latin American Perspectives* 3.2 (spring 1976): 5–29.

Durán-Cogan, Mercedes F., and Antonio Gómez-Moriana, eds. *National Identities and Sociopolitical Changes in Latin America.* New York: Routledge, 2001.

Dussel, Enrique. "Eurocentrism and Modernity (Introduction to the Frankfurt Lectures)." Beverley, John, Michael Aronna, and José Oviedo, eds. *The Postmodernism Debate in Latin America.* Durham-London: Duke University Press, 1995.

———. "Europa, modernidad y eurocentrismo." *La colonialidad del saber.* Lander 41–54.

Eckermann, Anne-Katrin. *One Classroom, Many Cultures: Teaching Strategies for Culturally Different Children.* St Leonards: Allen and Unwin, 1994.

Educación Maya: Experiencia y expectativas en Guatemala. Guatemala: UNESCO, 1995.

Fabian, Johannes. *Time and the Other: How Anthropology Makes Its Object.* New York: Columbia UP, 1983.

———. *Time and the Work of Anthropology: Critical Essays, 1971–1991.* Chur; Philadelphia: Harwood Academic, 1991. Studies in Anthropology and History 3.

Falla, Ricardo. "El movimiento indígena." *Estudios Centroamericanos* 353 (1978): 438–61.

Fanon, Frantz. *Black Skin, White Masks.* 1952. Trans. Charles Lam Markmann. New York: Grove, 1967.

———. *The Wretched of the Earth.* 1963. Trans. Richard Philcox. New York: Grove, 2004.

Favre, Henry. *Indigenismo.* México: Fondo de Cultura Económica, 1998.

Fazio, Carlos. "El juego del poder, y el contenido geopolítico del Plan Puebla–Panamá." *Construyendo Alternativas* 181–82 (diciembre 2001–enero 2002): 51–65.

————. "Plan Puebla–Panamá: El istmo de Tehuantepec, imán para la superexplotación." *Construyendo Alternativas* 181–82 (diciembre 2001–enero 2002): 25–36.

Ferman, Claudia. *Política y posmodernidad: Hacia una lectura de la anti-modernidad en lati-noamérica.* Buenos Aires: Almagesto, 1994.

Fischer, Edward F., and R. McKenna Brown, eds. *Maya Cultural Activism in Guatemala.* Austin: U of Texas P, Institute of Latin American Studies, 1996.

Fitch, Nancy. "The Conquest of Mexico: An Annotated Bibliography." Aug. 2000. 16 June 2003. <http://www.theaha.org/tl/LessonPlans/ca/Fitch/ conquestbib.pdf>.

Flores, Marco Antonio. "El montaje del farsante (I)." Memoria del disidente. *Siglo veintiuno* 29 Aug. 2004, "Magazine 21." 29 Aug. 2004. <http://www.sigloxxi.com>.

————. "El montaje del farsante (II)." Memoria del disidente. *Siglo veintiuno* 5 Sept. 2004, "Magazine 21." 5 Sept. 2004. <http://www.sigloxxi.com>.

————. "El montaje del farsante (III)." Memoria del disidente. *Siglo veintiuno* 12 Sept. 2004, "Magazine 21." 12 Sept. 2004. <http://www.sigloxxi.com>.

————. "El montaje del farsante (IV)." Memoria del disidente. *Siglo veintiuno* 19 Sept. 2004, "Magazine 21." 19 Sept. 2004. <http://www.sigloxxi.com>.

Florescano, Enrique. *Memoria indígena.* México: Taurus, 1999.

Forster, Cindy. "Rigoberta Menchú: A Witness Discredited?" *Against the Current* 80 (May–June 1999). 4 Apr. 2001. <http://www.solidarity-us.org/node/893>.

Foucault, Michel. "Orders of Discourse: Inaugural Lecture Delivered at the College de France." *Social Science Information* 10.2 (1970): 7–30.

Foucault, Michel, and Colin Gordon. *Power/Knowledge: Selected Interviews and Other Writings, 1972–1977.* Brighton: Harvester, 1980.

Franch, José Alcina. *Indianismo e indigenismo en América.* Madrid: Alianza Editorial, 1990.

Freire, Paulo. *Pedagogía del oprimido.* 1970. México: Siglo Veintiuno Editores, 1996.

Fried, Jonathan L., Marvin Gettleman, Deborah Levenson, and Nancy Peckenham, eds. *Guatemala in Rebellion: Unfinished History.* New York: Grove, 1983.

Friedan, Betty. *The Feminine Mystique.* New York: Norton, 2001.

————. *It Changed My Life: Writings on the Women's Movement.* Cambridge: Harvard UP, 1998.

Galeano, Eduardo. *The Open Veins of Latin America: Five Centuries of the Pillage of a Continent.* 1971. Trans. Cedric Belfrage. New York: Monthly Review, 1974.

Gálvez Borrell, Víctor, and Claudia Dary. *¿Qué sociedad queremos? Una mirada desde el movimiento y las organizaciones Mayas.* Guatemala: FLACSO, 1997.

Gandhi, Leela. *Postcolonial Theory: A Critical Introduction.* New York: Columbia UP, 1998.

García Canclini, Néstor. *Hybrid Cultures: Strategies for Entering and Leaving Modernity.* 1989. Trans. Christopher L. Chiappari and Silvia L. Lopez. Minneapolis; London: U of Minnesota P, 2005.

George, Susan. "A Short History of Neoliberalism: Twenty Years of Elite Economics and Emerging Opportunities for Structural Change." *Global Finance: New Thinking on Regulating Speculative Capital Markets.* Ed. Walden Bello, Nicola Bullard, and Kamal Malhotra. London; New York: Zed, 2000. 27–35.

González Amador, Roberto, and Rosa Elvira Vargas. "La cumbre de Cancún: Rechaza la cumbre la declaración final que sugiere México." *La jornada* 14 Sept. 2003, economy sec. 14 Sept. 2003. <http://www.jornada.unam.mx>.

González, Gaspar Pedro. "Una interpretación de *Hombres de maíz* desde la óptica de un escritor Maya contemporáneo." Paper presented at XVIII Simposio Internacional de Literatura: Asturias y Borges. Instituto literario y cultural Hispánico, Guatemala. 9–11 Aug. 1999. Paper accessed 6 July 2001. <http://www.yaxte.org/simposio.htm>.

————. *Kotz'ib', nuestra literatura Maya.* Rancho Palos Verdes: Fundación Yax Te', 1997.

————. *A Mayan Life.* Trans. Elaine Elliot. Rancho Palos Verdes: Yax Te' Press, 1995.

————. *La otra cara*. Rancho Palos Verdes: Yaxte', 1996.

————. *El retorno de los Mayas*. Guatemala: Fundación Myrna Mack, 1998.

González Ponciano, Jorge Ramon. *Esas sangres no están limpias: El racismo, el estado y la nación en Guatemala (1944–1997)*. Tuxtla Gutiérrez: U de Ciencias y Artes, 1998.

Gordon, Lewis R. "Fanon, Philosophy, and Racism." *Racism and Philosophy*. Ed. Susan Babbitt and Sue Campbell. Ithaca; London: Cornell UP, 1999. 32–49.

Graff, Gerald. "Teach the Conflicts." *The Politics of Liberal Education*. Ed. Darryl J. Gless and Barbara Herrnstein Smith. Durham: Duke UP, 1992. 57–74.

Gramsci, Antonio. *Selections from the Prison Notebooks of Antonio Gramsci*. Trans. Quintin Hoare and Geoffrey Nowell-Smith. New York: International Publishers, 1971.

Grandin, Greg. *The Blood of Guatemala: A History of Race and Nation*. Durham: Duke UP, 2000. Latin America Otherwise.

Gruzinski, Serge. *La colonización de lo imaginario: Sociedades indígenas y occidentalización el México español. Siglos XVI–XVIII*. 1988. México: Fondo de Cultura Económica, 2000.

————. *Images at War: Mexico from Columbus to Blade Runner (1492–2019)*. Trans. Heather MacLean. Durham: Duke UP, 2001. Latin America Otherwise.

Guatemala, memoria del silencio: Resumen del informe para el esclarecimiento histórico. Guatemala: Programa de Derechos Humanos y Reconciliación USAID, 2001.

Gugelberger, Georg M., ed. *The Real Thing: Testimonial Discourse and Latin America*. Durham: Duke UP, 1996.

————. "Remembering: The Post-testimonio Memoirs of Rigoberta Menchú Tum." *Latin American Perspectives* 25.6 (Nov. 1998): 62–68.

————. "*Stollwerk* or Bulwark? David Meets Goliath and the Continuation of the Testimonio Debate." Latin America Perspectives 26.6 (Nov. 1999): 47–52.

Guha, Ranajit. *Elementary Aspects of Peasant Insurgency in Colonial India*. Delhi: Oxford, 1983.

————. "The Small Voice of History." *Subaltern Studies IX: Writings on South Asian History and Society*. Ed. Shahid Amin and Dipesh Chakrabarty. Delhi: Oxford UP, 1996. 1–12.

Gutiérrez, Natividad. *Mitos nacionalistas e identidades étnicas: Los intelectuales indígenas y el estado mexicano*. México: Consejo Nacional para la Cultura y las Artes, 2001.

Guzmán Böckler, Carlos, and Jean-Loup Herbert. *Guatemala: Una interpretación histórico-social*. México: Siglo Veintiuno Editores, 1970.

Hale, Charles R. *Más que un Indio: Racial Ambivalence and Neoliberal Multiculturalism in Guatemala*. Santa Fe: School for Advanced Research, 2006.

————. "Rethinking Indigenous Politics in the Era of the 'Indio Permitido.'" *NACLA Report on the Americas* 38.2 (Sept.–Oct. 2004): 16–21.

Hale, Charles R., and Rosamel Millamán. "Cultural Agency and Political Struggle in the Era of the Indio Permitido." *Cultural Agency in the Americas*. Ed. Doris Sommer. Durham: Duke UP, 2006. 281–304.

Harss, Luis, and Barbara Dohmann. *Into the Mainstream: Conversations with Latin-American Writers*. New York: Harper and Row, 1967.

Heckt, Meike. *Guatemala, pluralidad, educación y relaciones de poder. Educación intercultural en una sociedad étnicamente dividida*. Guatemala: Asociación para el Avance de las Ciencias Sociales (AVANCSO), 2004.

Hinton, Alexander Laban, ed. *Annihilating Difference: The Anthropology of Genocide*. Berkeley: U of California P, 2002.

————. *Genocide: An Anthropological Reader*. Oxford; Malden: Blackwell, 2002.

Hobsbawn, Eric. "Introduction: Inventing Traditions." *The Invention of Tradition*. Ed. Eric Hobsbawn and Terence Ranger. 1983. Cambridge: Cambridge UP, 2003. 1–14.

hooks, bell. *Black Looks: Race and Representation*. Boston: South End, 1992.

Hurtado Heras, Saúl. *¿Cuál entonces mi creación? Reflexiones para una poética narrativa en Miguel Ángel Asturias*. Guatemala: Editorial Cultura, Dirección de Arte y Cultura, 1999.

Icaza, Jorge. *Huasipungo. The Villagers: A Novel.* Trans. Bernard Dulsey. Carbondale: Southern Illinois UP, 1964.

Imágenes homogéneas en un país de rostros diversos: El sistema educativo formal y la conformación de referentes de identidad nacional entre jóvenes guatemaltecos. Ciudad de Guatemala: Asociación para el Avance de las Ciencias Sociales (AVANCSO) en Guatemala, 1998.

Iverson, Katherine. "Civilization and Assimilation in the Colonized Schooling of Native Americans." *Education and Colonialism.* Ed. Philip G. Altbach and Gail P. Kelly. New York: Longman, 1978. 149–80.

Jaimes, Annette M., ed. *The State of Native America: Genocide, Colonization, and Resistance.* Boston: South End, 1992. Race and Resistance.

Jaimes, Annette M., and Theresa Halsey. "American Indian Women at the Center of Indigenous Resistance in Contemporary North America." Jaimes 311–44.

Jara, René, and Nicholas Spadaccini. *1492–1992: Re/Discovering Colonial Writing.* Minneapolis: Prisma Inst., 1989. Hispanic Issues 4.

Jara, René, and Hernán Vidal. *Testimonio y literatura.* Minneapolis: Inst. for the Study of Ideologies and Literature, 1986.

Jiménez Turón, Simeón. "Muerte cultural con anestesia." *América Indígena* 44.1 (enero–marzo 1984): 95–99.

Johnson, David E. "The Limits of Community: How 'We' Read *Me Llamo Rigoberta Menchú.*" *Discourse* 23.1 (winter 2001): 154–69.

Jonas, Susanne. *The Battle for Guatemala: Rebels, Death Squads, and US Power.* Boulder: Westview, 1991.

Kelly, Gail, and Philip G. Altbach, eds. *Education and the Colonial Experience.* New Brunswick: Transaction, 1984.

Kempen, Laura Charlotte. *Mariama Bâ, Rigoberta Menchú, and Postcolonial Feminism.* New York: P. Lang, 2001. Currents in Comparative Romance Languages and Literatures 97.

King, Martin Luther, Jr. "Conscience and the Vietnam War." *The Trumpet of Conscience.* By King Jr. New York; London: Harper and Row, 1968. 18–34.

Klor de Alva, Jorge. "Colonialism and Postcolonialism as (Latin) American Mirages." *Colonial Latin American Review* 1.1–2 (1992): 3–23.

Landa, Fray Diego de. *Relación de las cosas de Yucatán.* 1959. Introd. Angel María Garibay K. México: Editorial Porrua, 1986.

Lander, Edgardo, ed. *La colonialidad del saber: Eurocentrismo y ciencias sociales. Perspectivas Latinoamericanas.* Caracas: Facultad de Ciencias Económicas y Sociales (FACES-UCV); Instituto Internacional de la UNESCO para la Educación Superior en América Latina y el Caribe (IESALC), 2000.

———. "Modernidad, colonialidad y posmodernidad." *Democracia sin exclusiones ni excluidos.* Ed. Emir Sader. Caracas: Nueva Sociedad, 1998. 83–97.

Lemus, Juan Carlos. "Ak'abal: 'No gracias.' El poeta explica por qué rechaza el Premio Nacional de Literatura." *Prensa Libre* 25 Jan. 2004, culture sec. 25 Jan. 2004. <http://www .prensalibre.com>.

Liano, Dante. "Vida nueva, nación nueva: Indígenas y ladinos en Asturias." *1899/1999: Vida, obra y herencia de Miguel Ángel Asturias.* Madrid; Nanterre: ALLCA XX; Université Paris, UNESCO Editions, 1999. 53–73.

———. *Visión crítica de la literatura Guatemalteca.* Quetzaltenango: Editorial U de San Carlos de Guatemala, 1997.

Lienhard, Martín. "Antes y después de *Hombres de maíz*: La literatura ladina y el mundo indígena en el área Maya." *Hombres de maíz, edición crítica.* Asturias 571–92.

———. "Kalunga o el recuerdo de la trata esclavista en algunos cantos Afro-americanos." *Revista Iberoamericana* 65.188–89 (julio–diciembre 1999): 505–17.

———. *La voz y su huella: Escritura y conflicto étnico-cultural en América Latina, 1492–1988.*

1990. Lima: Editorial Horizonte, 1992.

Lineamientos curriculares para la educación primaria bilingüe intercultural. Guatemala: Cooperación Técnica Alemana; GTZ, 1998.

Loomba, Ania. *Colonialism/Postcolonialism.* London; New York: Routledge, 1998.

López, Luis Enrique. "La diversidad étnica, cultural y lingüística latinoamericana y los recursos humanos que la educación requiere." *Revista Iberoamericana de Educación* 13 (enero–abril 1997): 47–98.

Lorand de Olazagasti, Adelaida. *El indio en la narrativa Guatemalteca.* San Juan: Editorial Universitaria, 1968.

Lovell, George W. "Surviving Conquest: The Maya of Guatemala in Historical Perspective." *Latin American Research Review* 23.2 (1988): 25–57.

Lovell, George, and Christopher Lutz. "The Primacy of Larger Truths: Rigoberta Menchú and the Tradition of Native Testimony in Guatemala." *The Rigoberta Menchú Controversy.* Arias 171–97.

Lozano Vallejo, Ruth, Kathe Meentzen, and Jorge Agusto Aguilar, eds. *Interculturalidad: Desafío y proceso en construcción (Manual de capacitación).* Lima: SINCO Editores, 2005.

Lund, Joshua. *The Impure Imagination: Toward a Critical Hybridity in Latin American Writing.* Minneapolis: U of Minnesota P, 2006.

Lux de Cotí, Otilia. "Educación Maya, perspectiva para Guatemala." *Educación Maya: Experiencia y expectativas en Guatemala.* Guatemala: UNESCO, 1995. 104–15.

Macaulay, Thomas. "Minute on Indian Education." 1835. *The Post-colonial Studies Reader.* Ed. Bill Ashcroft, Gareth Griffiths, and Helen Tiffin. London; New York: Routledge, 1994. 428–30.

Macías, Julio César. *La guerrilla fue mi camino: Epitafio para César Montes.* 3rd ed. Guatemala: Editorial Piedra Santa Arandi, 1999. Colección Afluentes de Modernidad.

Mallon, Florencia. "The Promise and Dilemma of Subaltern Studies: Perspectives from Latin American History." *The American Historical Review* 99.5 (Dec. 1994): 1491–1515.

Marcos, Subcomandante. "El otro jugador." *Los caminos de la dignidad: Derechos indígenas, memoria y patrimonio cultural.* Escuela Nacional de Historia y Antropología (ENHA), México. 12 Mar. 2001. Lecture. 13 Mar. 2001. <http://www.ezln.org/marcha/20010312.es.htm>.

———. *Relatos de El Viejo Antonio.* México: Centro de Información y Análisis de Chiapas, 1998.

Martin, Gerald. *Journeys through the Labyrinth: Latin American Fiction in the Twentieth Century.* London; New York: Verso, 1989.

Martínez, Jorge Mario. "La crítica obsoleta." *La Ermita* 5.21 (enero–marzo 2001): 17–28.

Martínez, Osvaldo. "ALCA: El proyecto de anexión de América Latina a Estados Unidos en el siglo XXI." *Construyendo Alternativas* 181–82 (diciembre 2001–enero 2002): 7–23.

Martínez Peláez, Severo. *La patria del criollo: Ensayo de interpretación de la realidad colonial Guatemalteca.* Guatemala: Editorial Universitaria, 1971.

Marx, Karl. *Capital: A Critique of Political Economy.* Vol. 1. Trans. Ben Fowkes. New York: Penguin, 1990.

Mazzotti, José Antonio, and Ulises Juan Zevallos Aguilar, eds. *Asedios a la heterogeneidad cultural: Libro de homenaje a Antonio Cornejo Polar.* Philadelphia: Asociación Internacional de Peruanistas, 1996.

McClintock, Anne, Aamir Mufti, and Ella Shohat, eds. *Dangerous Liaisons: Gender, Nations, and Postcolonial Perspectives.* Minneapolis: U of Minnesota P, 1997.

McConaghy, Cathryn. *Rethinking Indigenous Education: Culturalism, Colonialism, and the Politics of Knowing.* Flaxton: Post Pressed, 2000.

Menchú, Rigoberta. "Discourse of Acceptance and Nobel Lecture." 10 Dec. 1992. 13 Oct. 2007. <http://www.nobelprize.org/nobel_prizes/peace/laureates/1992/tum-lecture.html>.

———. "Por Elían, por la justicia [Selected Letters from Well-Known Writers and Activists Regarding the Elían González Affair]." *Casa de las Américas* 218 (Jan.–Mar. 2000): 154–56.

———. "Rigoberta Menchú pide a las Naciones Unidas que se cumplan los derechos del Pueblo Saharaui tras visitar los campos de refugiados." *Rebelión* 10 Feb. 2003. 10 Feb. 2003. <http://www.rebelion.org/africa/menchu100203.htm>.

———. "Rigoberta Menchú's Open Letter to George W. Bush." 29 Sept. 2001. Center for Research and Globalization. 29 Sept. 2001. <http://www.globalresearch.ca/articles/MEN109A.html>.

Menchú, Rigoberta, and Elizabeth Burgos. *I, Rigoberta Menchú, An Indian Woman in Guatemala*. 1983. Trans. Ann Wright. London; New York: Verso, 1984.

Menchú, Rigoberta, and Comité de Unidad Campesina (CUC). *Trenzando el futuro: Luchas campesinas en la historia reciente de Guatemala*. Guatemala: Tercera Prensa–Hirugarren Prentsa, 1992.

Menchú, Rigoberta, with Dante Liano and Gianni Miná. *Crossing Borders*. Trans. Ann Wright. London: Verso, 1998.

———. *Rigoberta Menchú, la nieta de los Mayas*. Madrid: Aguilar, 1998.

Mignolo, Walter. "Are the Subaltern Studies Postmodern or Postcolonial? The Politics and Sensibilities of Geo-cultural Locations." Rabasa, Sanjinés, and Carr 45–74.

———. "Colonial and Postcolonial Discourse: Cultural Critique or Academic Colonialism?" *Latin American Research Review* 28.3 (1993): 120–34.

———. *The Darker Side of the Renaissance: Literacy, Territoriality, and Colonization*. Ann Arbor: U of Michigan P, 1995.

———. "Literacy and Colonization: The New World Experience." *1492–1992: Re/Discovering Colonial Writing*. Ed. René Jara and Nicholas Spadaccini. Minneapolis: Prisma Inst., 1989. 51–96. Hispanic Issues 4.

———. *Local Histories/Global Designs: Coloniality, Subaltern Knowledges, and Border Thinking*. Princeton: Princeton UP, 2000.

Millar, Marilyn Grace. *Rise and Fall of the Cosmic Race: The Cult of Mestizaje in Latin America*. Austin: U of Texas P, 2004.

Moller, Jonathan. *Our Culture Is Our Resistance: Repression, Refuge, and Healing in Guatemala*. New York: PowerHouse Books, 2004.

Montejo, Victor. *Maya Intellectual Renaissance: Identity, Representation, and Leadership*. Austin: U of Texas P, 2005.

———. *El Q'anil: Man of Lightning*. Tucson: U of Arizona P, 2001.

———. *Testimony: Death of a Guatemalan Village*. Willimantic: Curbstone, 1987.

———. "Truth, Human Rights, and Representation: The Case of Rigoberta Menchú." *The Rigoberta Menchú Controversy*. Arias 372–91.

Montenegro, Gustavo Adolfo. "Luis de Lión: 'Yo siempre tuve un cielo.'" Revista Domingo. *Prensa Libre* 9 May 2004: 8–11.

Morales, Mario Roberto. "A fuego lento: El dilema identitario de los ladinos." *Siglo veintiuno* [Guatemala] 4 Nov. 2003, opinion sec. 4 Nov. 2003. <http://www.sigloxxi.com>.

———. *La articulación de las diferencias, o, el síndrome de Maximón: Los discursos literarios y políticos del debate interétnico en Guatemala*. Guatemala: FLASCO Guatemala, 1998.

———. "Luis de Lión, el indio por un indio." *Conversatorio: Homenaje imaginario a la obra literaria de Luis de Lión*. 3–11.

———. "Matemos a Miguel Ángel Asturias." *El Señor Presidente: Miguel Ángel Asturias*. 1973. Coord. Gerald Martin. Barcelona; Nanterre: Galaxia Gutenberg; ALLCA XX, 2000. 853–64.

———. "El neomacartismo estalinista (o la cacería de brujas en la academia 'posmo')." *Encuentro* [Madrid] 19 (2000–2001): 47–58.

———, ed. *Stoll–Menchú: La invención de la memoria*. Guatemala: Consucultura, 2001.

———. "Sujetos interétnicos y moda posmo en xela." *Siglo veintiuno* [Guatemala] 19 June 2000, opinion sec. 19 June 2000. <http://www.sigloxxi.com>.

Morales Santos, Francisco. "Introducción." *La puerta del cielo y otras puertas*. By de Lión. Guatemala: Fundación Guatemalteca para las Letras; Editorial Artemis y Edinte, 1995. 1–3.

———. "Luis de Lión, poeta de la cotidianidad y de la tierra." *Conversatorio: Homenaje imaginario a la obra literaria de Luis de Lión*. 29–32.

Moraña, Mabel, ed. *Ángel Rama y los estudios Latinoamericanos*. Pittsburgh: Inst. Internacional de Literatura Iberoamericana, U de Pittsburgh, 1997. Serie Críticas.

Moreiras, Alberto. "José María Arguedas y el fin de la transculturación." *Ángel Rama y los estudios Latinoamericanos*. Ed. Mabel Moraña. Pittsburgh: Inst. Internacional de Literatura Iberoamericana, U de Pittsburgh, 1997. 213–34. Serie Críticas.

Moya, Ruth. "Interculturalidad y reforma educativa en Guatemala." *Revista Iberoamericana de Educación* 13 (enero–abril 1997): 129–55.

"Mujeres Mayas abriendo caminos." *La Cuerda: Una mirada feminista de la realidad* 6.57 (junio 2003). 23 Mar. 2008. <http://www.geocities.com/lacuerda_gt/eds/2003/lc200357.htm#lamedula2>.

Muyulema Calle, Armando. "De la 'cuestión indígena' a lo 'indígena' como cuestionamiento. Hacia una crítica del latinoamericanismo, el indigenismo y el mestiz(o)aje." *Convergencia de tiempos: Estudios subalternos/contextos latinoamericanos, estado, cultura, subalternidad*. Ed. Ileana Rodríguez. Ámsterdam; Atlanta: Ediciones Rodopi, 2001. 327–63.

Nakata, Martin. "Better." *Republica* 2 (1995): 61–74.

Nash, June C. *Mayan Visions: The Quest for Autonomy in an Age of Globalization*. New York: Routledge, 2001.

Nebrija, Antonio de. *Gramática Catellana, 1492*. Ed. José Rogerio Sánchez. Madrid: Casa Editorial Hernando, 1931.

Nelson, Diane M. *A Finger in the Wound: Body Politics in Quincentennial Guatemala*. Berkeley: U of California P, 1999.

Newland, Carlos. "La educación elemental en Hispanoamérica: Desde la independencia hasta la centralización de los sistemas educativos nacionales." *The Hispanic American Historical Review* 71.2 (mayo 1991): 335–64.

Noriega, Jorge. "American Indian Education in the United States: Indoctrination for Subordination to Colonialism." Jaimes 371–402.

O'Gorman, Edmundo. *Cuatro historiadores de Indias, siglo XVI: Pedro Mártir de Anglería, Gonzalo Fernández de Oviedo y Valdés, Bartolomé de las Casas, Joseph de Acosta*. México: Secretaría de Educación Pública, 1972.

———. *La invención de América: El universalismo de la cultura de occidente*. México: Fondo de Cultura Económica, 1958.

Oliva García, Julio. "Entrevista a Rigoberta Menchú Tum: 'La doble moral de Estados Unidos.'" *Rebelión* 4 Nov. 2001. 4 Nov. 2001. <http://www.rebelion.org/ddhh/menchu0441101.htm>.

Ortiz, Fernando. *Contrapunteo cubano del tabaco y el azúcar*. 1940. Caracas: Biblioteca Ayacucho, 1987.

———. *Cuban Counterpoint: Tobacco and Sugar*. Trans. Mauricio A. Font and Alfonso W. Quiroz. New York: Random House, 1970.

Pastor Bodmer, Beatriz. *The Armature of Conquest: Spanish Accounts of the Discovery of America, 1492–1589*. Trans. Lydia Longstreth Hunt. Stanford: Stanford UP, 1992.

Payeras, Mario. *Days of the Jungle: The Testimony of a Guatemalan Guerrillero, 1972–1976*. New York: Monthly Review Press, 1983.

Peña, Guillermo de la. "La construcción de la identidad nacional: La experiencia mexicana." *De la etnia a la nación: Textos para debates #11*. Guatemala: AVANCSO, 1996. 19–30.

Penny, Sarah. Rev. of *Crossing Borders*, by Rigoberta Menchú. *Bulletin of Latin American Research* 18.4 (Oct. 1999): 514–16.

Pérez Ruíz, Maya L. "Disyuntivas del movimiento indígena en México: Algunas reflexiones." *Mundialización y diversidad cultural: Territorio, identidad, y poder en el medio rural mexicano*. Comp. María Tarrío García, Sonia Comboni Salinas,and Roberto Diego Quintana. México: U Autónoma Metropolitana, 2007. 277–300.

Plan Puebla–Panamá: Por el desarrollo sustentable y socialmente incluyente [PPP]. México: Presidencia de la República, Secretaria de Relaciones Exteriores, 2000.

Platt, Tristan. "La escritura, el Chamanismo y la identidad o voces de Abya-Yala." *Nuevo Texto Crítico* 9.18 (July–Dec. 1996): 75–91.

Pop, Amanda. "¿Qué hará doctor Cojti?" *Siglo veintiuno* 14 Oct. 2003, opinion sec. 14 Oct. 2003. <http://www.sigloxxi.com>.

Popol Vuh: Las antiguas historias del Quiché. Ed. Adrián Recinos. San José: Editorial Universitaria Centroamericana, 1976.

Porpora, Douglas V. *How Holocausts Happen: The United States in Central America*. Philadelphia: Temple UP, 1990.

Powell, T. G. "Mexican Intellectuals and the Indian Question, 1876–1911." *Hispanic American Historical Review* 48.1 (Feb. 1968): 19–36.

Pratt, Mary Louise. "I, Rigoberta Menchú, and the 'Culture Wars.'" *The Rigoberta Menchú Controversy*. Arias 29–48.

Prensa Libre. "En el día de los pueblos indígenas." Editorial. 9 Aug. 2003: 14.

———. "Universidad Maya, idea controversial." Editorial. 22 Jan. 2004. 22 Jan. 2004. <http://www.prensalibre.com/pls/prensa/imprimir.jsp?p_cnoticia=79220&p_fedicion=22-01>.

———. "Universidad Maya, una universidad para todos." Opinion sec. 29 Jan. 2004. 29 Jan. 2004. <http://www.prensalibre.com>.

Prera Flores, Ana Isabel, y Lucrecia Méndez de Penedo. "Asturias, guatemalteco visionario." *1899/1999: Vida, obra y herencia de Miguel Ángel Asturias*. 19–25.

Prescott, William Hickling. *History of the Conquest of Mexico, with a Preliminary View of the Ancient Mexican Civilization, and the Life of the Conqueror Hernando Cortez*. 1853. 22nd ed. Ann Arbor: University of Michigan; Harper. Making of America Project. 15 Oct. 2007. <http://www.name.umdl.umich.edu/ABE2471>.

"Presidentes de C.A. satisfechos con resultados de la cita con Bush: 'TLC para quienes están mal.'" Politica. *Siglo veintiuno* 11 Apr. 2003. 11 Apr. 2003. <http://www.sigloxxi.com>.

Prieto, René. "Tamizar tiempos antiguos: La originalidad structural de *Hombres de maíz*." *Men of Maize (Critical Edition)*. Asturias 617–44.

Programa de las Naciones Unidas para el Desarrollo (PNUD). *Desarrollo humano y pacto fiscal*. Guatemala: Edisur, 2002.

Proyecto Interdiocesano Recuperación de la Memoria Histórica (Guatemala). *Guatemala, Never Again!* Maryknoll: Orbis Books, 1999.

Puiggrós, Adriana. *Imperialismo y educación en América Latina*. México: Editorial Nueva Imagen, 1980.

Quijano, Aníbal. "Coloniality and Modernity/Rationality." *Cultural Studies* 21.2 (2007): 168–78.

———. "Coloniality of Power, Eurocentrism, and Latin America." *Nepantla: Views from the South* 1.3 (2000): 533–80.

———. "'Raza,' 'etnia' y 'nación' en Mariátegui: Cuestiones abiertas." *Encuentro Internacional José Carlos Mariátegui y Europa: El otro aspecto del descubrimiento*. Lima: Empresa Editora Amauta, 1993. 167–87.

Quispe, Felipe. "Bolivia: Después de la renuncia, ¿Qué hacer? Entrevista a Felipe Quispe." *Rebelión* 21 Oct. 2003. 21 Oct. 2003. <http://www.rebelion.org>.

Rabasa, José. *Inventing America: Spanish Historiography and the Formation of Eurocentrism*. 1st ed. Norman: U of Oklahoma P, 1993. Oklahoma Project for Discourse and Theory 11.

Rabasa, José, Javier Sanjinés, and Robert Carr, eds. "Subaltern Studies in the Americas." Spec. issue of *Disposition* 9.46 (1996).

Rama, Ángel. *La ciudad letrada*. Montevideo: Comisión Uruguaya pro Fundación Internacional Ángel Rama, 1984. Serie Rama.

————. *The Lettered City*. Trans. and ed. John C. Chasteen. Durham: Duke UP, 1996. Post-contemporary Interventions.

————. *Transculturación narrativa en América Latina*. México: Siglo Veintiuno Editores, 1982.

Ramírez, Alberto, Julieta Sandoval, and Luisa Rodríguez. "Visita de Fox, entre acuerdos y protestas. Encuentro: Presidentes prometen beneficios para las mayorías." Nacional. *Prensa Libre* 24 Mar. 2004. 24 Mar. 2004. <http://www.prensalibre.com>.

Rivera Cusicanqui, Silvia. *"Oprimidos pero no vencidos," Luchas del campesinado aymara y qhechwa, 1900–1980*. La Paz: Ediciones Yachaywasi, 2003.

————. *Pachakuti: Los Aymara de Bolivia frente a medio milenio de colonialismo*. Chukiyawu: Ediciones Aruwiyiri, 1991.

Rivera Cusicanqui, Silvia, and Rossana Barragán, comps. *Debates post coloniales: Una introducción a los estudios de la subalternidad*. La Paz: Ediciones Aruwiyiri, 1997.

Robinson, William I. *Transnational Conflicts: Central America, Social Change, and Globalization*. London; New York: Verso, 2003.

Rodas, Ana María. "La virgen y la puta." *Conversatorio: Homenaje imaginario a la obra literaria de Luis de Lión*. 11–14.

Rodríguez, Ileana, ed. *The Latin American Subaltern Studies Reader*. Durham: Duke UP, 2001.

Rodríguez, Luisa. "'Los compromisos deben trasladarse en acciones,' Vicente Fox, mandatario mexicano." Nacional. *Prensa Libre* 24 Mar. 2004. 24 Mar. 2004. <http://www.prensalibre.com>.

Rorty, Richard. "The Demonization of Multiculturalism." *Journal of Blacks in Higher Education* 0.7 (spring 1995): 74–75.

Rus, Jan, coord. "If Truth Be Told: A Forum on David Stoll's *Rigoberta Menchú and the Story of All Poor Guatemalans*." Spec. issue of *Latin American Perspectives* 26.6 (Nov. 1999).

Said, Edward W. *Covering Islam: How the Media and the Experts Determine How We See the Rest of the World*. New York: Pantheon Books, 1981.

————. *Culture and Imperialism*. New York: Vintage Books, 1994.

————. *Orientalism*. New York: Vintage Books, 1979.

————. "Preface to *Orientalism*." *Al-Ahram* 7–13 Aug. 2003. 3 Mar. 2009. <http://weekly.ahram.org.eg/2003/650/op11.htm>.

Sam Colop, Luis Enrique. *Jub'aqtun Omay Kuchum K'aslemal: Cinco siglos de Encubrimiento, a propósito de 1992*. Guatemala: Editorial Cholsamaj, 1991. Seminario Permanente de Estudios Mayas, Cuaderno 1.

Sanford, Victoria. *Buried Secrets: Truth and Human Rights in Guatemala*. New York: Palgrave Macmillan, 2003.

————. "From *I, Rigoberta* to the Commissioning of Truth: Maya Women and the Reshaping of Guatemalan History." *Cultural Critique* 47 (winter 2001): 16–52.

————. "The Silencing of Maya Women, from Mamá Maquín to Rigoberta Menchú." *Social Justice* 27.1 (2000): 128–51.

Sarmiento, Domingo Faustino. *Conflicto y armonía de las razas en América: Conclusiones*. México: UNAM Coordinación de Humanidades Centro de Estudios Latinoamericanos Facultad de Filosofía y Letras; Unión de Universidades de América Latina, 1978. Latinoamérica, cuadernos de cultura Latinoamericana 27.

————. *Facundo: Civilization and Barbarism*. 1845. Trans. Kathleen Ross. Berkeley: U of California P, 2004.

Schirmer, Jennifer G. "Decir la verdad: La dimensión militar en la controversia Stoll–Menchú." Morales, Mario Roberto, ed. *Stoll–Menchú: La invención de la memoria.* Guatemala: Consucultura, 2001. 165–80.

———. *The Guatemalan Military Project: A Violence Called Democracy.* Philadelphia: U of Pennsylvania P, 1998.

———. "Whose Testimony? Whose Truth? Where Are the Armed Actors in the Stoll–Menchú Controversy?" *Human Rights Quarterly* 25 (2003): 60–73.

Schlesinger, Stephen C., and Stephen Kinzer. *Bitter Fruit: The Story of the American Coup in Guatemala.* 2001. 2nd ed. Cambridge: Harvard UP, 2005.

Schmidt, Friedhelm. "¿Literaturas heterogéneas o literature de la transculturación?" *Asedios a la heterogeneidad cultural. Libro de homenaje a Antonio Cornejo Polar.* Ed. José Antonio Mazzotti and U. Juan Zevallos Aguilar. Philadelphia: Asociación Internacional de Peruanistas, 1996. 37–46.

Schutte, Ofelia. "Race, Gender, and Sexuality: Indigenous Issues and the Ethics of Dialogue in LatCrit Theory." *Rutgers Law Review* 54 (2002): 1021–30.

Seed, Patricia. "Colonial and Postcolonial Discourses." *Latin American Research Review* 26.3 (1991): 181–200.

———. "More Colonial and Postcolonial Discourses." *Latin American Research Review* 28.3 (1993): 146–52.

Seijo, Lorena. "Indígenas se hacen escuchar en caminata. Protesta: Miles marcharon por la ciudad para exigir sus derechos." Nacional. *Prensa Libre* 27 Nov. 2003. 27 Nov. 2003. <http://www.prensalibre.com>.

Shohat, Ella, and Robert Stam. *Unthinking Eurocentrism: Multiculturalism and the Media.* London; New York: Routledge, 1994.

Smith, Carol A. ed. *Guatemalan Indians and the State, 1540 to 1988.* Austin: U of Texas P, 1990.

———. "Maya Nationalism." *Report on the Americas* 25.3 (Dec. 1991): 29–33.

———. "Why Write an Exposé of Rigoberta Menchú?" *The Rigoberta Menchú Controversy.* Arias 141–55.

Sobrevilla, David. "Transculturación y heterogeneidad: Avatares de dos categorías literarias en América Latina." *Revista de Crítica Literaria Latinoamericana* 27.54 (2001): 21–33.

Sommer, Doris, ed. *Cultural Agency in the Americas.* Durham: Duke UP, 2006.

Spivak, Gayatri Chakravorti. "The Post-modern Condition: The End of Politics?" *The Post-colonial Critic: Interviews, Strategies, Dialogues.* Ed. S. Harasym. New York: Routledge, 1990. 17–34.

Stam, Robert. "Multiculturalism and the Neoconservatives." McClintock, Mufti, and Shohat 188–203.

Stoll, David. "The Battle of Rigoberta." *The Rigoberta Menchú Controversy.* Arias 392–410.

———. *Between Two Armies in the Ixil Towns of Guatemala.* New York: Columbia UP, 1993.

———. "Rigoberta Menchú and the Last-Resort Paradigm." *Latin American Perspectives* 26.6 (Nov. 1999): 70–80.

———. *Rigoberta Menchú and the Story of All Poor Guatemalans.* 1999. Boulder: Westview, 2008.

Stoltz Chinchilla, Norma. "Of Straw Men and Stereotypes: Why Guatemalan Rocks Don't Talk." *Latin American Perspectives* 26.6 (noviembre 1999): 29–37.

Taracena, Arturo. *Etnicidad, estado y nación en Guatemala.* 2 vols. Guatemala: CIRMA, 2002–2004.

Taussig, Michael T. *The Devil and Commodity Fetishism in South America.* Chapel Hill: U of North Carolina P, 1980.

Tierney, Patrick. *Darkness in El Dorado: How Scientists and Journalists Devastated the Amazon.* New York: Norton, 2000.

"TLC para los mas pobres. Promesa: Presidentes centroamericanos pidieron protección de sectores a EE.UU." Económicas. *Prensa Libre* 11 Apr. 2003. 11 Apr. 2003.

<http://www.prensalibre.com>.

Torres-Rivas, Edelberto. *Las izquierdas, Rigoberta Menchú, la historia.* Guatemala: F y G Editores, 2007. Colección: Cuadernos de la izquierda imperfecta.

Torres Valenzuela, Artemis. *El pensamiento positivista en la historia de Guatemala, 1871–1900.* Guatemala: Talleres Caudal, SA, 2000.

United Nations. *Recopilación de los Acuerdos de Paz.* Chimaltenango: Saqb'e, 1997.

Varese, Stefano. "The Ethnopolitics of Indian Resistance in Latin America." *Latin American Perspectives* 23.2 (spring 1996): 58–71.

———. *Proyectos étnicos y proyectos nacionales.* México: Fondo de Cultura Económica, 1983.

Vargas Llosa, Mario. "Questions of Conquest: What Columbus Wrought, and What He Did Not." *Harper's Magazine* Dec. 1990: 45–53.

———. *La utopía arcaica: José María Arguedas y las ficciones del indigenismo.* México: Fondo de Cultura Económica, 1996.

Vasconcelos, José. *The Cosmic Race: A Bilingual Edition.* 1925. Trans. Didier Tisdel Jaén. Baltimore: Johns Hopkins UP, 1997.

Vaughan, Mary Kay. *Cultural Politics in Revolution: Teachers, Peasants, and Schools in Mexico, 1930–1940.* Tucson: U of Arizona P, 1997.

Velásquez Nimatuj, Irma Alicia. *La pequeña burguesía indígena comercial de Guatemala.* Guatemala: AVANCSO, 2002.

Verso. "The Attack on Rigoberta Menchú." Editorial. 23 Dec. 1998. 15 May 2001. <http://www.versobooks.com/verso_info/menchu.shtml>.

Villoro, Luis. *Los grandes momentos del indigenismo en México.* 1950. México: El colegio de México; El colegio Nacional; Fondo de Cultura Económica, 1998.

Wald, Alan. *The Responsibility of Intellectuals: Selected Essays on Marxist Traditions and Cultural Commitment.* Atlantic Highlands: Humanities Press, 1992.

Walsh, Catherine. "Interculturality and the Coloniality of Power. An 'Other' Thinking and Positioning from the Colonial Difference." *Coloniality of Power, Transmodernity, and Border Thinking.* Ed. Ramon Grosfoguel, Jose David Saldivar, and Nelson Maldonado-Torres. Durham: Duke UP, n.d.

Warren, Kay B. *Indigenous Movements and Their Critics: Pan-Maya Activism in Guatemala.* Princeton: Princeton UP, 1998.

———. "Telling Truths: Taking David Stoll and the Rigoberta Menchú Exposé Seriously." *The Rigoberta Menchú Controversy.* Arias 198–218.

Warren, Kay B., and Jean E. Jackson. *Indigenous Movements, Self-Representation, and the State in Latin America.* Austin: U of Texas P, 2002.

Watanabe, John, and Edward Fischer, eds. *Pluralizing Ethnography: Comparison and Representation in Maya Cultures, Histories, and Identities.* Santa Fe: School for Advanced Research, 2004.

West, Cornell. "The New Cultural Politics of Difference." *The Cultural Studies Reader.* Ed. Simon During. London; New York: Routledge, 1993. 256–70.

Wideman, John Edgar. Introd. *Live from Death Row.* By Mumia Abu-Jamal. Reading; Menlo Park: Addison-Wesley, 1995.

Williams, Patrick, and Laura Chrisman. *Colonial Discourse and Post-colonial Theory: A Reader.* New York; London: Harvester Wheatsheaf, 1994.

Willinsky, John. *Learning to Divide the World: Education at Empire's End.* London; Minneapolis: U of Minnesota P, 1998.

Wilson, Richard. *Resurgimiento Maya en Guatemala (Experiencias Q'eqchi'es).* Antigua: Centro de Investigaciones Regionales de Mesoamérica (CIRMA), 1999.

Yáñez, Aníbal. "The Quicentenary, a Question of Class, Not Race: An Interview with Rigoberta Menchú." *Five Hundred Years of Colonization: Struggles for Emancipation and Identity.* Spec. issue of *Latin American Perspectives* 19.3 (summer 1992): 96–100.

Zapatista Army of National Liberation. "First Declaration from the Lacandon Jungle: Today We Say 'Enough Is Enough!'" 1994. 4 Mar. 2009. 26 Apr. 2009. <http://www.struggle.ws/mexico/ezln/ezlnwa.html>.

Zapeta, Estuardo. *Las huellas de B'alam*. Guatemala: Editorial Cholsamaj, 1999.

———. "Liberación Maya: Entre el mito y el ridículo." *Siglo Veintiuno* 11 Apr. 2000, opinion sec. 11 Apr. 2000. <http://www.sigloxxi.com>.

Zimmerman, Marc. *Literature and Resistance in Guatemala: Textual Modes and Cultural Politics from El Señor Presidente to Rigoberta Menchú*. 2 vols. Athens: Ohio U Center for International Studies, 1995. Monographs in International Studies. Latin America 22.

———. "Rigoberta Menchú after the Nobel: From Militant Narrative to Postmodern Politics." Rodríguez 111–28.

Index

to endorse politics of, 117. *See also* class; culture; race

disappearance, of Luis de Lión in 1984, 35

El Diseño de reforma educativa (Runuk'ik jun K'ak'a Tijonik 1998), 139–56

diversity, neoliberalism and Zapeta's model of, 117–18

D'Souza, Dinesh, 175n11

Dupuy, Alex, 115

Dworkin, Kenny, 85

Eckermann, Anne-Katrin, 185n26

economics: and Zapeta on indigenous entrepreneurship, 113–15; free trade agreements and model of for Latin America, 163–66, 186n3–6. *See also* neoliberalism

education: discursive and epistemological practices of coloniality of power, 128; and illiteracy rate in Guatemala, 182n2; and indigenous boarding schools in Mexico, 133–37, 183n11; liberal discourse on category of, 129–30; Maya intellectuals and initiatives for change, 137–38; and practices of colonial period, 130–31, 136; reform movement and bilingual intercultural forms of, 139–56, 184n16, 184n18, 185n23, 185n29; and reproduction of relations of power and subordination, 129, 138–39; as theme in study of Maya movement, 12–13

El Periódico (newspaper), 89

enlightenment, Kant's definition of, 115–16

environment: and free trade agreements, 163–64; and nature in Asturias's later works, 32

Esquivel, Adolfo Pérez, 83

essentialism: in discourse on Eurocentrism, 13–14; identity politics and interethnic debate in Guatemala, 122

Eurocentrism: and concept of "coloniality of power," 8, 9, 11; essentialism in discourse on, 13–14; and Latin Americanist intellectual tradition, 103–104

Fabian, Johannes, 20, 64–65

Facundo: Civilization and Barbarism (Sarmiento 1845), 162–63

Fanon, Frantz, 15, 42–43, 44, 45, 116–17

Fazio, Carlos, 164

feminism: in Guatemala and role of Maya women, 177n35; indigenous movements and critiques of, 74–76; and Menchú's link between struggles of women and indigenous peoples, 73

"First Declaration from the Lacandon Jungle" (Zapatistas), 123

Flores, Francisco, 159

Flores, Marco Antonio, 180n15

Florescano, Enrique, 44

foquismo, ideology of in Cuba and Nicaragua, 67, 175n6

Foucault, Michel, 182n3

Fox, Vicente, 160, 165

Free Trade Agreement of the Americas (FTAA), 31–32, 160

Friedman, Betty, 75

Galeano, Eduardo, 78, 116, 153

Gandhi, Mahatma, 84

Gante, Pedro de, 130–31, 134, 183n7

Garifuna: and educational reform, 142; and future of Guatemala, 158; history and current population of, 170n20; and Maya experience, 16

General Directorate of Bilingual Intercultural Education (DIGEBI), 143, 144, 147–48

genocide, and Guatemalan civil war, 49, 60, 63, 66, 108

Gerardi, Juan José, 175n8

globalization: and anti-globalization movements, 182n27; educational reform in context of, 141; Menchú's *Crossing Borders* as meditation on, 78–79, 82, 85; Morales's reading of in context of interethnic question, 90–93, 99, 103; use of term in context of Maya movement, 8; and Zapeta's neoliberalism, 115. *See also* modernity

Gonzáles, Gaspar Pedro, 16, 180n12

González Casanova, Pablo, 183n12

Gordon, Lewis R., 3

Graff, Gerald, 12, 154

Gramsci, Antonio, 177n37

Grandin, Greg, 180n8

Gruzinski, Serge, 41, 182n4

Guatemala: feminism and role of Maya women in, 177n35; interethnic debate and identity politics in, 87–89, 119–25; overview of recent history, 174n2; works of Rigoberta Menchú and intercultural relations in, 66–86. *See also* civil war; culture; economics; education; Maya movement; politics

Guatemalan Commission for Historical Clarification (CEH), 175n8

Guatemalan Communist Party (PGT), 88

Guatemalan Institute for Tourism (INGUAT), 94

Guatemalan National Revolutionary Unity (URNG), 4

Guatemalan Republican Front (FRG), 5

Guatemalan Workers Party (PGT), 173n27

Guerilla Army of the Poor (EGP), 54, 59–62, 63, 65, 68

Guevara, Ernesto "Che," 175n6

Gugelberger, Georg, 72

Guha, Ranajit, 43, 168n11
Gutiérrez, Natividad, 137
Guzmán, Jacobo Arbenz, 173n29

Hale, Charles, 2–3, 117
Hall, Edward T., 169n15
Harss, Luis, 24
Herbert, Jean-Loup, 179n4
hooks, bell, 46
Horowitz, David, 51
Las huellas de B'alam (Zapeta 1999), 88, 106–19
Huidobro, Vicente, 171n12
human rights, and ideological tendencies in Maya movement, 5

Icaza, Jorge, 31
identity: education and imposition of Ladino, 132; and Guatemala's interethnic debate in context of identity politics and modernity, 87–89, 119–25; and Maya cosmovision, 85; and Morales on difference and intercultural relations, 89–105. See also indigenismo/indigenista; Ladino; mestizaje; mestizo
ideology: and cultural representation in Stoll's exposé on Rigoberta Menchú, 50–66; de Lión's radical attitude toward Ladino, 45; Eurocentrism as implied form of, 14; and Latin Americanist intellectual tradition, 104, 105; and tendencies in Maya movement, 4–6
images, Gruzinski's analysis of role of in colonial Mexico, 41–42
Indian: clarification of use of category, 15; economic capitalist logic and figure of Indio permitido (the permissible Indian), 177; and education reform, 152; representations of in literature, 19–23; stereotypical representation by Asturias in Men of Maize, 25, 26. See also indigenous peoples
indigenismo/indigenista: as conceptual and theoretical frame for category of the Indian in literature, 20–23; Menchú's demystification of discourse on, 69, 73; and mestizaje, 170n1; and new aesthetic paradigm of Asturias, 31
indigenous movements: and criticism of Marxist and feminist paradigms, 74–76; development of concept, 6; increasing prominence of in recent decades, 1–2; and resistance to free trade agreements, 164–65. See also Maya movement
indigenous peoples: clarification of use of category, 15; and concepts of authenticity among Maya intellectuals, 93–96; and inverse transculturation, 98; and Menchú on feminism, 73; Morales on globalization and cultural hybridity, 92, 120–121; Zapeta on role of agency in popular protests, 111–12. See also

Garifuna; Indian; indigenous movements; Maya; Xinka
Institutional Revolutionary Party (PRI), 1
Inter-American Development Bank (IDB), 161
interculturality: and articulation of differences by Morales, 89–105; and education reform, 139–56; history of concept, 169n15; and interethnic debate in Guatemala, 87–89, 119–25; as theme in study of Maya movement, 15; works of Rigoberta Menchú and movement toward in Guatemala and Latin America, 66–86; and Zapeta on modernity, 106–19. See also culture; difference
International Indian Treaty Consul, 64
International Labor Organization (ILO), Agreement 169 on the Indigenous and Tribal Peoples of, 4
International Monetary Fund (IMF), 161
International Year of the Indigenous Peoples (United Nations 1993), 4, 52
I, Rigoberta Menchú: an Indian Woman in Guatemala (Menchú 1983): and debates on multiculturalism, 175n11; "intercultural mestizaje" and Morales's reading of, 177–78n38; and intercultural relations in Guatemala and Latin America, 66–72; Stoll's criticism of, 49–66; as testimonio, 175n4
"It Seems like a Story [Parece cuento]" (in Los zopilotes de Lión 1966), 34
Iverson, Katherine, 130

Kalsmith, Alfred, 51
Kant, Emmanuel, 115–16
Kelly, Gail, 183n12
Kempen, Laura Charlotte, 76
King, Martin Luther, Jr., 83–84
knowledge, and indigenista representations of "Indian," 22

Ladino: de Lión and ideology of, 45, 172n21; education and imposition of new identity, 132; and idea of authenticity in Asturias's Men of Maize, 28–29; identity politics and interethnic debate in Guatemala, 120, 121; and interculturality in educational reform, 147–48, 152; Morales on differences between Mayas and, 119; and Morales on Ladino-globalization relationship, 99, 103; and stereotyped constructions of identity, 145–46; use of term, 167n2. See also mestizo
La Hora (newspaper), 89
Landa, Diego de, 130
land tenure, and Stoll's criticism of Vicente Menchú, 55–58, 63, 65
language(s): and coloniality in education after independence, 131–32; and Cojtí's logic of

authenticity, 180n11; debates about standardization of Maya, 185n20; education and attempts to eliminate indigenous, 135; educational reform and indigenous, 143; interculturality and attitudes toward indigenous, 147–51

Lansing, Robert, 184n14

Latin America: category of "internal colonialism" in, 183n12; and Latin Americanist tradition, 98–99, 103–105; and neoliberalism, 178–79n1; and postcolonialism, 13; works of Rigoberta Menchú and intercultural relations in, 66–86. *See also* Bolivia; Cuba; Guatemala; indigenismo/indigenista; Ladino; mestizaje; Mexico

Law of the Constitutional Congress (1824), 131

Left: and critiques of Marxist and feminist paradigms by indigenous movements, 74–76; and interethnic debate in Guatemala, 88; and Zapeta on interculturality, 107–108

León, Juan, 173–74n37

Liano, Dante, 77–78, 171n16

liberation movements, Menchú's criticism of in *Crossing Borders*, 73

Lienhard, Martin, 30–31, 105

Linguistic Project Francisco Marroquín (PLFM), 185n20

literature: *costumbrimo* and *vanguardia* as styles of, 30, 171n12; and definition of *testimonio* as genre, 175n4; Maya nationalism and political decolonization in works of de Lión, 34–48; and mestizaje in works of Asturias, 23–33; representation of "Indian" and "indigenous problem" in, 19–23; and *testimonio* as theme in study of Maya movement, 12

Llosa, Mario Vargas, 97, 173n34, 176n23

López Alvarado, Manuela, 111, 128–29, 147

Lorand de Olazagasti, Adelaida, 23–24

Lux de Cotí, Otilia, 148, 150, 167n5, 185n27

Macaulay, Thomas B., 184n14

Maduro, Ricardo, 159

Maguire, Mairead Corrigan, 83

Mahuad, Jamil, 1

Marcos, Subcomandante, 96–97, 98, 124–25, 171n14

Marighella, Carlos, 67

Martin, Gerald, 32, 171n10

Martínez, Osvaldo, 164

Marx, Karl, 114

Marxism: and criticism of paradigms by indigenous movement, 74–76; and interethnic debate in Guatemala, 88. *See also* Left

Matto de Turner, Clorinda, 20

Maya: and creation myths in de Lión's *El tiempo principia en Xibalbá*, 44; and debates about standardization of languages, 185n20; and indigenous point of view in de Lión's *El tiempo principia en Xibalbá*, 170n7; Menchú on as historical identity, 81. *See also* Maya cosmovision; Maya movement; Maya nationalism

Maya cosmovision: Asturias's perspective on, 31; and intercultural subaltern epistemology, 158; Menchú's ideal of reaffirming and promoting, 70–71, 72, 80; use of term and reconceptualization of, 14–15

Maya movement: and educational reform, 137–38, 140–41; and focus on racism rather than class, 181n23; and future of Guatemala, 157–66; Menchú's cultural and political contribution to, 66–86; and Morales on intercultural relations and identity politics, 89–105; overview of themes in study of, 2–17; promotion of indigenous cultural revitalization compared to Asturias's politics of mestizaje, 31; revival of for revolutionary purpose, 84–85; and Zapeta on interculturality and modernity, 106–19, 167–68n6. *See also* indigenous movements; Maya; Maya cosmovision; Maya nationalism

Maya nationalism: and political decolonization in works of Luis de Lión, 22, 34–48; and Zapeta on interculturality, 109–10. *See also* Maya; Maya movement

Maya University, 185n28

McClintock, Anne, 43

McCloud, Janet, 74

McConaghy, Cathryn, 146–47

Means, Lorelei DeCora, 74

media: Menchú on role of as cultural mediator, 80; and Morales on intercultural relations, 91. *See also* newspapers

Menchú Tum, Rigoberta: and construction of new Maya epistemology, 154–55, 158; *Crónica* (magazine) issue on, 2–3; and interculturality in Guatemala and Latin America, 66–86, 178n43; and *I, Rigoberta Menchú* as *testimonio*, 175n4; and Maya cosmovision, 31; and Morales on intercultural relations, 100, 101–102; and participation in politics, 1, 85, 175n13; and Stoll's reading of *I, Rigoberta Menchú*, 48, 49–66; use of category "Indian," 15; on use of technology and science by indigenous peoples, 79–80, 178n41; and world leadership of indigenous movements, 4

Menchú, Vicente, 50, 52, 55–66, 70

Mendoza, Carlos, 179n5

Men of Maize (Asturias 1949), 22, 23–33, 46, 163–64

mestizaje: and concept of inverse transculturation, 98–100; concept of in *Men of Maize* by
Asturias, 23–33; de Lión and "Mayanization"
in *El tiempo*, 46–47, 48; and indigenismo,
170n1; and "indigenous problem" in literature, 20, 47; and Latin Americanist intellectual tradition, 103–105; Menchú on problem
of in Latin America, 80–81; Millar's study of
"cult of," 180n17; and Morales's reading of *I,
Rigoberta Menchú*, 177–78n38; and Zapeta
compared to Morales, 118, 119. *See also*
Ladino; mestizo
mestizo: and Arguedas on cultural identity, 98;
and Latin Americanist tradition, 99; and
Morales on intercultural relations, 91, 100,
103; and national imaginary in post-revolu-
tionary Mexico, 133; use of term, 167n2. *See
also* Ladino; mestizaje
Mexican Revolution (1911–1917), 20, 133
Mexico: free trade agreements and Zapatista
rebellion, 164; Gruzinski's analysis of role of
images in colonial period, 41–42; internal
colonialism and imperialist educational project in, 183–84n14; and mestizo national
imaginary after Revolution, 132–33; and
Zapeta's approach to Zapatista rebellion, 111
Mignolo, Walter, 8, 11, 119
Millamán, Rosamel, 117
Millar, Marilyn G., 180n17
Minà, Gianni, 77, 78
Ministry of Education, 143
modernity: and coloniality of power, 11; and
Guatemala's interethnic debate in context of
identity politics in Latin America, 87–89;
indigenous languages and interculturality in
education, 150–51; and Menchú's condemnation of state sponsored violence, 79; and
Menchú's discussion of Maya spirituality, 71;
Morales and Cojtí on authenticity of indigenous cultures, 94–96, 99; Morales's rejection
of colonial project of, 102; and representation of Indian by Asturias in *Men of Maize*,
26, 28–29; use of term in context of Maya
movement, 8; and Zapeta on interculturality
and modernity, 106–19. *See also* globalization
Montejo, Victor, 15–16, 89, 106, 168n6,
176–77n24
Morales, Mario Roberto: and concept of interculturality, 149, 150; criticism of Menchú and
reading of *I, Rigoberta Menchú*, 111,
177–78n38; on definition of Ladino, 167n2;
on de Lión's relationship with Asturias, 34,
36; difference and intercultural relations in
La articulación de las differences, 88, 89–105;
on indigenous languages and modernity,

150, 151; on indigenous traditions as cul-
tural mixture, 120–21; and unresolved ten-
sions between Ladinos and Mayas, 87;
Zapeta compared to, 118, 119, 123
Moreiras, Alberto, 97–98
motives, of Stoll's discussion of *I, Rigoberta
Menchú*, 50, 51, 54–55, 63
Moya, Ruth, 139, 146
Muyulema, Armando, 104

Nakata, Martin, 65
naming, colonial practices of, 9–10, 93
National Coordination of Guatemalan Widows
(CONAVIGUA), 5
National Coordinator of Peasant Organizations
(CONIC), 179n2, 186n6
National Indigenist Institute (INI), 95
National Institute for Agrarian Transformation
(INTA), 55–58
nationalism, use of term in Maya context, 6–7.
See also Maya nationalism
Nayrapacha, and Andean concept of past, 44
Nebrija, Antonio, 10
Nelson, Diane, 109
neoliberalism: and free trade agreements, 165,
179n2; origins and influence of in Latin
America, 178–79n1; and Zapeta on intercul-
turality, 108, 113–15, 117
Neruda, Pablo, 171n12
Newland, Carlos, 183n9
newspapers: and interethnic debate in
Guatemala, 89; internet sites of, 179n5. *See
also* media
Nicaragua, and ideology of foquismo, 67, 175n6
Nimatuj, Irma Alicia Velázquez, 16, 89
Nobel Peace Prize, and Rigoberta Menchú, 52,
53, 70–71, 77
North American Free Trade Agreement (NAFTA),
164

objectivity, and Stoll's interpretation of Menchú's
testimonio, 50, 59, 65
October Revolution (1944–1954), 88, 133
orientalism: and concept of indigenismo, 22, 47;
and Stoll's strategy of misappropriation, 60
Ortiz, Fernando, 29, 171n11
Other Conquest, The (film), 173n33, 183n6

Pacheco, Abel, 159
Palma, Ricardo, 171n12
Parity Commission for Educational Reform
(COPARE), 184n18
past: and Andean concept of Nayrapacha, 44;
and literary representations of Indians,
20–21
Pastor Bodmer, Beatriz, 162

paternalism, and representation of Indian by
Asturias in *Men of Maize*, 26–27
Payeras, Mario, 67
Paz, Rigoberto Juárez, 16, 89
Peace Accords (1996), 4, 52, 89, 141, 167n4
Peláez, Severo Martínez, 179n3
Penny, Sarah, 78
performance, of political ideals in literature, 36
Plan Puebla-Panamá: Por el desarrollo sustenable y socialmente incluyente (2000), 31, 160–61, 165
politics: and Guatemala's interethnic debate in context of modernity, 87–89, 119–25; Menchú's participation in presidential, 85, 175n13; and Morales on difference and intercultural relations, 89–105; and Stoll's revisionism on civil war in Guatemala, 54, 58, 59, 63; and Zapeta on difference, 117. *See also* conservatism; democracy; Left; neoliberalism; resistance
Pop, Amanda, 6
Popul Wuj, 24, 44, 47, 85
popular rights, and ideological tendencies in Maya movement, 3, 6
Portillo, Alfonso, 159, 170n7
positivism, and Austurias's politics of mestizaje, 33
postcolonialism, use of concept in context of Latin America, 13
Powell, T. G., 136
power, coloniality of: description of model, 8–11; de Lión's insight into in *El tiempo principia en Xibalbá*, 39, 45; education and discursive or epistemological practices of, 128; and Maya relations with state, 58–59; Morales on hegemonic power of Ladinos in Guatemala, 103; and role of Maya movement in future of Guatemala, 166; Zapeta on Maya movement and symmetrical relations of, 109
Prensa Libre (newspaper), 89, 149, 150, 181n19, 185n28
Professional Development of Human Resources, 143
Program of Bilingual Bicultural Education (PRONEB), 143–44
Pueblo enfermo: Contribución a la psicologia de los pueblos Hispano-Americanos (Arguedas 1910), 21
La puerta del cielo y otras puertas (de Lión 1995), 37–38, 47
Pulg, José Manuel, 133

Quijano, Anibal, 8–11, 119

Rabinal Achí (ballet-drama), 91, 180n10
race: and concept of "coloniality of power," 8, 9,

11; education and reproduction of essentialized categories of, 133; and indigenous boarding schools, 135. *See also* indigenous peoples; racism
racism: Maya movement's position on class and, 181n23; and paternalism of Asturias in *Men of Maize*, 26–27; shared views of Zapeta and Rorty on, 119; Zapeta's response to latent racism in Guatemala, 110. *See also* indigenous peoples; race
Rama, Ángel, 29–30, 97, 98, 120
Reagan, Ronald, 53
Recovery of the Historical Memory (REMHI), 175n8
religion, role of in dividing Maya communities during Ríos Montt's regime, 59. *See also* Catholic Action
resistance: to free trade agreements, 164–65, 186n4, 186n6; to indigenous boarding schools, 136–37; Maya cosmovision as narrative of, 85
Revolutionary Armed Forces (FAR), 68, 173n27
Revolutionary Organization of People in Arms (ORPA), 68
Rigoberta Menchú and the Story of All Poor Guatemalans (Stoll 1999), 49–66
Ríos Montt, Gen. Efraín, 5, 58, 59
Rivera Cusicanqui, Silvia, 44
Robinson, William I., 186n5
Rodas, Ana María, 40
Rorty, Richard, 118–19
Rosa, Rodrigo Rey, 169n18
Rosaldo, Renato, 122
Rother, Larry, 54
Ruíz, Maya Pérez, 6
Ruiz, Samuel, 78

Said, Edward, 22, 47, 61, 65, 145, 155, 176n22, 182n3
Sánchez, Gonzalo, 1
"Sandal Wearer, The" (de Lión in *Su segunda muerte* 1970), 37
Santos, Francisco Morales, 35, 172n21, 173n30, 173n36
Sarmiento, Domingo Faustino, 10, 26, 162–63, 176n23
Sartre, Jean-Paul, 3
Schirmer, Jennifer, 64
Schutte, Ofelia, 81
science, Menchú on use of by indigenous peoples, 79–80, 178n41
Siglo veintiuno (newspaper), 89, 107
Smith, Carol, 36, 59
social movements: and concept of "indigenous movement," 6; Maya movement and nationalist politicocultural agendas of other,

Emilio del Valle Escalante (Maya K'iche', Guatemala) is Assistant Professor of Latin American literatures and cultures at the University of North Carolina at Chapel Hill. His research focuses on contemporary indigenous literatures and social movements in the Americas.